THE ENVIRONMENT ACT 2021

A GUIDE FOR PLANNERS AND DEVELOPERS

Tom Graham

Published May 2022

ISBN 978-1-9163023-1-0

Text © Tom Graham

Typography © Bath Publishing

All rights reserved. No part of this publication may be reproduced in any material form (including photocopying or storing it in any medium by electronic means and whether or not transiently or incidentally to some other use of this publication) without the written permission of the copyright holder except in accordance with the provisions of the Copyright, Designs and Patents Act 1988 or under the terms of a licence issued by the Copyright Licensing Agency (www. cla.co.uk). Applications for the copyright owner's written permission to reproduce any part of this publication should be addressed to the publisher.

Tom Graham asserts his right as set out in ss77 and 78 of the Copyright Designs and Patents Act 1988 to be identified as the author of this work wherever it is published commercially and whenever any adaptation of this work is published or produced including any sound recordings or films made of or based upon this work.

The information presented in this work is accurate and current as at 30 April 2022 to the best knowledge of the author. The author and the publisher, however, make no guarantee as to, and assume no responsibility for, the correctness or sufficiency of such information or recommendation. The contents of this book are not intended as legal advice and should not be treated as such.

Contains public sector information licensed under the Open Government Licence v3.0.

Bath Publishing Limited

27 Charmouth Road

Bath

BA1 3LJ

Tel: 01225 577810

email: info@bathpublishing.co.uk

www.bathpublishing.com

Bath Publishing is a company registered in England: 5209173

Registered Office: As above

TO

Thomas, my favourite grandson

and

Linda, my favourite wife!

About the author

Tom Graham is a barrister and former solicitor with over 40 years experience in town & country planning and highway law. He has advised, and continues to advise, in both the private and public sectors and taken the lead in a number of major public inquiries.

Tom has been a lecturer in a range of topics for over 20 years.

He has a particular interest in climate change and currently writes and lectures on the topic. He is, also, writing a book on contaminated land and the planning process[1] (having written a book on the same topic in 1995).

---

[1] Due to be published by Bath Publishing.

Acknowledgments

I need to proffer some acknowledgements, and there are a number of them. First, of course I must thank my long-suffering wife, Linda, for putting up with my writing yet another book. Then I would like to thank David Chaplin and Helen Lacey at Bath Publishing. Once again, David and Helen have had the confidence to risk the publication of a new book on my behalf and Helen has performed her usual miracles in turning the manuscript into the finished product. I also thank Peter Smith for his considerable help in editing the manuscript.

I have, along the way, participated in a number of webinars and seminars in working up the book and learned a lot from my fellow speakers in doing so.

Finally, my thanks to Linda Jackson and Umi Filby for choosing the cover to this book.

Tom Graham

CONTENTS

Chapter 10: Local Biodiversity Reports

Chapter 11: Conservation Covenant Agreements

List Of Acronyms

Biodiversity Unit (BU)

Breeding Bird Survey (BBS)

British Trust for Ornithology (BTO)

Chartered Institute of Ecology and Environmental Management (CIEEM)

Clean Air Zones (CAZ)

Common Birds Census (CBC)

Ecological Clerk of Works (ECoW)

Ecological Impact Assessment (EcIA)

Environmental Impact Assessment (EIA)

Freedom of Information (FOI)

Geographical Information System (QGIS)

Habitats Regulations Assessment (HRA)

Joint Nature Conservation Committee (JNCC)

Local Nature Recovery Strategies (LNRS)

National Capital Committee (NCC)

National Character Area (NCA)

Office for Environmental Protection (OEP)

Preliminary Ecological Appraisal (PEA)

Sites of Importance for Nature Conservation (SINCs)

Sites of Special Scientific Interest (SSSI)

Small Sites Metric (SSM)

Special Protection Areas (SPAs)

Suitable Alternative Natural Greenspace (SANG)

Sustainable Urban Drainage Systems (SUDS)

UK Environmental Law Association (UKELA)

Bibliography

25 Year Environment Plan Progress Report, April 2019 to March 2020 (11 June 2020) (HMG)

A Green Future: Our 25 Year Plan to Improve the Environment (Defra) (2018)

A Practical Guide to Planning, Highways and Development, Tom Graham (Bath Publishing, 2019)

Begon, Townsend and Harper Ecology: From Individuals to Ecosystems (Fourth Edition) (Blackwell Publishing, 2006)

Biodiversity: A Beginners Guide (revised and updated edition) (Beginners Guides), John Spicer (One World, May 2021)

Biodiversity 2020: A strategy for England's wildlife and ecosystem services (Defra) (CD 9.2)

Biodiversity in the UK: bloom or bust? - First Report of Session 2021–22", (the *"Commons Audit Report"*) (June 2021)

Biodiversity Offsetting Pilot – Technical Paper: the metric for the biodiversity offsetting pilot in England (March 2012), (published for Defra)

Biodiversity Offsetting Pilots, Guidance for Developers (March 2012). A joint publication by Natural England and Defra

Capacity crunch: do councils have the expertise to deliver their biodiversity goals? (ENDS Report)

Communication from the Commission on the Precautionary Principle (Brussels, 2.2.2000 COM(2000) 1 final)

Consultation on Biodiversity Net Gain Regulations and Implementation (Defra) (The *"Consultation Document"*) (January 2022)

Design Manual for Roads and Bridges (DMRB) Volume 11,LA115

Guidelines for Preliminary Ecological Appraisal" (2nd edition) (CIEEM) (December 2017)

Habitats regulations HRGN 3 guidance note (English Nature) (1999)

Handbook for Phase 1 habitat survey – a technique for environmental audit (JNCC) (2010)

Handbook of the Convention on Biological Diversity - including its Cartagena Protocol on Biosafety 3rd edition - Secretariat of the Convention on Biological Diversity (2005)

Information paper on the Policy Statement on Environmental Principles (Defra) (December 2018)

Interpreting the NPPF, Alistair Mills (Bath Publishing, 2018)

"Judicial Ignorance of the Parliamentary Process Implications for statutory interpretation" – Daniel Greenberg, Judicial Power Project (March 2017)

Late lessons from early warnings II: science, precaution and innovation (EEA Report, 1/2013)

Measuring Environmental Change: Outcome Indicator Framework for the 25 Year Environment Plan (Defra) (May 2019)

"*Modern Statutory Interpretation*": Lord Justice Sales, Lecture at Society of Legal Scholars Conference (September 2016)

National Planning Policy Framework (2021)

Put a price on nature? We must stop this neoliberal road to ruin - George Monbiot SPERI Annual Lecture 2014

Quantifying biodiversity (Steve Buckland, Royal Statistical Society) (August 2009)

Scrutiny of the Draft Environment (Principles and Governance) Bill (Environmental Audit Committee) (October 2019)

Shaping the future of Nature Recovery: Developing Local Nature Recovery Strategies, Jo Traill-Thompson (27 August 2021)

Small Sites Metric Calculation Tool: User Guide – Beta Test (Natural England Joint Publication JP040. First published July 2021

Species diversity or biodiversity? Journal of Environmental Management, 75(1):89–92, Hamilton, A J (2005)

"*Statutory Interpretation – the Myth of Parliamentary Intent*" (Sir John Laws Renton Lecture, November 2017)

Summary of changes from Biodiversity Metric 2.0 to version 3.0" (Natural England Joint Publication JP039 – July 2021)

The Biodiversity Metric 3.0 – auditing and accounting for biodiversity – USER GUIDE (Natural England Joint Publication JP039), first published 7 July 2021 (currently under revision)

The Green Book (2020) (publishing. service.gov.uk)

The Law Commission - (LAW COM No 349) – "*CONSERVATION COVENANTS*" (23 June 2014)

Towards a Framework for Defining and Measuring Changes in Natural Capital, Working Paper, 1 March 2014 (Natural Capital Committee)

UK Biodiversity Indicators 2021 Revised (Defra) (2021)

Understanding Legislation: A Practical Guide to Statutory Interpretation, David Lowe and Charlie Potter (Hart Publishing, 2018)

United Nations Environment Programme document "*What is Biodiversity?*" (February 2010)

United Nations Environmental Programme Convention on Biological Diversity (5 June 1992)

Table Of Cases

Table Of Statutes

Table Of Statutory Instruments

Table Of Directives

Table Of Frameworks And Guidance

Introduction – *"Why Bother"*?[1]

The Environment Act was given Royal Assent on 9 November 2021, and, as is usual with most legislation, almost all of the provisions have yet to come into force. So far as those relating to biodiversity net gain are concerned, the general consensus appears to be that the relevant transition period will be in the order of two years from that date. To put it another way, the clock has already started ticking towards a fixed point in the not-too-distant future. One option is, of course, to sit back and do nothing until the mandatory *"biodiversity net gain condition"* and associated provisions are triggered. This would not be, it is submitted, a particularly sound course of action for any developer or local planning authority. This observation generates many causes for concern which need to be addressed over the period leading to the trigger date(s), and they include:

- lead times;

- resources;

- staffing levels and expertise; and

- training.

Lead times

The Environment Act has been given Royal Assent and is rapidly heading towards a trigger date for its biodiversity net gain provisions. It would, therefore, be sensible to compare this timeline in the critical path of any modest or large development. The nominal period of 18 months for a lead time to the grant of planning permission would be unusual in the first case and improbable in the second. The developer must, first, secure the development site, either by acquisition or by way of an option to purchase. This alone could take some months.

The prudent developer would engage in pre-application discussions with the local planning authority and, if the site is in any way contentious, in some form of public relations exercise. If the site is likely to have a significant impact on land which is subject to the Habitat Regulations, it might be the case that a screening application has to be made and, then, an appropriate assessment produced. This time-consuming assessment and reporting exercise might, of course, be conditioned or constrained by things which are outside the control of the developer and local planning authority, such as breeding seasons. If the land is suspected of being contaminated, a desktop study will need to be provided to the local planning authority and, perhaps, a more extensive *"Phase II Report"* where there are

---

[1] The title of this introduction may seem a bit provocative in a formal textbook and I did spend some time wondering whether it was appropriate. However, I normally dwell on the slide with exactly this title when talking about biodiversity net gain in webinars or seminars in order to catch the audience's attention and, it seems to me, that the same logic might apply a connection with this book because it goes to the core of why it is published now instead of waiting until the dust has been settled on by publication of the details of the 2021 Act.

legitimate concerns about the suitability of the site for development. If the site is a large one, an environmental impact assessment might be necessary. It might also be the case that the local planning authority and the developer need to negotiate heads of terms for a relevant section 106 agreement before the proposals are put before the planning committee. Only an incurable optimist would proceed on the basis that all of this can be done in less than 18 months.

Even then, if the planning committee is minded to grant planning permission, it will normally be necessary to settle and execute the section 106 agreement, and this exercise could be time-consuming in itself.

These matters turn (in part) on local planning authority staffing levels and material resources as much as inbuilt constraints. Plus, there will, as usual, be the last-minute rush by developers to see if they can push their proposals through when they suddenly realise that they are heading towards a hard trigger date. The reality, of course, is that such trigger dates have a propensity for creating inevitable logjams.

In short, neither developer nor local planning authority stands a reasonable chance of achieving this particular trigger date unless the application is given some form of expedited treatment to avoid it. Then, of course, there might be objections that this process of speeding the application along implies some sort of bias in favour of the developer in order to avoid an onerous obligation.

One answer is, of course, that the prudent developer will seek to incorporate biodiversity net gain into any new scheme proposals henceforth, but this then brings one to the question of whether the local planning authority has the resources to respond to it.

Finally, and perhaps cynically, some local planning authorities might be tempted to drag their heels as the trigger date approaches, so as to gain the benefit of the statutory condition and scheme. One hopes that this will not be the case, but worldly developers should plan on the basis of reality as opposed to pious optimism. They can gauge the temperature by early research on, and involvement with, the relevant authority by pre-application discussions and, now, viewing "*YouTube*" videos of the actual committee in action on similar applications.[2]

Resources
In the document entitled "*Biodiversity in the UK: bloom or bust? - First Report of Session 2021–22*", (the "*Commons Audit Report*"), the Environmental Audit Committee of the House of Commons had this to say on the capacities of local authorities to deliver biodiversity net gain:

---

[2]   To be blunt, this is the advice I would give my clients! Getting to committee at the last minute, and with a positive officer recommendation, is no guarantee that some members might not seek to defer the item for "*further research*" or a site visit when it comes before them. Such ploys are not unknown in the world of planning committees.

> *"184. The biodiversity net gain policy is proposed to be implemented by 'local decision makers' who would agree net gain plans with developers. The majority of these local decision makers will be local authorities. The Government estimated that the cost to local Government of implementing net gain will be £9.5m per year."*

Thus, one has to ask where the money is coming from and how it will be spent.

Staffing levels and expertise

A relatively recent ENDS Report survey[3] showed that the majority of UK councils do not have in-house ecologists:

> *"Exclusive figures show only a quarter of English councils employed in-house ecological experts in 2018. But this figure falls to 16% for experts who hold chartered status in ecology – currently only available from the Chartered Institute of Ecology and Environmental Management (CIEEM). ENDS' figures were obtained following a freedom of information (FOI) request to all 353 councils in England, to which 307 authorities provided responses."*

The ENDS Report went on to say that the identification of ecologists who achieve chartered status is essential. CIEEM's chief executive officer Sally Hayns told ENDS that:

> *"Chartered status for ecology is reserved for those practitioners who have demonstrated a high technical level of competencies like ecological assessment, designing or habitat creation over and above someone who is non-chartered."*

She added:

> *"We believe more local authorities should have access to in-house ecological expertise because without that we think they are vulnerable to challenge – in strategic plan-making and development decision-making. That can make planning authorities risk averse, but also non-compliant with legislation and policy."*

The ENDS report added that:

> *"Our findings paint a similar picture to research carried out by the Association for Local Government Ecologists (ALGE), which in a report in 2013 found that only one-in-three councils had access to in-house ecological expertise. At the time, ALGE said: 'An average capacity of only one ecologist for every three local planning authorities in England would appear to be inadequate to deal with the relevant workload'.*
>
> *ENDS' own figures indicate there has been a small increase only in the number of ecological experts employed in the six years after ALGE's 2013 report. In 2018, the*

---

[3]   *Capacity crunch: do councils have the expertise to deliver their biodiversity goals?* (www.endsreport.com/article/1585763/capacity-crunch-councils-expertise-deliver-biodiversity-goals?utm_source%3Dwebsite&utm_medium%3Dsocial).

> *number of ecological experts, chartered and non-chartered, employed by the 307 authorities that responded to our FOI request was 142, up from 124 in 2013 – a 14% rise."*

The Commons Audit Report went on to say that Philip Glanville[4] summarised the issue around local planning authority capacities to deliver biodiversity net gain:

> *"185. [Local authorities] have had 10 years of funding challenges. We face a significant funding gap as we go forward. Planning authorities have borne the brunt of that. Nearly 40% of funding loss is at planning authorities. That expertise around biodiversity, conservation, ecology has fallen away ...* **two-thirds of authorities do not have an in-house capacity on this,** *so if local Government should and needs to have that role, it also needs to be invested into."* (Emphasis added).

These reports might suggest that there is or will be a staffing shortage when set against the demands of implementing the biodiversity net gain condition. If this staffing gap continues, the consequences could include the creation of bottlenecks or, in desperation, developers covering the costs of employing independent external ecologists. If the latter, these costs must be added to viability assessment for schemes and the worst case might be a developer arguing that they cannot afford to cover these costs unless there is a reduction in the local planning authority's aspirations for affordable housing or other benefits. In large part, the answer lies in the hands of the local planning authorities and those who fund them and, again, this suggests that the problem should be put on the table now, rather than leaving it until too late in the day.

The position is not necessarily bleak. The information technology which is central to biodiversity net gain is generally free; this is to say, the biodiversity metric and the geographical information system (QGIS) – likewise, the relevant regulations and guidance. One would expect that the local planning authority would not have any difficulty in this aspect of the exercise, provided that staff are dedicated to capturing and distributing these materials. The wise local planning authority would also invest in specialist books, journals, etc – some of which are expensive, some of which are not.

Training
None of the above discussion is of any practical use unless developers, officers and members are trained to the apposite degree.

The Commons Audit Report stated:

> *"185 ... Philip Glanville's comments are supported by the CIEEM and the Association of Local Environmental Records Centres (ALERC) who both recommended that considerable investment in training and skills in ecology will be necessary for local authorities to implement BNG."*

---

[4]   Member of the Local Government Association's Environment, Economy, Housing and Transport Board, and Mayor of Hackney.

Training is essential and training takes time and the commitment of scarce resources.

The Environment Act 2021 is, among other things, intended to cause a sea-change in the way that the development industry delivers its products by setting out a framework within which they and local planning authorities tackle the difficult topic of protecting and, in some cases, enhancing the environment.

In days gone by, a developer's promise to deliver *"ecological improvements"* was not given great importance and, certainly, the planning obligations which accompanied the grant of permissions did little, if anything, to provide that those promises were transmuted into measurable and enforceable results. The modern reality is that such a promise will, in future, carry great weight in the consideration of the application and should therefore be secured by legal mechanisms which provide measurable and enforceable outcomes. This sea-change means that all professionals involved in the property development process must learn a new language and tackle subject areas which had, previously, been of peripheral concern. The change is a challenging one. Planners, developers and lawyers now spend as much time talking about ecology, chemistry and engineering as they do about pure planning. They have to steep themselves in esoteric books on these subjects in order to keep up.

It is also necessary that the appropriate skills are applied to particular tasks within the process. For example, it is difficult to see how ecologists would have the necessary legal skills to draft management plans which are enforceable in a court of law. This means that lawyers should have some understanding of how the Biodiversity Metric operates in order to draft the necessary legal documentation (e.g. section 106 agreements). This is particularly the case where a large scheme is brought forward in phases and sophisticated documentation is needed to provide clarity and enforceability. The seemingly straightforward process of settling a *"section 106 agreement"* requires close collaboration between ecologist, planner and lawyer and, so far as the lawyer is concerned, there is little point in tackling a planning obligation without a basic understanding of ecology. Likewise, there is little point in a planning advocate attempting to cross-examine an expert in ecology unless the advocate has a good grasp of topics such as the Biodiversity Metric and, hopefully, the computer-based mapping and information system which underpins it. Ecologists need to keep up-to-date with a rapidly changing paradigm which includes policy, law and science.

Hopefully, local planning authorities will not take the view that officers are autodidacts and can learn these difficult matters in their own time and at their expense.[5] No doubt there are many different views as to how training can be achieved, but all involve the expenditure of time and many will also involve expenditure of money.

Turning to members, many local planning authorities provide training courses for members and, indeed, some will not allow members to sit on committees until they have attended prescribed courses. This is important not only because members need to understand the

---

[5] Perhaps by watching YouTube videos!

discussions in front of them but also to make their decisions robust in the event of judicial challenges.

My oft-repeated advice is *"Training ... Training ... Training ..."!*

Tempus fugit

The harsh reality is that, sitting back on some sort of *"wait and see"* platform is not a prudent approach for either developer or local planning authority. There is a need to grapple with all of the topics mentioned above as a matter of urgency. Not only is the publication of books such as this one justifiable but also it is essential to this task. This book is intended to provide some brief guidance to those who are, or will be, involved in this changing paradigm in the hope that it, in some ways, eases the passage. And so, happy reading!!

Some preliminary points

First, there is the inevitable *"health warning"*; namely, that (whilst we have striven for accuracy) this book is no substitute for reading the source materials, and its contents are not intended as advice to be applied to any specific case. Ergo, it is no substitute for specific expert advice on a case-by-case basis.

The *"Consultation Document"*

Secondly, a bit of an apology to those who bought this book on a pre-publication basis. Thank you for your patience. There was a slight delay in my getting the manuscript to Bath Publishing because Defra published a consultation document entitled *"Consultation on Biodiversity Net Gain Regulations and Implementation"* in January 2022.[1] This document is very important in this context and I had two choices. One was to make reference to it in an annex, and the other was to integrate the document into the narrative. I chose the latter course for reasons of navigation and readability, but it took some time to achieve. Ergo, I blame the Government!

---

[1]   Referred to as the *"Consultation Document"* in this book.

Chapter 1

Interpretation Of The Environment Act

1.1   Introduction

The Act is a difficult one to construe because it contains many expressions which are either undefined or are only partially defined. For example, the preamble to the Act contains the word "*biodiversity*", and the notions of protecting and enhancing are central to the parts of the Act which seek to do so by way of the planning system. Yet, the term is not defined: see Chapter 3. Likewise, the vague phrase "*species abundance*" is used in a context which creates a significant statutory approach to this topic: see Chapter 3. The problem is made doubly difficult by the fact that these phrases are of uncertain meaning, even among experts. Lawyers prefer, of course, to find robust definitions in legislation,[1] but it might be the case that Parliament has left these expressions open-ended for just this reason; namely, that fixing a settled legal meaning might place the legislation out of step with iterations in science or terminology. One answer is that the provision of particularity in these cases could have been accommodated by "*Henry VIII clauses*", which provide a minister with power to set and then vary such definitional materials from time to time and as these things evolve, but the Act is infrequent in its use of such devices. Hence, it is necessary to consider the principles which assist in construing words and phrases which appear, at first reading, to be ambiguous.

The Act is not a standalone document. It is accompanied by a set of Explanatory Notes and, also, by various *ex post facto* commentaries in the National Planning Policy Framework and the National Planning Practice Guidance. There is the temptation to resort to these various extrinsic materials when seeking to interpret these new provisions, but this could be a mistake. It is, therefore, prudent to consider, albeit very briefly, the complex principles which apply in seeking to construe a statute.

1.2   The "*canons of interpretation*"

Lawyers should, normally, be taught the "*canons of interpretation*" at an early stage in their training because, nowadays, most of the law which the Courts are called on to apply is statutory. Whether this happens in practice is debatable. Lord Justice Sales once opined:

> "*Yet statutory interpretation languishes as a subject of study. For the most part, law students are expected to pick it up by a sort of process of osmosis. It's more fun and engaging to study cases, as vignettes of real life. So the common law and common law method wins out.*"[2]

---

[1]   Albeit some might seek to exploit ambiguity!

[2]   Lord Justice of Appeal, Court of Appeal of England and Wales – *Modern Statutory Interpretation*. The article was based on the text of a lecture delivered at the Society of Legal Scholars conference at St Catherine's College, Oxford in September 2016 and first published in the Statute Law Review.

As is often the case, these *"canons"* or *"rules"* are not so much rules as guidelines. The complexity of language is such that it is necessary to deploy a degree of judgement while seeking to understand and apply statutory language.

1.3 The *"golden rule"*

The traditional starting point is to say that the words in a statute are normally given their ordinary or natural meaning. This is sometimes known as the *"golden rule"*. It is said that one should seek to understand the *"plain meaning"* of the words in question. There is, however, the difficulty where the subject matter of the statute is a highly technical one. For example, there is no *"plain meaning"* for the word *"biodiversity"*, because the phrase will have different meanings to different people and will vary according to the specific context within which it is used.[3]

1.4 The *"intention of Parliament"*

Lawyers have adopted the fiction that they would, in seeking to understand legislation, try to divine the mind of Parliament when it formed that legislation. Sir John Laws once said:

> *"1. Time without number judges have referred to the intention of Parliament. The intention of Parliament is seen as the key to the interpretation of statutes. Indeed, the interpretation of statutes is thought to consist in ascertaining the intention of Parliament.*
>
> *2. Like all or most of my recent colleagues, I have used this kind of language in judg-ments. But I have come to think it is misleading and unhelpful. It is misleading because there is no such thing as the intention of Parliament; I will explain why. And it is unhelpful because all too often it has turned the interpretation of statute into a futile quest for this non-existent chimera, causing various quite unnecessary problems ..."[4]*

One answer is not to look to the logic of language, but to the authors themselves. Which brings us (hopefully neatly) to the decision of the House of Lords in *Pepper v Hart* [1993] A.C. 593, a taxation case.

There, teachers appealed against a decision concerning the basis for the tax treatment of benefits in kind received by them, namely the education of their children on payment of concessionary school fees.

The Judicial Committee held (*inter alia*)[5] that the rule prohibiting references to Parliamentary material by the Courts as an aid to the construction of legislation was relaxed. The rule was relaxed, but only so far as to permit such references where: (a) the wording of legislation was ambiguous or obscure or its literal meaning led to absurdity; (b) the material relied upon consisted of one or more statements by the Minister or other promoter of the relevant

---

[3] See Chapter 3 for some of these varying definitions in the context of environmental law.

[4] *Statutory Interpretation – the Myth of Parliamentary Intent* (Renton Lecture, November 2017).

[5] Lord Mackay of Clashfern LC dissenting in part.

Act, together (if necessary) with such other Parliamentary material as was necessary to understand such statements and their effect; and (c) the statements relied on were clear.

It is fair to say that, whilst the decision was made in 1992, it still remains the subject of vigorous debate within the legal community. Many very senior lawyers have argued, and are still arguing, that *Pepper v Hart* causes more problems than it actually solved. Arguably, it simply stands one fiction of top of another.[6]

Pepper v Hart was intended to inform the judiciary about the state of mind of an assembly of differing minds; namely, Parliament. However, Parliament does not have a hive mind akin to the Borg collective.

Sir John Laws continued his lecture by saying:

> "5. *Parliament is a many-headed body. Intention is a characteristic of a single mind. The members of a group of persons may in theory have the same intention, in the sense that each may intend to act in the same way as each of the others. Or each may intend that he and all of the others should together achieve a common plan. But all of these cases are merely instances of members of the group individually intending the same result as each of the others. In neither circumstance does the group (as a whole) entertain an intention in the paradigm sense, that is, a state of mind of a single individual. A group does not have a mind, and therefore cannot possess a state of mind.*"

Without wishing to digress too much, there is a great danger in seeking to deploy sophisticated devices when attempting to unpack the historical meaning attributed to a word or phrase by its author; namely, that it is an exercise in retro-engineering. It will only take you back to the true intent of the author if that author used exactly the same devices when he packaged up the message in the first place.[7] The path out of a labyrinth might be to follow the string that somebody laid down to the entrance, but what if there is more than one piece of string and multiple entrances? Each of those paths must work, but you get back to a different starting point with each one. Why should one presume that an author has deployed one set of semantic algorithms over another?

In *Pepper v Hart*, Lord Griffiths said (page 617):

> "*The object of the court in interpreting legislation is to give effect so far as the language permits to the intention of the legislature. If the language proves to be ambiguous I can see no sound reason not to consult Hansard to see if there is a clear statement of the meaning that the words were intended to carry. The days have long passed when the courts adopted a strict constructionist view of interpretation which required them to*

---

[6]   To adopt the old story from science, it might be an infinite regression of *Turtles, turtles all the way down*. See Professor Stephen Hawking, *A Brief History of Time* (1988).

[7]   Hence why Shakespeare is difficult when not read in Middle English and against the sociological, political and religious backdrop of the time.

adopt the literal meaning of the language. The courts now adopt a purposive approach which seeks to give effect to the true purpose of legislation and are prepared to look at much extraneous material that bears upon the background against which the legislation was enacted. **Why then cut ourselves off from the one source in which may be found an authoritative statement of the intention with which the legislation is placed before Parliament?**" (Emphasis added).

The flaw in this reasoning is that Hansard is not a perfect record of deliberations in Parliament. Hansard does not present as a verbatim transcript, with all the imperfections and repetitions of normal speech, and it is, therefore, not a completely authoritative record. It is an edited version of Parliamentary proceedings which are, in many cases, the result of *extempore* speeches rather than written submissions.[8] Nor would it assist if judges were provided with audio recordings or verbatim transcripts because there is still the problem of the silent minority. As anyone with experience of planning committees will know, many members vote without having taken part in the debate. Some simply abstain without giving reasons.

It is said that the intention of Parliament is an objective concept, not a subjective one, and is to be deduced from what the Court reasonably imputes to Parliament by virtue of the language used. This, slightly circular, argument was developed by Lord Nichols of Birkenhead in *R (On the application of Spath Holme Ltd) v SSETR* [2001] 2 A.C. 349 at pp 397–398:

> "*Statutory interpretation is an exercise which requires the court to identify the meaning borne by the words in question in the particular context. The task of the court is often said to be to ascertain the intention of Parliament expressed in the language under consideration. This is correct and may be helpful, so long as it is remembered that the 'intention of Parliament' is an objective concept, not subjective. The phrase is a shorthand reference to the intention which the court reasonably imputes to Parliament in respect of the language used. It is not the subjective intention of the minister or other persons who promoted the legislation. Nor is it the subjective intention of the draftsmen, or of individual members or even of a majority of individual members of either House. These individuals will often have widely varying intentions. Their understanding of the legislation and the words used may be impressively complete or woefully inadequate. Thus, when courts say that such and such a meaning 'cannot be what Parliament intended', they are saying only that the words under consideration cannot reasonably be taken as used by Parliament with that meaning. As Lord Reid said in Black-Clawson International Ltd v Papierwerke Waldhof-Aschaffenburg AG [1975] AC 591, 613: 'We often say that we are looking for the intention of Parliament, but that is not quite accurate. We are seeking the meaning of the words which Parliament used'.*"

---

[8] See *Judicial Ignorance of the Parliamentary Process Implications for statutory interpretation* – Daniel Greenberg, Judicial Power Project, March 2017 (https://judicialpowerproject.org.uk/daniel-greenberg-judicial-ignorance-of-the-parliamentary-process-implications-for-statutory-interpretation/). Nor is there some form of "*iambic pentametre*" to guide the tenor of spoken words which are transcribed into written form.

1.5   External aids to interpretation

If, notwithstanding the application of these basic rules of interpretation, the meaning of a statutory provision remains ambiguous then the Courts may, reluctantly, turn to sources outside the legislation itself. This is often called resorting to *"external aids to interpretation"* or *"extrinsic aids to interpretation"*. Clearly, this raises the question of whether or not external documents such as the National Planning Policy Framework and the National Planning Practice Guidance can be brought into play when seeking to construe the provisions of the 2021 Act.

In his lecture, Lord Justice Sales said:[9]

> *"With a re-balancing of statutory interpretation in favour of accommodating purpose and background understandings as against text, the arguments for recourse to interpretive aids outside the statute became correspondingly stronger. The courts now accept that reference to law commission and Governmental reports which provide guidance regarding purpose is legitimate; ..."*[10]

In *Pepper v Hart*, Lord Browne-Wilkinson said (page 634):

> *"In my judgment, subject to the questions of the privileges of the House of Commons, reference to Parliamentary material should be permitted as an aid to the construction of legislation which is ambiguous or obscure or the literal meaning of which leads to an absurdity. Even in such cases references in court to Parliamentary material should only be permitted where such material clearly discloses the mischief aimed at or the legislative intention lying behind the ambiguous or obscure words. In the case of statements made in Parliament,* **as at present advised I cannot foresee that any statement other than the statement of the Minister or other promoter of the Bill is likely to meet these criteria** *..."* (Emphasis added).

These references to antecedent documents are puzzling. To quote Sir John Laws again:

> *"12. ... But first – in principle – why should the Bill's promoters be the sole representatives of the intention of Parliament? What about other MPs who supported the Bill? As I have suggested, it is surely highly likely that the supporters of any Bill will have mixed motives and intentions, some more moved by the party whips than anything else. What about Members of Parliament who opposed the Bill, or abstained? The intention of the legislature is presumably supposed to be the intention of the legislature as a whole: the intention of Parliament, not the intention of this or that Member of Parliament."*

Be that as it may, it is sometimes appropriate to have regard to extrinsic aids in seeking to attribute meaning to statutory words.

---

[9]   Ibid.

[10]   *Black-Clawson International v Papierwerke AG* [1975] A.C. 591.

1.6   Existing legislation

For example, it may be possible to use existing legislation as an aid to interpretation. This is based on the premise that Parliament must be presumed to have been aware of the relevant pre-existing law when it passed an Act and would have sought consistency between statutes. This principle will encompass both the pre-existing legislation and also any relevant caselaw. This is particularly so when the Parliamentary draftsman was, clearly, gaining guidance from other legislation when drafting the provisions in question. It will be saying that those drafting the Environment Act had certain other legislation in mind when doing so. There are two (perhaps obvious) shortcomings in this approach.

First, it may be presumed that Parliament is omniscient and was not only aware of an open-ended provision but also inserted it intentionally, perhaps to provide flexibility and avoid over-prescription. This point may be seen by the discussion in paragraph 3.2 below.

Secondly, there is the argument that the apparently *"cognate"* legislation does not, on analysis, go to the same objective and, therefore, the context within which the word appears is different to that given by the Act which stands to be construed. This breaks down into two separate subheadings:

- If a new statute inserts wording into an existing statute, then it should be the case that the said new wording takes its meaning from the context provided by the existing statute into which it was inserted.[11] This is the approach which has been taken in this book in relation to those provisions of the Environment Act which have amended the Town and Country Planning Act 1990.

- If the new statute creates wording which, whilst it stands outside an existing statute, appears to relate to the scheme of the existing statute, then it might be the case that the highly technical concept expressed by the maxim *"in pari materia"* comes into play. If the words in the newer statute are open to different meanings, then the older provisions might be prayed in aid in construing the latter.[12] However, the courts are reluctant to resort to this principle, save in clear cases. It has been said that the *"in pari materia"* principle should be taken with *"a pinch of salt"*.[13]

1.7   Explanatory Notes

Turning to the Explanatory Notes which accompany the Act, and the extent to which they can be taken into account as external aids.

The first draft of a set of Explanatory Notes will be produced at the same time as the relevant Bill is introduced into Parliament, and they will follow the Bill as it goes through the Parliamentary process to its final adoption. If the Bill receives Royal Assent, a final

---

[11]   See discussion in *Nottingham County Council v Secretary of State for the Environment* [1986] 1 All E.R. 199.

[12]   See *Re MacManaway [1951] A.C. 161* and *Re Billison's Settlement Trusts* [1984] 2 All E.R. 401.

[13]   See *Littlewoods Mail Order Stores Limited v IRC* [1961] Ch 597 (CA).

copy of the Explanatory Notes will be published alongside the new Act. The Explanatory Notes to an Act are admissible aids to construction insofar as they cast light on the objective setting or contextual setting of the statute and the mischief at which it is aimed. However, the caselaw is unclear as to the precise application of this principle.

In *Westminster City Council v National Asylum Support Service* [2002] 1 W.L.R. 2956, Lord Steyn said (at para 6):

> *"What is impermissible is to treat the wishes and desires of the Government about the scope of the statutory language as reflecting the will of Parliament. The aims of the Government in respect of the meaning of clauses as revealed in the Explanatory Notes cannot be attributed to Parliament. The object is to see what is the intention expressed by the words enacted."*

However, in *Mucelli v Government of Albania* [2009] UKHL 2, Lord Rodger said (at para 9):

> *"... I pay no attention whatsoever to the explanatory notes as an indication of their meaning. In this case the notes do not identify the mischief behind the enactments. Nobody outside Government knows who drafted them, or revised them or on what basis. They cannot be regarded as any kind of authoritative guide as to the meaning of the provisions. The focus must be on the words of the provisions themselves."*

The point about the anonymous authorship of these notes is worth dwelling on. As will be discussed below, paragraphs 920 to 927 of the Explanatory Notes refer to section 102 of the 2021 Act. This has to do with the Natural Environment and Rural Communities Act 2006. Section 102 allegedly introduces a *"general duty to conserve and enhance biodiversity"*. Paragraph 920 of the Explanatory Notes states that section 102 *"makes textual amendments to section 40 of that Act, to avoid repeating definitions"*. Paragraph 923 of the notes then goes on to say:

> *"This extends the duty of public authorities beyond the NERC Act, which referred only to conservation, so that it includes the enhancement of biodiversity in England. The aim is to provide for enhancement or improvement of biodiversity, not just its maintenance in its current condition."*

The problem with these paragraphs from the Explanatory Notes is that they are, quite simply, wrong!

Section 40(1) of the 2006 Act provided that a public authority must, in exercising its functions, have regard, so far as is consistent with the proper exercise of those functions, *"to the purpose of <u>conserving</u> biodiversity"*. Section 40(3) goes on to provide that *"conserving biodiversity"* includes, in relation to a living organism or type of habitat, *restoring or enhancing* a population or habitat. Thus, the word *"conserving"* is a term of art with an extended meaning which includes restoration and enhancement, and it is completely wrong to say that section 40 of the 2006 Act is limited to conservation only or the maintenance of a site in its current condition.

Arguably, Explanatory Notes cannot be taken into account in the detailed interpretation of an Act as a matter of law, and they are of dubious accuracy in any event. Accordingly, it is submitted that they may be taken into account, albeit with a degree of circumspection and caution, in seeking to understand the broad purpose of the legislation.

1.8 *Ex post facto* materials

It is necessary to distinguish between the use of materials which pre-dated the Act and those which were produced after the legislative process had been concluded.

Documents which have been produced after the legislation has been passed should not, normally, be used as external aids to interpretation as such. It has been said that they do not enjoy any particular legal status and do not differ in their influence from a statement by an academic in a textbook or article. The force of the latter is derived, in part, from the reputation and experience of their authors and, in part, from the persuasiveness of their reasoning. And therein lies the problem with post-2021 statements about the Environment Act in both the National Planning Policy Framework and the National Planning Practice Guidance. This is to say that the authors of both of these documents are unknown. It might be argued that they should be given weight because they are drafted by civil servants employed in the relevant minister's department; however, they still remain as unnamed civil servants. If they are, indeed, lawyers, one is still left to ponder whether they have sufficient gravitas to assist experienced judges.

One clear exception is where the legislation uses technical words, the meanings of which may change from time to time as science or technology evolves. This is discussed below.

1.9 Antecedent or contemporary materials

In *Greenwich London Borough Council v Powell and Another* [1989] A.C. 995, the House of Lords had regard to a circular (Circular 28/77) issued by the Department of the Environment to local authorities in England in 1977, in tackling the question of whether a gypsy caravan site fell within the definition of "*protected site*" for the purposes of the Mobile Homes Act 1983. Lord Bridge of Harwich stated:

> *"The Bill which became the Act of 1983 was a Government Bill and it would be quite unrealistic not to recognise that the distinction between the two classes of site made in the statute must have been made with full knowledge of the policy which had been followed since 1970 with regard to the performance by local authorities of their duty under section 6 of the Act of 1968. That policy, whilst technically inadmissible as an aid to the construction of the definition of 'gipsies' in section 16 of the Act of 1968, is, in my opinion, fully cognizable as a powerful pointer to the intention of the legislature in excluding local authority sites 'providing accommodation for gipsies' from the definition of 'protected site' in the Act of 1983."*

R v SSE ex p Nottinghamshire CC [1986] A.C. 240 is an example of the *"contemporary exposition"* principle.[14] There the House of Lords had to tackle the phrase *"principles applicable to all local authorities"* in the Local Government, Planning and Land Act 1980 (as amended by the Local Government Finance Act 1982) and in connection with the Rate Support Grant. In part, the grant system involved setting expenditure targets for all local authorities for the coming year which they could then only exceed at risk of suffering a reduction in the amount they will receive by way of grant from central Government. Three local authorities thought their expenditure targets had been set at unfairly low levels. The Act of 1982 received Royal Assent on 13 July 1982. The Rate Support Grant Report for the year 1982–83 had been submitted to the House of Commons on 5 February 1982 and in due course approved by resolution of the House. That report referred to the anticipated enactment of section 8 of the Act of 1982, then embodied in a Bill before Parliament. One issue concerned whether reference could be made to the report. Lord Bridge of Harwich stated that it could:

> *"The point is a novel one and must, therefore, be determined by resort to principle. ... The reality is that the Rate Support Grant Report for 1982–83, which contained the relevant guidance and secured the approval of the House of Commons, was submitted to the House by the Secretary of State whose department was concurrently promoting the money Act which became the Act of 1982. Is there any principle which requires us to put on blinkers and ignore this reality? I know of none. If we can regard the reality, then it seems to me that, to the extent that the meaning of provisions given retrospective force is open to doubt, the nature of the guidance by reference to which those provisions will operate, having been set out in a report submitted to and approved by the House of Commons before the enactment of the statute, is available as a contemporanea expositio of the draftsman's purpose."*

1.10   Technical words

One need only glance at the Environment Act to see that it abounds with words and phrases which are technical terms of art. For example, the notion of an *"aerodynamic diameter"* in connection with particulate matter[15] in Part 4 of the Act is derived from those who measure air quality, but it can be confused with the use of the same expression by those who study the aerosol properties of medications and the like.[16]

Hence the need to have regard to the meanings of technical words in context. In 1881, Fry J stated:[17]

---

[14]   The Latin name being *"contemporanea expositio"*.

[15]   See Chapter 3 below.

[16]   The latter has nothing to do with a common-sense or legalistic idea of what the dimensions of such a material might be, because it is the description of a virtual particle which derives its properties from a real one, but not its shape.

[17]   See also Jessel M.R.; *Taylor v Corporation of St Helens* (1877) 6 Ch D 264, 270.

"If it is a word which is of a technical or scientific character then it must be construed according to that which is its primary meaning, namely, its technical or scientific meaning. But before you can give evidence of the secondary meaning of a word, you must satisfy the Court from the instrument itself or from the circumstances of the case that the word ought to be construed not in its popular or primary signification but according to its secondary intention."[18]

1.11   Hortative words

Some statutory provisions that might appear, at first blush, to be merely hortative might be found to impose an enforceable duty.

The classic case, for those in practice in the 1980s, must be *Steinberg v Secretary of State* (1988). This turned on what is now section 72 of the Planning (Listed Buildings and Conservation Areas) Act 1990, and what is now called the *"conservation area test"*.

It is possible to find current statutory provisions which fall on either side of the line.

Section 40 of the Natural Environment and Rural Communities Act 2006 bears a striking similarity to the tenor of the *"conservation area test"*.

The message would appear to be that something which appears in statute might not be as robust as one might believe. In many cases, provisions are hortative and not intended to be enforced through the Courts. With others, they are dependent on delivery by administrative means. Some are directly enforceable. There is nothing wrong with this division of labour, but it is important that those who place weight on statute are aware of it so that their expectations match the reality.

1.12   The effect of international treaties

Many of the concepts which arise in the context of environmental law have their roots in the domestic application of international treaties. The provisions of the Environment Act are no different, and so it is important to consider the principles which apply to the treatment of treaty obligations within domestic law. Of course, the UK has withdrawn from the European Union; however, it does not follow that all treaty obligations with European countries have thereby been dispensed with.

The application of international law is, not surprisingly, an extremely complex topic and this chapter can merely touch on it.

The interpretation of domestic legislation in the light of treaties is discussed by Lowe and Potter:[19]

---

[18]   Per Fry J in *Holt & Co v Collyer* (1881) 16 Ch D 718, at p 720.

[19]   David Lowe and Charlie Potter, *Understanding Legislation: A Practical Guide to Statutory Interpretation* (Hart Publishing, 2018).

"[920] It is important to note that, even when treaty provisions have by legislation been incorporated into or otherwise given effect in English law, it is not the treaty provisions of cells which form part of domestic law, only the domestic legislation ...

[921] Nevertheless, rules of international law can have a very significant effect on the interpretation of domestic legislation. ... they have effect in particular through: (i) the presumption of conformity; (ii) the presumption of compatibility; and (iii) contributing more generally to the context in which legislation falls to be interpreted. ..."

In *R (Adams) v Secretary of State for Justice* [2011] UKSC 18, it was stated that there is a presumption that, where a statute is passed in order to give effect to the obligations of the United Kingdom and there is an international convention, the statute should be given a meaning that conforms to that of the convention: per Lord Phillips. This principle applies where the statute in question is reasonably capable of bearing that meaning; however, it cannot apply where the expression in domestic legislation is cast in terms which clearly and unambiguously differ from the meaning ascribed to it by a treaty obligation: see *SerVaas Inc v Rafidain Bank* [2010] EWHC 3287 (Ch). Arguably, the meaning of *"biodiversity"* may be influenced by the definition of that term in the Rio Declaration of 1992 (see Chapter 4). As noted above, this word is not defined in the Environment Act itself. Notwithstanding, it is reasonably capable of bearing the meaning given by the Rio Declaration[20] without doing any great violence to the word or compromising the use of the word within the Act itself.

The *"presumption of compatibility"* expresses the, possibly, self-evident proposition that it is presumed that Parliament does not intend to legislate in conflict with the UK's international obligations unless it does so in very clear terms.

As to the notion of contribution to context, a number of cases support reference to international obligations when seeking to construe UK domestic legislation: see *R (Carson) v Secretary of State for Work and Pensions* [2005] UKHL 37. Again, however, this type of exercise is viable only where the domestic legislation is, in some way, in need of interpretation beyond that which is otherwise obvious in the plain words of the statute itself.

The obvious problem is that treaty obligations are usually cast in high-level language and so may be misused if applied in the determination of ordinary planning applications. There is, also, the dilemma which may be created by a planning committee seeking to *"double-count"* treaty obligations which have, already, been crystalised in national planning policy or statute. Ergo, these difficult legal matters are best left to the Courts.

---

[20]   Deriving from the UN Conference on Environment and Development, Rio de Janeiro, Brazil, 3-14 June 1991: see paragraph 3.2 below.

Chapter 2

Territorial Extent

This book is concerned with the provisions of the 2021 Act which apply to England and Wales only. Notwithstanding, it is worthwhile to note the overall territorial extent of the provisions of the Act. These are set out in section 146 and summarised by the Explanatory Notes (pages 24 to 25).

The extent of an Act is the legal jurisdiction where it forms part of the law. The extent of an Act can be different from its application. Application refers to where it has practical effect.

Subject to a small number of exceptions, the Act forms part of the law of England and Wales and applies to England. About half of the Act's provisions extend and apply to Wales with a significant number of provisions extending to Great Britain, the UK or England, Wales and Northern Ireland. Sections 48, 59, 61, 65, 67, 71, 91 and Schedule 2 form part of the law of Northern Ireland and apply to Northern Ireland only. Sections 90 and 95 apply to Wales only.

Chapter 3

Overarching Principles

3.1   Introduction

Part 1 of the Environment Act sets out a number of overarching principles which relate to environmental improvement policies and governance and, in particular, improving the natural environment. Many of these may interact with town and country planning, and it is likely that the achievement of the environmental targets set out in them will be material considerations in the determination of planning applications. This is to say, a development scheme which will promote any of these objectives should, thereby, gain additional credit when the balancing exercise is carried out in evaluating the application. For example, section 2(1) provides that the Secretary of State must set a target for particulate matter in the ambient air and it should be the case that, if an application goes to the reduction of particulate matter in the air, then this benefit should carry additional weight because it will go to a national objective. Notwithstanding this, there is little point in studying the specific provisions for property developments within the Act without, first, gaining an understanding of the broad conceptual context within which they have been introduced.

3.2   What is "*biodiversity*"?

It is sensible to start this chapter with a basic question, namely "*What is 'biodiversity'?*". There is little point in repeatedly using the expression without gaining an understanding of what it means and how it may be crystallised for the purposes of administrative actions. It follows that one needs to get this on the table at the outset.

The expression "*biodiversity*" comes up repeatedly in discussions of the topic areas which are of concern in connection with the Act. Somewhat surprisingly, the Act does not, itself, provide any form of definition of the phrase.[1] The meaning of "*biodiversity*" is left as open-ended. Arguably, there is something very odd about an Act of Parliament, which, in its preamble, states that it is making provision for "*biodiversity*", but then does not go on to explain the meaning it attributes to this otherwise ambiguous word for the purposes of the Act.[2] It is, therefore, necessary to examine it by reference to external sources.

This devolves into three separate tasks for the property practitioner. First, finding a workable legal description of "*biodiversity*". Secondly, finding a way of measuring biodiversity or, in the absence of direct measurements, finding a reasonable proxy. Finally, attributing

---

[1]   Albeit, the Act is not alone in so doing. The word comes up in a number of statutes without any discernible description of what it is intended to mean – for example, the Natural Environment and Rural Communities Act 2006, the Marine and Coastal Access Act 2009, the Wildlife and Natural Environment Act 2011, the Localism Act 2011 and the Environment (Wales) Act 2016.

[2]   Given that, for all practical purposes, the Secretary of State was the sponsor for the Environment Bill during its very long gestation period, it might be argued that he had every opportunity to seek to come to grips with defining this central concept in the Bill instead of leaving it at large.

relative values to the various constituent elements of a biota[3] when set against any degradation which may result from a proposed development scheme.[4] None of this is particularly straightforward.

It might appear that assistance can be gained from apparently cognate legislation. Section 40(3) of the Natural Environment and Rural Communities Act 2006 provides a partial definition: *"Conserving biodiversity includes, in relation to a living organism or type of habitat, restoring or enhancing a population or habitat"*. Amendments to the Wildlife and Countryside Act 1981 introduced a definition of *"species"* in new Schedule 9A; namely, to mean *"any kind of animal or plant"*. By contrast, section 58 of the Nature Conservation (Scotland) Act 2004 provides an attractive definition of *"biodiversity"* as having the same meaning as *"biological diversity"* in the United Nations Environmental Programme Convention on Biological Diversity of 5 June 1992 as amended from time to time (or in any United Nations Convention replacing that Convention).[5] However, such assistance might be of limited value when it comes to interpreting the Act and three observations can be made. First, it may be presumed that Parliament is omniscient and was not only aware of the omission but did so intentionally, perhaps to provide flexibility and avoid over-prescription. This argument gains weight from the fact that the notion of *"biodiversity"* is a new one and definitions may vary and change from time to time. Secondly, there is the argument that the apparently *"cognate"* legislation does, on analysis, go to a different objective and, therefore, the context within which the word appears is different from that given by the Act. Finally, the two preceding observations might be mitigted by the fact that, so far as is reasonable, the Courts will continue domestic legislation so as to accord with obligations in international treaties. These points are discussed in more detail in paragraphs 1.6 and 1.12 in Chapter 1 above.

As to non-legal definitions, Spicer[6] has this to say: *"There are a number of reasonable definitions of biodiversity – over 80 of them in fact! Many have merit or offer a slightly different take on the notion."*

The difficulty in finding a meaning for this word is compounded by the fact that it is a relatively new one. For example, the somewhat massive[7] compact edition of the Oxford English Dictionary, which was compiled up to 1971, does not mention the word at all. Likewise, it does not appear in the Oxford Reference Dictionary which was published in 1986.[8]

---

[3] The simple definition of a *"biota"* is the flora and fauna of a region: per Merriam-Webster. If one adds the temporal dimension, this can be expanded to the types of plant and animal life found in specific regions at a specific time or the organisms that occupy an ecological niche or ecosystem at a particular time.

[4] And, of course, for measuring *"biodiversity net gain"* where this is required of a developer (see below).

[5] Article 2: *"the variability among living organisms from all sources including, inter alia, terrestrial, marine and other aquatic ecosystems and the ecological complexes of which they are part: this includes diversity within species, between species and of ecosystems"*: see below. See also the Handbook of the Convention on Biological Diversity - including its Cartagena Protocol on Biosafety 3rd edition - Secretariat of the Convention on Biological Diversity (2005).

[6] John Spicer in *Biodiversity: A Beginners Guide (revised and updated edition) (Beginners Guides)* (One World, May 2021). This book provides a useful introduction to this topic (notwithstanding that there is a quotation from Greta Thunberg at the beginning).

[7] My copy runs to over 4,000 pages!

[8] Oxford University Press, 1986.

The origin of the word appears to be attributable to Walter G Rosen,[9] when seeking a generic name for the *"National Forum on BioDiversity"*, which was held in Washington, DC, in 1986, under the auspices of the National Academy of Sciences and Smithsonian Institution.

Spicer states: *"Fortunately, there is one definition that has gained international currency, signed by up to 150 nations that put together the Convention on Biological Diversity at Rio de Janeiro, Brazil, in 1992"*. This is one of the documents produced by the UN Earth Summit[10] in 1992 and entitled *"Convention on Biological Diversity"*, which defined *"biological diversity"* as meaning:

> *"the variability among living organisms from all sources including, inter alia, terrestrial, marine and other aquatic ecosystems and the ecological complexes of which they are part: this includes diversity within species, between species and of ecosystems."*

In 2004, Hamilton[11] had this to say:

> *"Species diversity and biodiversity are widely used terms in ecology and natural resource management. Despite this, they are not easily defined and different authors apply these terms with varying connotations. The term biodiversity, in particular, has the dubious honour of being widely used but rarely defined. Is it simply the number of species or is it something more?."*

The book *"Ecology: From Individuals to Ecosystems"*[12] stated, in 2006:

> *"The term biodiversity makes frequent appearances in both the popular media and the scientific literature – but it often does so without an unambiguous definition. At its simplest, biodiversity is synonymous with species richness. Biodiversity, though, can also be viewed at scales smaller and larger than the species. For example, we may include genetic diversity within species, recognising the value of conserving genetically distinct sub-populations and sub-species. Above the species level, we may wish to ensure that species without close relatives are afforded special protection, so that the overall evolutionary variety of the world's biota is maintained as large as possible. At a larger scale still, we may include in biodiversity the variety of community types present in a region – swamps, deserts, early and late stages in a woodland succession and so on. Thus 'biodiversity' may itself, quite reasonably, have a diversity of meanings. **Yet it is necessary to be specific, if the term is to be of any practical use.**"*
> (Emphasis added).

---

9   Senior Program Officer in the Board on Basic Biology – a unit of the USA's Commission on Life Sciences, National Research Council/National Academy of Sciences.

10   The United Nations Conference on Environment and Development, Rio de Janeiro, Brazil, 3–14 June 1992 (aka the *"Rio Conference"*).

11   Hamilton, A J (2005) *Species diversity or biodiversity? Journal of Environmental Management*, 75(1):89–92.

12   Begon, Townsend and Harper *Ecology: From Individuals to Ecosystems* (Fourth Edition) (Blackwell Publishing, 2006), page 602.

The discussion within the relevant chapter is then narrowed to species richness.

It might, quite reasonably, be argued that the purpose of the Act is to make the term *"biodiversity"* of practical use and that, therefore, it was necessary to be specific when inserting this wording into the legislation. It might be the case that the Secretary of State will provide guidance on the point; however, this runs the risk of being excluded from the interpretation of the statute on the basis that it is *ex post facto* external evidence: see Chapter 1. It might be that some clue can be gained from the definition of *"natural environment"* in section 44 of the Environment Act; not least because it is close to the definition *"biological diversity"* in the UN Convention cited above. This means plants, wild animals and other living organisms, their habitats, land (except buildings or other structures), air and water, and the natural systems, cycles and processes through which they interact. But the interpretational difficulty lies in the fact that the phrase *"natural environment"* is used in a very specific way elsewhere in the Act and it is arguable that it should not be stretched to cover other provisions, even as an aid to interpretation.

Be that as it may, it might be that this word could be described as being a technical one, which allows the introduction of external evidence when it comes to the interpretation of it: see Chapter 1 above. If so, then there are a number of high-level publications which offer their varying opinions as to the ambit of this subject. For example, the United Nations Environment Programme document *"What is Biodiversity?"* (February 2010)[13] states:

> *"However, the word 'Biodiversity' is relatively new, and is thought to have first been coined as a contraction of the term 'biological diversity' in 1985 and then popularised by a number of authors.*
>
> *Biodiversity is the variety of life on Earth, it includes all organisms, species, and populations; the genetic variation among these; and their complex assemblages of communities and ecosystems. It also refers to the interrelatedness of genes, species, and ecosystems and in turn, their interactions with the environment.*
>
> *Three levels of biodiversity are commonly discussed – genetic, species and ecosystem diversity.*
>
> *1. Genetic diversity is all the different genes contained in all the living species, including individual plants, animals, fungi, and microorganisms.*
>
> *2. Species diversity is all the different species, as well as the differences within and between different species.*
>
> *3. Ecosystem diversity is all the different habitats, biological communities and ecological processes, as well as variation within individual ecosystems."*

---

[13]   https://www.unesco.pl/fileadmin/user_upload/pdf/BIODIVERSITY_FACTSHEET.pdf.

The 2018 publication on behalf of the Department for Environment, Food and Rural Affairs entitled "*A Green Future: Our 25 Year Plan to Improve the Environment*" states (at page 58):

> "*Biological diversity, or 'Biodiversity', is* **simply** *the variety of life on Earth – the variety of ecosystems or habitats, of species and of the genetic diversity they contain. We value wildlife in its own right but biodiversity also underpins much of the economic and social benefit we gain from nature.*" (Emphasis added).

Many might say that there is no "*simply*" about it and that this is a matter of considerable complexity and refinement: see above. At first glance, this formulation might seem to follow on from the Rio Declaration; however, the tail-piece is a departure: "*but biodiversity also underpins much of the economic and social benefit we gain from nature*". These words introduce a troublesome ethnocentric element which invokes the somewhat contentious notion of "*natural capital*", and the "*accounting*" of it, in notional monetary terms, when proposed development schemes are assessed by way of a cost-benefit approach.

At page 146, the document states that:

> "*Housing and infrastructure developers can invest in habitat creation projects as a cost-effective way of fulfilling their obligations to compensate for habitat loss under the National Policy Planning Framework. Natural England's metric does this by converting damage to biodiversity into a comparable unit.*"

As the discussion of the Biodiversity Metric in Chapter 9 will disclose, this is a loose use of language in a document of national import: see below. The metric does not convert "*damage to biodiversity into a comparable unit*", but provides for habitats only.

There are further publications, but it is questionable whether they would be admissible in the Courts or as to the weight to be attributed to them in the determination of planning applications and in public inquiries

The fulsome document which was published on behalf of the Department for Environment, Food and Rural Affairs and entitled "*Biodiversity 2020: A strategy for England's wildlife and ecosystem services*" does not provide a concise definition, but it might be argued that the ambit of the phrase is readily drawn from a reading of the document as a whole.

Finally, there is another publication, again on behalf of the Department for Environment, Food and Rural Affairs, entitled "*UK Biodiversity Indicators 2021 Revised*" and compiled by the Joint Nature Conservation Committee,[14] which provides a concise definition as follows:

> "*Biodiversity is the variety of all life on Earth: genes, species and ecosystems. It includes all species of animals and plants, and the natural systems that support them. Biodiversity*

---

[14] This document, with additional supporting data and text, is available to be downloaded on the Joint Nature Conservation Committee website: jncc.gov.uk/ukbi.

> *matters because it supports the vital benefits humans get from the natural environment.*
> *It contributes to the economy, health and well-being, and it enriches our lives.*"[15]

The document contains a wealth of information; but, again, one has to ask how it would be received in the Courts or in public inquiries.

Section 4(1) of the Act provides that, before making regulations under sections 1 to 3, the Secretary of State must seek advice from persons whom the Secretary of State considers to be independent and to have relevant expertise. Thus it might be the case that this will be the point of entry for extra-statutory interpretational materials.

Drawing these threads together, it is probably safe to say that "*biodiversity*" can properly be described for working purposes as being composed of the following:

- **Genetic diversity**: all the different genes contained in all living species, including individual plants, animals, fungi, and micro-organisms.

- **Species diversity**: all the different species, as well as the differences within and between different species.

- **Ecosystem diversity**: all the different habitats, biological communities and ecological processes, as well as variation within individual ecosystems.

This sounds reasonable for a working description, but then this leads to the matter of measurement.

In his article "*Quantifying biodiversity*",[16] Buckland[17] referred to the 2002 World Summit on Sustainable Development in Johannesburg, where nearly 200 nations agreed to strive for "*a significant reduction in the current rate of loss of biological diversity*" by 2010 and said:

> "*What the summit did not address is how to determine whether its objective gets met. How can you find a meaningful number that represents biodiversity?*"

Therein lies the dilemma. His summary included the following comments:

> "*The monitoring of regional trends in biodiversity is in its infancy. No doubt the 2010 target will be met for some ecological communities and not for others, but we are unlikely to be able to tell the hits from the misses: very few nations will be in a*

---

[15]   Page 2.

[16]   https://rss.onlinelibrary.wiley.com/doi/full/10.1111/j.1740-9713.2009.00371.x.

[17]   Steve Buckland is Professor of Statistics at the University of St Andrews and Co-Director of the National Centre for Statistical Ecology. His research interests include "*computer-intensive statistical methods, wildlife resource management and biodiversity monitoring*".

position to demonstrate that the target has been met even for one [ecological] community let alone for [ecological] communities in general.

Given the diversity of measures that are readily evaluated using inappropriate data, many nations will claim to have met the target by careful selection of trend estimates. However, in true Darwinian style, better schemes will evolve. Some existing schemes will become extinct and others will mutate to become more successful and relevant. The process will be slow and painful and many will use statistical arguments to resist change. The most compelling of these is that long time series of data should not be compromised by changing the scheme. The BTO[18] addressed this when they replaced the CBC[19] with the BBS[20] by having the schemes operate in parallel from 1994 to 2000. This allowed them to calibrate one against the other and to assess whether species trends were comparable for the two schemes.

The BBS showed that it is possible to monitor changes in biodiversity for birds, effectively and economically, over areas as large as nation states. It is an encouraging example. What can be done for birds can be done for other species. Where there is a will there is a way."

Spicer states:[21]

"This sounds quite satisfying until we ask the million-dollar question. The question that reveals the extent to which the study of biodiversity is a science: how do we measure it? This is not so straightforward. And yet it goes to the very heart of what we mean when we talk about biodiversity or when we refer to the biodiversity of a particular area, country or region."

Spicer then goes on to give the example of a rocky shore called *"Bird Rock"* which is part of a Marine Conservation Area at La Jolla, north of San Diego in California: *"Here we have life, and life in abundance"*. He then went on to ask how one could measure biodiversity at Bird Rock:

"Could simply counting how many different types of living things there are do? This sounds like a possibility – but it's no mean task. It could potentially take not just weeks and months but years, even for such a small area – and that's leaving out all of the land animals, plants and microbes that form the larger landscape that is La Jolla."

One compounding problem is, of course, that populations tend to fluctuate, either by season or as they react to changes in their habitats.

---

18   The British Trust for Ornithology (BTO).
19   The Common Birds Census (CBC).
20   The UK Breeding Bird Survey (BBS).
21   Ibid page 5.

This discussion brings us back to the original questions relating to framing these complicated and extensive topics in such a way that, when a proposed development is in contemplation, those involved in the process of bringing it forward have the ability to bring some measurability and objectivity to the exercise. Clearly, the importation of a mechanism for doing so will also allow those who have an extrinsic interest in the proposed project (for example, local residents, or nature conservation groups) to access and interrogate the materials which have been brought into play in the administrative processes.

The harsh reality is that no economically viable mechanism could possibly capture all of the ecological information which could be derived from a particular biota which may be affected by a proposed development, and so it is necessary to reduce the matter to the adoption of a proxy or series of proxies. So far as development control is concerned, the Biodiversity Metric is a system which measures habitat and then takes habitat as being a proxy for those other aspects of biodiversity which may adopt the given habitat. More controversially, this metrication of habitat types provides a basis for the system of ecological trading by way of a biodiversity credit system. But the Biodiversity Metric does not stand alone, in that there is extensive legislation relating to the conservation and protection of sensitive habitats which, again, goes to the habitat, as opposed to the relevant biota as a whole.[22] None of these comments should be viewed as criticisms because one has to operate in the real world, and this means having proper regard to hard constraints such as finances and the expenditure of time.

3.3   The "*long-term*" targets

Section 1 of the Act provides that the Secretary of State *may*, by regulations, set "*long-term targets*"[23] in respect of any matter which relates to the "*natural environment*" or "*people's* (sic) enjoyment of the natural environment.*"[24]

The use of the word "*may*" in section 1 makes this a statutory discretion, and not a duty; however, section 1(2) goes on to provide that the Secretary of State *must* exercise the power in subsection (1) so as to set a long-term target in respect of at least one matter within each "*priority area*", and this is a statutory duty. By section 1(4) a target set under this section must specify:

(a)   a standard to be achieved, which must be capable of being objectively measured (the "*specified standard*"),[25] and

---

[22]   See Chapters 8, 9 and 10 below.

[23]   15 years – see below. The Government has, at time of writing, commenced a consultation process in respect of the environmental targets within the Act. This consultation started on 16 March 2022 and closed on 11 May 2022. See https://consult.defra.gov.uk/natural-environment-policy/consultation-on-environmental-targets/consultation/subpage.2022-03-15.6135362752/.

[24]   By section 44, the "*natural environment*" means plants, wild animals and other living organisms, their habitats, land (except buildings or other structures), air and water, and the natural systems, cycles and processes through which they interact.

[25]   Section 1(8).

(b)   a date by which it is to be achieved (the "*specified date*").[26]

A target is a "*long-term*" target if the specified date is no less than 15 years after the date on which the target is initially set: section 1(6).

The "*priority areas*" are air quality, water, biodiversity, resource efficiency and waste reduction: section 1(3). The phrases "*air quality*" and "*biodiversity*" are not defined and this observation raises significant matters of interpretation.

The phrase "*air quality*" is open-ended and so need not be limited to air-borne particulate matter. This leaves the question of what might or might not be included under the rubric "*air quality*" within this section. The first point would appear to be that "*air quality*" should be construed as relating back to the overarching provision in section 1(1); that is to say, it should relate to the natural environment or people's enjoyment of the natural environment, and this begs the question of whether it should be construed to include gases and particulates which may directly affect human beings or impact on climate change. In particular, of course, there is the question of whether "*air quality*" in this connection includes emissions of carbon dioxide and other gases which are said to be associated with global warming.

Section 1(4) provides that a target set under this section must specify a standard to be achieved, which must be capable of being objectively measured, and a date by which it is to be achieved. Section 1(5) provides that regulations under this section may make provision about how the matter in respect of which a target is set is to be measured. These provisions would seem to go to matters of quantification and measurement rather than allowing the Secretary of State to make regulations which define what is and is not to be measured. Accordingly, it is difficult to know whether these regulations will attempt to provide some particularity to the generic expression "*biodiversity*"; if, indeed, this exercise falls within the rule-making power of the Secretary of State under this provision in any event.

Be that as it may, the notion that a target set under these provisions must specify a standard to be achieved, which must be capable of being objectively measured, opens up the question of how these matters can be objectively measured in real life and on a national scale.

3.4   The "*air quality*" target

Turning to particular provisions relating to air quality, section 2(1) of the Act provides that the Secretary of State *must* by regulations set a target for particulate matter (the "*$PM_{2.5}$ air quality target*") in respect of the annual mean level of $PM_{2.5}$ in ambient air.[27] The use of the word "*must*" makes this a mandatory duty.

---

[26]   Section 1(8).

[27]   By section 2(3), "*$PM_{2.5}$*" means particulate matter with an "*aerodynamic diameter*" not exceeding 2.5 micrometres, but "*ambient air*" is not defined. This also begs the further question of what is meant by "*aerodynamic diameter*".

The key distinction between section 1 and section 2 on this point is that, in section 2, the $PM_{2.5}$ air quality target may, but need not, be a long-term target unless it is selected as a priority area for section 1(2): see section 2(2). This duty is in addition to (and does not discharge) the duty in section 1(2) to set a long-term target in relation to air quality: section 2(5).

The regulations setting the $PM_{2.5}$ air quality target may make provision defining *"ambient air"*. The meaning of *"ambient air"* can be contentious because it will determine those areas which are within and outwith the input data for the specified target. The current definition is in the Air Quality Standards Regulations 2010 (S.I. 2010/1001):

> *"'Ambient air' means outdoor air in the troposphere[28] excluding workplaces where members of the public do not have regular access."*

To put it another way, workplaces and construction sites are not included. This is despite the fact that they are major sources of air pollution. If the regulations made by the Secretary of State do not include construction sites, it is arguable that local planning authorities may have to fill the gap – for example, where a house building site is proceeding in stages and incoming residents may be moving into dwellings as the scheme is progressing.

It is the duty of the Secretary of State to ensure that targets set under section 1 are met, that the $PM_{2.5}$ air quality target set under section 2 is met and that the *"species abundance"* environmental target (see below) is met: section 5.

3.5 The *"species abundance"* target

Section 3 provides for a *"species abundance"* environmental target. By section 3(1), the Secretary of State *must* by regulations set a target (the *"species abundance"* target) in respect of a matter relating to the abundance of species. There are a number of interpretational points in this subsection.

First, the use of the phrase *"in respect of a matter"* is difficult to construe. Presumably, the intent is that the *"matter"* in question is intended to mean something which furthers species abundance. This flexibility of meaning is important in the interpretation of the statutory provision, because a *"matter"* could include, for example, the provision of a favourable habitat, as opposed to something which relates directly to the specie itself.

Secondly, there is the question of what is meant by the phrase *"species abundance"* in any event. Presumably, this phrase was intended to relate to the enhancement of a specie to be specified by regulations; however, this leads to something of a knot in terms of ecological science. One of the points being, and it is an obvious one, is that the favouring of one specie over another within a given habitat may have the result of reducing the resources available to all species within the habitat, thereby having an impact which goes beyond the favoured specie. This is to say, the precursor to carrying out a strategy which favours a

---

[28] The troposphere is the lowest portion of the atmosphere. This layer contains most of the Earth's clouds and is the location where weather primarily occurs: www.britannica.com/science/atmosphere/troposphere.

particular specie should be an assessment of the ecological capacity of the relevant habitat in question. Ergo, this is a site-specific exercise, which evaluates habitats individually (as opposed to *en masse*), and leads to the comment that it is difficult to see how this duty is suited to nationally applicable regulations.

As to the specification of targets, the lead document might be a revision of "*UK Biodiversity Indicators 2021 Revised*"[29] which states:

> "*it is expected that these will be agreed in spring 2022 ... To allow for a thorough review of these indicators it is anticipated that there will be a pause in publication in 2022, with the next update in 2023.*"

The specified delivery date for the species abundance target is 31 December 2030: section 3(2).

The species abundance target is not a long-term target, and the duty in section 3(1) is in addition to (and does not discharge) the duty in section 1(2) to set a long-term target in relation to biodiversity: section 3(3). By way of an interpretational point relating to the meaning of the word "*biodiversity*" within the context of the Act, this "*for the avoidance of doubt*" coda might suggest that the draftsman had species diversity in mind when referring to species abundance which, in turn, might suggest that species diversity falls within the contemplation of "*biodiversity*" as a priority area in section 1(3).

By section 4(9), drafts of statutory instruments containing regulations setting each of the targets required by section 1(2), the $PM_{2.5}$ air quality target, and the species abundance target, must be laid before Parliament on or before 31 October 2022.

3.6 Environmental improvement plans

The Act requires the Secretary of State to prepare and maintain an "*environmental improvement plan*" and creates a new statutory cycle of monitoring, planning and reporting to ensure continuing improvement to the environment.

An "*environmental improvement plan*" is a plan for significantly improving the "*natural environment*"[30] in the period to which the plan relates: section 8(2). An environmental improvement plan must set out the steps which the Government intends to take to improve the natural environment in the period to which the plan relates: section 8(4). It may also set out steps which the Government intends to take to improve people's enjoyment of the natural environment in that period (and, if it does so, references in this Part of the Act to

---

[29] https://data.jncc.gov.uk/data/31925413-3fa4-4382-962f-6ac2c168d542/ukbi2021-summary-booklet.pdf.

[30] By section 44, the "*natural environment*" means plants, wild animals and other living organisms, their habitats, land (except buildings or other structures), air and water, and the natural systems, cycles and processes through which they interact.

improving the natural environment, in relation to that plan, include improving people's enjoyment of it): section 8(5).[31]

The first environmental improvement plan will be the document called "*A green future: our 25 year plan to improve the environment*"[32] which was published on 11 January 2018: section 8(7). The environmental improvement plan sets out a key commitment to develop a comprehensive set of indicators, which collectively describes environmental change as it relates to 10 thematic goals (Page 10). These goals relate to:

(1)   Clean air.

(2)   Clean and plentiful water.

(3)   Thriving plants and wildlife.

(4)   A reduced risk of harm from environmental hazards such as flooding and drought.

(5)   Using resources from nature more sustainably and efficiently.

(6)   Enhanced beauty, heritage and engagement with the natural environment.

(7)   Mitigating and adapting to climate change.

(8)   Minimising waste.

(9)   Managing exposure to chemicals.

(10) Enhancing biosecurity.

The plan should now be read alongside the daughter document entitled "*Measuring Environmental Change: Outcome Indicator Framework for the 25 Year Environment Plan*"[33] and contains 66 indicators, arranged into 10 broad themes. This document states (page 2):

> "*The indicators will be used to check progress towards the long-term vision of the 25 Year Environment Plan. The framework was developed using the concept of natural capital. Natural capital is defined as the 'elements of the natural environment which provide valuable goods and services to people such as clean air, clean water, food and recreation'. The framework focuses on the outcomes and goals that we have set out to achieve. These outcomes and goals can be grouped together under: 1) reducing pressures*

---

[31]   The phrase "*improving the natural environment*", in relation to an environmental improvement plan, is to be read in accordance with section 8(5): section 47.

[32]   Published on behalf of Defra.

[33]   Published on behalf of Defra in 2019.

on natural capital (e.g. pollution or plant disease); 2) improving the state of natural capital assets (including air, water, land and seas); and 3) increasing the benefits that we get from those assets."

No doubt this document, and succeeding indicators, will be prayed in aid in respect of planning applications, but it is important to note that it goes on to say (page 2):

"The indicators within this framework are not targets, and they do not have specific end points, levels or trajectories attached to them. They are a way to monitor the changes happening in the environment and they enable us to then ensure we are taking appropriate action."

The first review of this first environmental improvement plan must be completed by 31 January 2023: section 10(3).

The Government produced a progress report on 11 June 2020.[34] The report describes progress made towards the 10 goals set out in the plan over the period between April 2019 and March 2020. For the purposes of this book, it is notable that the progress report addresses high-level indicators and, as such, might be of limited relevance to site-specific planning applications.

The Secretary of State must prepare annual reports on the implementation of the current environmental improvement plan: section 9(1).

On the first review of the first environmental improvement plan, the Secretary of State must set at least one interim target in respect of each *"relevant matter"*[35] and secure that there is, at all times until the end of the five-year period beginning with the *"relevant date"*,[36] an interim target set by the plan in respect of each relevant matter.

3.7   Policy Statement on Environmental Principles

The Act provides for *"environmental principles"* to protect the environment from damage by making environmental considerations central to the policy development process across Government. The principles work together to legally oblige policy-makers to consider choosing policy options which cause the least environmental harm. This means that, when making policy, Ministers of the Crown must have the correct level of regard to the content of the *"Policy Statement on Environmental Principles"*.

---

[34] *25 Year Environment Plan Progress Report, April 2019 to March 2020* (11 June 2020): https://assets.publishing. service.gov.uk/government/uploads/system/uploads/attachment_data/file/891783/25yep-progress-report-2020. pdf.

[35] A *"relevant matter"* means any matter in respect of which there is a target under sections 1 to 3: section 14(2)..

[36] The *"relevant date"* is the first day of the period to which the new plan relates: section 14(7).

Section 17(1) provides that the Secretary of State must prepare a *"Policy Statement on Environmental Principles"*. By section 17(5), the *"environmental principles"* means the following principles:

(a)   The principle that environmental protection should be integrated into the making of policies.

(b)   The principle of preventative action to avert environmental damage.

(c)   The precautionary principle, so far as relating to the environment.

(d)   The principle that environmental damage should, as a priority, be rectified at source.

(e)   The *"polluter pays"* principle.

This policy statement will explain how the environmental principles should be interpreted and proportionately applied by Ministers of the Crown when making policy: section 17(2). It may also explain how Ministers of the Crown, when interpreting and applying the environmental principles, should take into account other considerations relevant to their policy:[37] section 17(3). The Secretary of State must be satisfied that the statement will, when it comes into effect, contribute to the improvement of environmental protection, and sustainable development.

Furthermore, a Minister of the Crown must, when making policy, have due regard to the Policy Statement on Environmental Principles currently in effect: section 19(1).

> *"The legal duty is for Ministers of the Crown to 'have regard' to the policy statement. This means that Ministers of the Crown must consider the relevance of the policy statement for their given policy area and assess whether the policy statement applies."*[38]

The policy statement does not require Ministers to take, or refrain from taking, any action that would have no significant environmental benefit, or if the environmental benefit would be disproportionate when compared to other factors: section 19(2).

---

[37]   The word *"policy"* includes proposals for legislation, but does not include an administrative decision taken in relation to a particular person or case (for example, a decision on an application for planning permission, funding or a licence, or a decision about regulatory enforcement); and *"making policy"* includes developing, adopting or revising policy: section 47.

[38]   *Information paper on the policy statement on Environmental Principles* (December 2018), Department for Environment, Food and Rural Affairs: https://assets.publishing.service.gov.uk/government/uploads/system/uploads/attachment_data/file/766299/env-bill-information-paper.pdf.

Chapter 4

The *"Trickle-Down"* Effect

4.1 Introduction

The Policy Statement on Environmental Principles does not extend the determination of individual planning applications.

Section 47 of the Environment Act provides that administrative decisions taken in relation to a particular person or case (for example, a decision on an application for planning permission, funding or a licence, or a decision about regulatory enforcement) are not matters of *"policy"*.

This means that decisions such as a licensing decision or a decision about planning permission, regulatory enforcement or a grant of funding are outside the scope of the policy statement.

In its pre-legislative scrutiny report on the draft Environment (Principles and Governance) Bill,[1] the Environmental Audit Committee recommended that the environmental principles be put on an unqualified legal basis in relation to environmental policy and that all public bodies should have a duty to apply the principles as was then the case under EU law: paragraph 24. The Government responded by saying that:

> *"Placing a greatly expanded legal duty on public bodies would go significantly beyond equivalence with EU law and would place a large regulatory burden on public bodies. We therefore intend to continue to focus the duty on policy-making by Ministers. The influence of the principles will flow through to individual decisions by virtue of being included in policy and law. As is the case in the EU currently, we expect that if public bodies need to use the environmental principles in decision-making, the principles should be included in the relevant legislation or guidance and will therefore be used by public bodies in the exercise of their functions."*

Unfortunately, this statement is optimistic in that it does not acknowledge the conceptual problems which will attend any *"trickle-down"* of broad policy statements.

4.2 The problems

The problems with attempts at applying the five above principles directly to the development control stage can be seen by a consideration of the *"precautionary principle"*. NB: It is not the objective of this chapter to discuss the practical application of all five principles.

---

[1] The Environmental Audit Committee – Eighteenth Report of Session 2017–19, *Scrutiny of the Draft Environment (Principles and Governance) Bill* (HC 1951) on 25 April 2019. The Government's response was received on 15 October 2019.

There are, so far as the appropriation of this principle to individual planning applications is concerned, three initial problems. First, the iterations of it in various official publications tends to be at a high level and, as such, these publications are not particularly helpful when it comes to examining site-specific planning applications. Secondly, the principle was constructed to guide the creation of policies and rules in a proactive fashion; whereas, of course, the assessment of planning applications is reactive. Thirdly, a number of the oft-cited cases have to do with the question of the active banning of the use of particular substances as opposed to reactive refusals or grants of licences.

Having said this, there is a danger that those assessing or determining planning applications will seek to apply what they see as the precautionary principle to them and to, then, take an oversimplistic view which might turn on the slippery catachresis *"better safe than sorry"*. This phrase has been used in some professional journals; however, it fails to reflect the complexity of this principle and would, if applied generally, stultify much development which is otherwise acceptable by setting an ambiguous and unrealistic threshold of acceptability. Arguably, it would also involve a fundamental misunderstanding of the committee's role in this process (see below).

A layperson might understand the precautionary principle as meaning that an action should not be allowed if there is any risk of harm whatsoever to (in this case) the environment; hence *"better safe than sorry"*. This is not, however, the way in which the expression is usually used in a more formal context.

The definition of a *"precautionary approach"*[2] in the 1992 *Rio Declaration on Environment and Development* was:

> *"Where there are threats of serious or irreversible damage, lack of full scientific certainty shall not be used as a reason for postponing cost-effective measures to prevent environmental degradation" (UNEP 1992)*

This was an international treaty and not, in any way, a prescription for site-specific developments.

This is reflected in the following description of the precautionary principle so far as it relates to the environment:

> *"The precautionary principle is understood as the principle that where there are threats of serious or irreversible damage, lack of scientific certainty shall not be used as a reason for postponing cost-effective measures to prevent environmental degradation.*
>
> *This principle is included in many international treaties and is already embedded into UK policy areas, such as in fisheries or chemicals policy. If applied appropriately, the*

---

[2]   Query whether an *"approach"* differs from a *"principle"*.

precautionary principle can function to encourage innovation by incentivising policy makers to seek alternative options in policy design. The precautionary principle should be considered where there are reasonable grounds for concern and used in a proportionate manner, taking into account the available scientific evidence, and the associated costs and benefits of action and non-action."[3]

The adoption of the precautionary principle in the formulation of policies within the European Union was outlined in Article 191 of the Treaty on the Functioning of the European Union:[4]

"[2] ...Union policy on the environment shall aim at a high level of protection taking into account the diversity of situations in the various regions of the Union. It shall be based on the precautionary principle and on the principles that preventive action should be taken, that environmental damage should as a priority be rectified at source and that the polluter should pay."

The European Environment Agency provided a description in 2013:[5]

"The precautionary principle provides justification for public policy and other actions in situations of scientific complexity, uncertainty and ignorance, where there may be a need to act in order to avoid, or reduce, potentially serious or irreversible threats to health and/or the environment, using an appropriate strength of scientific evidence, and taking into account the pros and cons of action and inaction and their distribution."

Whilst including environmental protection, these varying expositions are pitched at the formulation of policy and at too high a level to be helpful in day-to-day planning decisions.

The flaw in planning committees and their advisors looking directly to the principles, and the treaty obligations which underlie them, is that they would be considering global statements which not only go to the making of policy but also should, by now, be embedded in national policy in any event. Accordingly, they would, in effect, be *"double-counting"* those matters which are listed in the principles.

However, these provisions are important because their effect will be that the Policy Statement on Environmental Principles must form one of the considerations to be taken into account by the relevant Minister when revisiting the National Planning Policy Framework. The National Planning Policy Framework is a material consideration in the formulation of

---

[3]   *Information paper on the policy statement on Environmental Principles* (December 2018), Department for Environment, Food and Rural Affairs: page 12. https://assets.publishing.service.gov.uk/government/uploads/system/uploads/attachment_data/file/766299/env-bill-information-paper.pdf.

[4]   Formerly Article 174 of the Treaty Establishing the European Community (TEC). See now the Consolidated version of the Treaty on the Functioning of the European Union (revised version from EUR-Lex dated 01/03/2020): www.legislation.gov.uk/eut/teec/contents.

[5]   *Late lessons from early warnings II: science, precaution and innovation* (EEA Report, 1/2013), page 648.

local development plan policies and in development control. It should, therefore, follow that the principles in the Statement will filter down to a local level by way of this linkage:

> *"The policy statement on environmental principles applies to Ministers of the Crown. This is because the majority of high-level and strategic policies relating to the environment are owned by central Government. Central Government sets the policy framework and legislation for any key policy decisions taken by other public bodies, for example in developing the National Planning Policy Framework. Therefore, the application of the policy statement to Ministers of the Crown will mean that environmental principles are also reflected in the operational policies, legislation and operating frameworks affecting the functions of a wide range of public bodies."[6]*

Furthermore, and perhaps more importantly, it should be noted that the UK Government committed to the above-mentioned international treaty obligations many years ago and these should be embedded in present-day national policy in any event. It should not matter that these national policies do not use phrases such as *"precautionary principle"*, so long as the national policies adopt this principle in effect.

4.3   The *"cost-benefit"* approach

Planning committees should be familiar with cost-benefit assessments as part of their reasoning on applications, and it might be argued that the precautionary and preventative principles can be construed in that connection, with the *"cost"* varying according to the standpoint of the observer. The refusal of planning permission could be construed as a measure to prevent environmental degradation in a particular case. The *"cost"* of refusal would include losing the benefits of the proposed scheme. Thus, with a residential scheme, it would be the loss of housing and, with an employment scheme, it would be the loss of economic activity. If one shifts perspective, then the *"cost"* of granting such a planning permission might involve environmental degradation.

This cost-benefit approach can be seen in paragraph 177 of the National Planning Policy Framework (2021) which states (among other things) that, when considering applications for development within National Parks, the Broads and Areas of Outstanding Natural Beauty, permission should be refused for major development other than in exceptional circumstances, and where it can be demonstrated that the development is in the public interest. Consideration of such applications should include an assessment of:

(a)   the need for the development, including in terms of any national considerations, and the impact of permitting it, or refusing it, upon the local economy;

(b)   the cost of, and scope for, developing outside the designated area, or meeting the need for it in some other way; and

---

[6]   *Information paper on the policy statement on Environmental Principles* (December 2018), Department for Environment, Food and Rural Affairs – page 5. https://assets.publishing.service.gov.uk/government/uploads/system/uploads/attachment_data/file/766299/env-bill-information-paper.pdf.

(c)   any detrimental effect on the environment, the landscape and recreational opportunities, and the extent to which that could be moderated.

Likewise, paragraph 180(b) states that, when determining planning applications, local planning authorities should (*inter alia*) apply the following principle:

> *"b) development on land within or outside a Site of Special Scientific Interest, and which is likely to have an adverse effect on it ... should not normally be permitted. The only exception is where the benefits of the development in the location proposed clearly outweigh both its likely impact on the features of the site that make it of special scientific interest, and any broader impacts on the national network of Sites of Special Scientific Interest."*

4.4   The "*risk management*" approach

In 2000 the Commission of the European Communities produced a document entitled "*Communication from the Commission on the Precautionary Principle*"[7] which could be described as setting out an approach which turns on risk management. It stated:

> *"4. The precautionary principle should be considered within a structured approach to the analysis of risk which comprises three elements: risk assessment, risk management, risk communication. The precautionary principle is particularly relevant to the management of risk."*

There is nothing new in the concept of risk management in the delivery of socially desirable objectives. To give a common example, in a metaphysical ideal world one could try to eliminate every whiff of radon gas from every residential development site, but the reality is that land is a very scarce resource in the UK, funding is not unlimited, and so all development sites cannot be models of environmental perfection. It is necessary to evaluate risks and, if they appear to exist at unacceptable levels, then to deploy commercially realistic remediation strategies to reduce them to acceptable levels. This is the crux of the pragmatic "*suitable for use*" approach which has been adopted for the purposes of town and country planning in the UK and which forms the basis of an exercise in risk management in connection with the development of sites affected by contamination.[8]

Paragraph 180(a) states that, when determining planning applications, local planning authorities should apply the following principle:

> *"if significant harm to biodiversity resulting from a development cannot be avoided (through locating on an alternative site with less harmful impacts), adequately mitigated, or, as a last resort, compensated for, then planning permission should be refused."*

---

[7]   Brussels, 2.2.2000 COM(2000) 1 final.

[8]   See paragraph 183 of the National Planning Policy Framework 2021.

The question of what is, or is not, "*significant harm*" is, of course, a matter of risk evaluation, and matters of mitigation and compensation go to risk management.

It is, perhaps, wrong for local planning authorities to seek to over-lay the principles which are (or will be) set out in legislation and national policy by imposing their own versions of the environmental principles, in particular the "*precautionary principle*" and the "*preventative principle*". The comment is made for a number of reasons including that (at least in theory) this exercise amounts to "*double-counting*" where those principles are already incorporated in those polices and that legislation. Also, and hopefully more persuasively, because planning committees are, already, overburdened with overly complicated tasks and adding another one will, simply, open up more potential for error in an already too litigious aspect of public law.

4.5   Air quality and the "*trickle-down*" effect

One of the key issues is whether there is a "*trickle-down*" effect in connection with air quality. It is, therefore, helpful to examine this topic in order to look at the way in which the "*effect*" might apply in the overall context of the planning system as a whole.

An apposite starting point might be the Environment Act 1995, which required local authorities to assess and manage the quality of the air in their areas. Where specified standards and objectives are not being met, they are required to declare Air Quality Management Areas and then prepare action plans. The Secretary of State has produced the National Air Quality Strategy, which specifies the standards and objectives that local authorities need to achieve. The Act is intended to strengthen these duties by giving greater clarity on the requirements of action plans enabling greater collaboration between local authorities and all tiers of local Government, as well as with Relevant Public Authorities, in the creation and delivery of those plans. It also requires the Secretary of State to regularly review the National Air Quality Strategy.

The National Planning Policy Framework (2021) states:

> "*181. Planning policies and decisions should sustain and contribute towards compliance with relevant limit values or national objectives for pollutants, taking into account the presence of Air Quality Management Areas and Clean Air Zones, and the cumulative impacts from individual sites in local areas. Opportunities to improve air quality or mitigate impacts should be identified, such as through traffic and travel management, and green infrastructure provision and enhancement. So far as possible these opportunities should be considered at the plan-making stage, to ensure a strategic approach and limit the need for issues to be reconsidered when determining individual applications.* **Planning decisions should ensure that any new development in Air Quality Management Areas and Clean Air Zones is consistent with the local air quality action plan.** "*(Emphasis added).*

Thus, the National Planning Policy Framework places Air Quality Management Areas and Clean Air Zones on the table when making planning decisions, albeit that the emphasis appears to be on trying to resolve air quality matters at the plan-making stage, presumably on the basis that this will place less of a burden on the development control stage. It should follow that overarching the national priorities in the Environment Act (such as the $PM_{2.5}$ target) will come into the decision-making process, if nothing else than on a "*direction of travel*" basis.

The problem is, of course, that plan-making is not a speedy process and decisions must be made whilst they are being prepared. Furthermore, local development plan policies are not without their own difficulties, as discussed below. Accordingly, one can foresee the pressure on local planning authorities to pre-empt their emerging local plans by making decisions on a site-by-site basis. To put this into practical terms, one would expect that most members of planning committees will be aware of these national priorities and might be asking officers for advice as to the weight to be attributed to them. One can also foresee this question coming up on a regular basis.

The National Planning Practice Guidance website also contains advice on this topic:[9]

> "**When could air quality considerations be relevant to the development management process?**
>
> *Whether air quality is relevant to a planning decision will depend on the proposed development and its location. Concerns could arise if the development is likely to have an adverse effect on air quality in areas where it is already known to be poor, particularly if it could affect the implementation of air quality strategies and action plans and/or breach legal obligations (including those relating to the conservation of habitats and species). Air quality may also be a material consideration if the proposed development would be particularly sensitive to poor air quality in its vicinity.*
>
> **What specific issues may need to be considered when assessing air quality impacts?**
>
> *Considerations that may be relevant to determining a planning application include whether the development would:*
>
> - *Lead to changes (including any potential reductions) in vehicle-related emissions in the immediate vicinity of the proposed development or further afield. This could be through the provision of electric vehicle charging infrastructure; altering the level of traffic congestion; significantly changing traffic volumes, vehicle speeds or both; or significantly altering the traffic composition on local roads. Other matters to consider include whether the proposal involves the development of a bus station, coach or lorry park; could add to turnover in a large car park; or*

---

[9]   As is often the case with the National Planning Practice Guidance, it is difficult to identify its target audience. If it is advice to experienced local planning authorities, much of it appears to be of the "*teaching grandmother to suck eggs*" kind. Be that as it may!

> *involve construction sites that would generate large Heavy Goods Vehicle flows over a period of a year or more;*
>
> - *Introduce new point sources of air pollution. This could include furnaces which require prior notification to local authorities; biomass boilers or biomass-fuelled Combined Heat and Power plant; centralised boilers or plant burning other fuels within or close to an air quality management area or introduce relevant combustion within a Smoke Control Area; or extraction systems (including chimneys) which require approval or permits under pollution control legislation;*
>
> - *Expose people to harmful concentrations of air pollutants, including dust. This could be by building new homes, schools, workplaces or other development in places with poor air quality;*
>
> - *Give rise to potentially unacceptable impacts (such as dust) during construction for nearby sensitive locations;*
>
> - *Have a potential adverse effect on biodiversity, especially where it would affect sites designated for their biodiversity value."*
>
> *Paragraph: 006 Reference ID: 32-006-20191101 - Revision date: 01 11 2019.*

The overarching principles in the Environment Act are not, therefore, feeding into a *carte blanche* in the matter of air quality but into a pre-existing framework. If nothing else, they may, at the lowest, be taken as an aid to the interpretation of national policies and guidance;[10] or they might (and perhaps should) be given weight as a material planning consideration in their own right.

The National Planning Practice Guidance advises:

> **"How can an impact on air quality be mitigated?**
>
> *Mitigation options will need to be locationally specific, will depend on the proposed development and need to be proportionate to the likely impact. It is important that local planning authorities work with applicants to consider appropriate mitigation so as to ensure new development is appropriate for its location and unacceptable risks are prevented. Planning conditions and obligations can be used to secure mitigation where the relevant tests are met.*
>
> *Examples of mitigation include:*

---

[10]   For a discussion of the relevance of legal provisions to the interpretation of national policy, see Alistair Mills, *Interpreting the NPPF* (Bath Publishing, 2018), page 24.

- *maintaining adequate separation distances between sources of air pollution and receptors;*

- *using green infrastructure, in particular trees, where this can create a barrier or maintain separation between sources of pollution and receptors;*

- *appropriate means of filtration and ventilation;*

- *including infrastructure to promote modes of transport with a low impact on air quality (such as electric vehicle charging points);*

- *controlling dust and emissions from construction, operation and demolition; and*

- *contributing funding to measures, including those identified in air quality action plans and low emission strategies, designed to offset the impact on air quality arising from new development."*

Paragraph: 008 Reference ID: 32-008-20191101 - Revision date: 01 11 2019.

The National Planning Practice Guidance goes on to add, to its list of considerations, whether the development would:

- *Expose people to harmful concentrations of air pollutants, including dust. This could be by building new homes, schools, workplaces or other development in places with poor air quality.*

- *Give rise to potentially unacceptable impacts (such as dust) during construction for nearby sensitive locations.*

- *Have a potential adverse effect on biodiversity, especially where it would affect sites designated for their biodiversity value.*

Paragraph: 006 Reference ID: 32-006-20191101 – Revision date: 01 11 2019.

The final bullet point flags up that air pollution can have a deleterious effect on ecology.

Thus, perhaps, the officer who is asked these questions by members, often without warning, during a committee meeting should be armed not only with a general knowledge of the Environment Act but also of the way in which its national priorities may interact with the context provided by the extant planning system. This is no small burden and brings to mind the old ironic saying: *"May you live in interesting times"*.[11]

---

[11] For those interested in such things, the philologist Garson O'Toole attributes the origin of the saying to a speech made by Joseph Chamberlain in 1898: *"I think that you will all agree that we are living in most interesting times. I never remember myself a time in which our history was so full, in which day by day brought us new objects of interest, and, let me say also, new objects for anxiety"*. Garson O'Toole, *May You Live in Interesting Times* (May You Live In Interesting Times – Quote Investigator).

Chapter 5

Environmental Governance

5.1   Overview

The Environment Act is intended to comprise two thematic parts. The first provides a legal framework for environmental governance. The second makes provision for specific improvements to the environment. Given that this book is aimed at development control, the first part is of limited relevance in the day-to-day determination of planning applications.

The first part of the Act fulfils a legal obligation set out in section 16 of the European Union (Withdrawal) Act 2018. This is to say, it acts to replace those matters relating to the environment which were the concern of directives from the European Union until 1 January 2021. This sought to satisfy a pledge in the Government's 2019 manifesto "*Get Brexit done: unleash Britain's potential*" which stated that the Government would protect and restore our natural environments after leaving the EU.

Part 1 of the Act, therefore, relates to environmental governance. It gives a number of overarching provisions, including to:

- allow the Government to set long-term targets (of at least 15 years' duration) in relation to the natural environment and people's enjoyment of the natural environment via statutory instrument;

- require the Government to meet long-term targets, and to prepare remedial plans where long-term targets are not met;

- require the Government to set at least one long-term target in each of the priority areas of air quality, water, biodiversity, and resource efficiency and waste reduction;

- require the Government to set and meet an air quality target for fine particulate matter in ambient air ($PM_{2.5}$);

- require the Government to periodically review all environmental targets to assess whether meeting them would significantly improve the natural environment in England;

- establish the process by which a long-term target is set and amended, as well as an enhanced process where a long-term target is lowered or revoked;

- require the Government to produce an annual report on the environmental improvement plan, to consider progress towards improving the natural environment and meeting the targets;

- require the Government to review the plan periodically, to consider progress and whether further or different steps are needed to improve the natural environment and meet the targets and, if appropriate, revise the plan;

- require the Government to collect and publish data used to measure progress in improving the natural environment and meeting the targets;

- require the publication of a policy statement on environmental principles setting out how environmental principles specified under the Act are to be interpreted and applied by Ministers of the Crown during the policy-making process;

- establish a new "*Office for Environmental Protection*";

- require the Government to publish a report on the impact of all new environmental primary legislation; and

- require the Government to undertake a report on environmental legislation across the world on a two-yearly basis.

The Act requires the Government to prepare and maintain an environmental improvement plan and is intended to create a new statutory regime of monitoring, planning and reporting to seek a continuing improvement to the environment. This will be a plan to significantly improve the natural environment, which sets out the steps the Government intends to take to improve the natural environment, and which sets out interim targets towards meeting long-term targets. The first environmental improvement plan is the 25-year environmental plan which was published in January 2018.[1]

Ministers will be required to make a statement to Parliament setting out the effect of new primary environmental legislation on existing levels of environmental protection.

For these purposes, "*environmental protection*" means:

(a)   protection of the natural environment[2] from the effects of human activity;

(b)   protection of people from the effects of human activity on the natural environment;

(c)   maintenance, restoration or enhancement of the natural environment; and

---

[1]   See now; https://assets.publishing.service.gov.uk/government/uploads/system/uploads/attachment_data/file/803266/25yep-progress-report-2019-corrected.pdf#:~:text=When%20the%2025%20Year%20Environment%20Plan%20was%20published,first%20progress%20report%20since%20the%20Plan%20was%20published.

[2]   In this Part, the "*natural environment*" means: (a) plants, wild animals and other living organisms; (b) their habitats; and (c) land (except buildings or other structures), air and water, and the natural systems, cycles and processes through which they interact.

(d)   monitoring, assessing, considering or reporting on anything in paragraphs (a) to (c).

In this Part of the Act *"environmental law"* means any legislative provision to the extent that it:

(a)   is mainly concerned with environmental protection, and

(b)   is not concerned with an excluded matter.[3]

This definition is of particular importance in the present context because it would appear to cover town and country planning. The planning regime covers all of the criteria set out in the definition of *"environmental protection"*, and it is arguable that it is mainly concerned with environmental protection. No doubt some might argue the contrary and say that environmental protection is one of the principal concerns of town and country planning but it is not the main one, in that it is a regime which concerns itself with the spatial distribution of development. Given that section 39(8) includes a definition of *"statutory review"* which is focused on the planning legislation,[4] it is difficult to see how such an argument could be sustained. Be that as it may, it is prudent to proceed on the basis that town and country planning is captured by this legislation.

5.2   The Office for Environmental Protection

The Act creates a new public body – namely, the Office for Environmental Protection (OEP) – with the ostensible purpose of holding the Government to account in respect of environmental law and its environmental improvement plan. The overarching objective of the OEP is to monitor progress in improving the natural environment in accordance with the Government's domestic environmental improvement plans and targets. It will be able to provide the Government with written advice on any proposed changes to environmental law.

It is intended that the OEP will be independent of Government. However, some have expressed concerns as to whether or not this will be the case in reality. The Secretary of State will be responsible for the appointment of non-executive board members and will provide the OEP's budget, neither of which suggests true independence. Furthermore, Ministers appear to have the ability to *"advise"* the new body. The form and content of this *"advice"* remains to be seen, but it is arguable that these concerns have some justification.[5]

Interesting though these provisions might be, they are unlikely to be of great relevance in the context of development control. However, the OEP will also have complaints and enforcement duties and powers and these may have significance for local planning authorities.

---

[3]   Excluded matters are: (a) disclosure of or access to information; (b) the armed forces or national security; and (c) taxation, spending or the allocation of resources within Government.

[4]   See below.

[5]   *Campaigners fear Office for Environmental Protection may be undermined by UK Government* (3 November 2020): https://cedrec.com/r/news/1120-campaigners-fear-the-independent-office-for-environmental-protection-may-be-undermined-by-the-uk-government. See also www.circularonline.co.uk/news/environment-bill-amendment-would-give-gov-get-out-of-jail-free-card/.

5.3   Enforcement mechanisms

By section 32, a person may make a complaint to the OEP if the person believes that a *"public authority"* has failed to comply with environmental law. A *"public authority"* will include a local planning authority.[6]

Those familiar with disputatious planning applications will, no doubt, be concerned as to whether this complaints procedure might or might not be used by disgruntled objectors in connection with proposed development schemes which, according to the objectors, have in some way been processed in breach of environmental law. Given that the wide definition of *"environmental law"* relates back to the even wider definition of *"environmental protection"*, this could be a legitimate concern. For example, the definition of environmental protection not only includes protection *per se* but also relates to maintenance, restoration and enhancement. One can easily foresee that a disgruntled objector might take the view that the scheme proposals failed to have regard to these matters. This is particularly so, given the revised content of section 40 of the Natural Environment and Rural Communities Act 2006 (see below).

Also, the OEP may carry out an investigation without having received such a complaint if it has information that, in its view, indicates that a public authority may have failed to comply with environmental law[7] and that the failure would be a serious failure.

The OEP must prepare a report on the investigation and provide it to the public authority. The OEP may give an *"information notice"* to a public authority if:

(a)   the OEP has reasonable grounds for suspecting that the authority has failed to comply with environmental law; and

(b)   it considers that the failure, if it occurred, would be serious.

The Act does not seek to set out any criterion upon which the question of seriousness might be evaluated, and this is left to the publication of an enforcement strategy by it. Section 23 provides that the OEP must prepare a strategy setting out how it intends to exercise its function. The strategy must contain an enforcement policy which will include the following:

•   how the OEP intends to determine whether failures to comply with environmental law are serious;

---

6   In this Part, *"public authority"* means a person carrying out any function of a public nature that is not a devolved function, a parliamentary function or a function of any of the following persons: (a) the OEP; (b) a Court or tribunal; (c) either House of Parliament; (d) a devolved legislature; or (e) the Scottish Ministers, the Welsh Ministers, a Northern Ireland department or a Minister within the meaning of the Northern Ireland Act 1998.

7   In this Part *"environmental law"* means any legislative provision to the extent that it (a) is mainly concerned with environmental protection, and (b) is not concerned with an excluded matter.

- how the OEP intends to determine whether damage to the natural environment or to human health is serious;

- how the OEP intends to exercise its enforcement functions in a way that respects the integrity of other statutory regimes; and

- how the OEP intends to prioritise cases.

In considering its enforcement policy, the OEP must have regard to the particular importance of prioritising cases that it considers have or may have national implications, and the importance of prioritising cases:

(a) that relate to ongoing or recurrent conduct;

(b) that relate to conduct that the OEP considers may cause (or has caused) serious damage to the natural environment or to human health; or

(c) that the OEP considers may raise a point of environmental law of general public importance.

Whilst this might, at first blush, appear to be a matter of legal draftsmanship, the reality is somewhat more difficult. If this means that the OEP will be concentrating on large-scale breaches of environmental law only, this raises the question of whether or not such a strategy would ignore the cumulative impact of multiple small-scale infractions. To put it another way, it is necessary to ask whether the environment will suffer a "*death by a thousand cuts*" whilst the OEP is overly focused on large infractions which, in reality, may be less significant than the cumulative effect of smaller ones. It might be the case that the principal determinant must be the economic one, because the OEP will not have an unlimited budget. Initiating proceedings in relation to multiple complaints is likely to require more resources than focusing on a lower number of complaints relating to larger matters. There is, of course, the usual sociological problem that a body which is resourced from Government, and is accountable to the public, will be tempted to concentrate on those cases which raise its public profile.

Sections 35 to 43 make provision about the functions of the OEP in relation to failures by public authorities to comply with environmental law. A reference to a public authority failing to comply with environmental law means the following conduct by that authority:

(a) unlawfully failing to take proper account of environmental law when exercising its functions; or

(b) unlawfully exercising, or failing to exercise, any function it has under environmental law.

The OEP may give a "*decision notice*" on a public authority if:

(a) the OEP is satisfied, on the balance of probabilities, that the authority has failed to comply with environmental law; and

(b) it considers that the failure is serious.

A decision notice is a notice that:

(a) describes a failure of a public authority to comply with environmental law; and

(b) sets out the steps the OEP considers the authority should take in relation to the failure (which may include steps designed to remedy, mitigate or prevent reoccurrence of the failure).

5.4 *"Environmental Review"*

Where the OEP has served a decision notice on a public authority, the OEP may apply to the High Court for an *"environmental review"*. An environmental review is a review of alleged conduct of the authority that is described in the decision notice as constituting a failure to comply with environmental law.

On an environmental review, the Court must determine whether the authority has failed to comply with environmental law, applying the principles applicable on an application for judicial review: section 38(5).[8]

If the Court finds that the authority has failed to comply with environmental law, it must make a statement to that effect (a *"statement of non-compliance"*): section 38(6). A statement of non-compliance does not affect the validity of the conduct in respect of which it is given. By section 38(9), where the Court makes a statement of non-compliance, it may grant any remedy that could be granted by the Court on a judicial review (other than damages) but only if satisfied that granting the remedy would not:

(a) be likely to cause substantial hardship to, or substantially prejudice the rights of, any person other than the authority; or

(b) be detrimental to good administration.

If the test in section 38(9) (*"Condition A"*) is not met, then the Court may grant a remedy if it is satisfied that:

(a) granting the remedy is necessary in order to prevent or mitigate serious damage to the natural environment or to human health; and

---

[8] The phrase *"the principles applicable on an application for judicial review"* means, in relation to an environmental review, the principles that would apply on an application for judicial review in the jurisdiction under which the environmental review arises.

(b)   there is an exceptional public interest reason to grant it.

Unlike the European Commission before it, the Court is not able to make an award of damages against a delinquent public body, and some commentators have seen this as a distinct lack of "*teeth*". However, it is worth bearing in mind that this would be a case of "*other people's money*"; namely, that the relevant body will be funded out of the public purse or, in the case of local authorities, by local residents. Imposing a financial penalty will not strike the public body in its own coffers, but will impact on otherwise innocent members of the public. Whilst the members of the European Commission might have been remote from the impact of their deliberations, the same cannot be said of domestic legislation.

If this procedure is triggered in connection with an application for planning permission, one can see the potential for considerable delay. Leaving aside the time consumed in the OEP's own procedures, any referral to the Court for an environmental review is likely to be not only time-consuming but also expensive.

5.5   "*Judicial Review*" or "*Statutory Review*"

Section 39(1) provides that the OEP may apply for judicial review, or a statutory review,[9] in relation to conduct of a public authority (whether or not it has given an information notice or a decision notice to the authority in respect of that conduct) if the OEP considers that the conduct constitutes a serious failure to comply with environmental law and the "*urgency condition*" is met; that is, if the OEP considers that it is necessary to make such an application (rather than proceeding under sections 35 to 38) to prevent, or mitigate, serious damage to the natural environment or to human health: sections 39(1) and 39(2).

It is doubtful whether this particular provision makes any change to the substantive law on judicial review, aside from giving the OEP the necessary standing to initiate such a review. The OEP will also be given standing to enter extant proceedings as an "*intervenor*". In the absence of any specific rules to the contrary, one would expect that the OEP will be entitled to invite the Court to apply any of the remedies which are available in the ordinary course of judicial review proceedings. The remedy of declaration would, no doubt, serve in the majority of cases. If a planning permission has been granted in breach of environmental law then, of course, the Court will need to consider whether or not it is appropriate to quash the permission.

If, on an application for judicial review or a statutory review made by the OEP, there is a finding that a public authority has failed to comply with environmental law, the authority must publish a statement that sets out the steps it intends to take in light of the finding. Thus, if the High Court quashes a decision of the public body, the matter does not end

---

9   The phrase "*statutory review*" means a claim for statutory review under: (i) section 287 or 288 of the Town and Country Planning Act 1990; (ii) section 63 of the Planning (Listed Buildings and Conservation Areas) Act 1990; (iii) section 22 of the Planning (Hazardous Substances) Act 1990; or (iv) section 113 of the Planning and Compulsory Purchase Act 2004.

there. The authority is obliged to publish a statement which, in practice, will mean that it should be driven to carry out the remedial steps mentioned in that statement.

Chapter 6

Local Nature Recovery Strategies

6.1 Introduction

The background to Local Nature Recovery Strategies is outlined in *"Consultation on Biodiversity Net Gain Regulations and Implementation"* (January 2022), at pages 94 and 95:

> *"Local Nature Recovery Strategies are locally produced spatial planning frameworks for nature, informed by national maps and priorities. Each strategy will, for the area it covers, agree priorities for nature's recovery, map the most valuable existing areas for nature and map specific proposals for creating or improving habitat for nature and wider environmental goals."*

The Glossary to the Consultation Document states:

> *"Local Nature Recovery Strategies: These will support local action by consistently mapping important existing habitats and identifying opportunities to create or restore habitat. Developed through a collaborative approach, LNRSs will also support the delivery of a Nature Recovery Network by acting as a key tool to help local partners better direct investment and action that improves, creates and conserves wildlife-rich habitat."*

Natural England had this to say in 2021:[1]

> *"It's not just about biodiversity. LNRSs are expected to include the wider environmental benefits of nature recovery, including nature-based solutions that counter the effects of climate change, such as natural flood management. The pilots[2] have shown the potential for LNRSs to bring together land use planning and land management. For example, they've identified woodland to store carbon, reduce flooding and cool urban areas; and peatlands, which absorb then store water while capturing carbon dioxide, contributing to Net Zero targets. This and more can be achieved by joining up nature recovery with wider environmental outcomes."*

6.2 Local Nature Recovery Strategies and development control

The Consultation Document states, at page 75, that:

> *"When identifying the appropriate combination of habitat features for a given parcel of land, landowners and managers should consider the relevant local nature priorities,*

---

[1] *Shaping the future of Nature Recovery: Developing Local Nature Recovery Strategies*, Jo Traill-Thompson, posted on 27 August 2021 – Natural England (blog.gov.uk)).

[2] Natural England carried out a series of pilot studies to assist in formulating these provisions.

such as those in Local Nature Recovery Strategies, as delivering the right kind of habitat in the right place will maximise the environmental outcomes."

Annex B to the Consultation Document sets out a proposed Biodiversity Gain Plan Template (working draft)[3] and part of the requested information is, *"What local plans or strategies have been used to inform strategic significance multipliers within metric? ... For example, Local Plan, **Local Nature Recovery Strategies, Green Infrastructure strategies.**"* (Emphasis added).

In September 2021, a Parliamentary Briefing paper[4] provided the following overview:

- "In the UK, around 41% of species have declined in abundance since 1970 due to environmental pressures like habitat loss.

- To help address this, the UK Government is creating Local Nature Recovery Strategies (LNRS) in England, a map of priority habitats to be improved and restored.

- Engaging landowners, land managers, and other key stakeholders to guide decisions on which habitats are included in LNRS, would ensure wider benefits are delivered to both nature and people.

- Effective delivery of the LNRS will require an understanding of the trade-offs between land uses, working across administrative boundaries, and addressing skills and capacity gaps.

- Funding for stakeholders, such as land managers, to deliver LNRS outcomes will be provided from a range of future environmental land management schemes together with private investment."

6.3   The statutory provisions

Sections 104 to 108 of the Environment Act provide for the creation of Local Nature Recovery Strategies in England, how the geographical coverage of each Local Nature Recovery Strategy will be determined, and the relationship between Local Nature Recovery Strategies and the *"biodiversity duty"* under section 40 of the Natural Environment and Rural Communities Act 2006.

The statutory objective is that, taken together, the whole of England will be covered by Local Nature Recovery Strategies: section 104(2). The area to be covered by each Local Nature Recovery Strategy will be determined by the Secretary of State: section 104(3).

---

[3]   At page 102 under heading: *E2: Baseline habitat data used to inform metric.*

[4]   POSTNOTE Number 652 September 2021: https://researchbriefings.files.parliament.uk/documents/POST-PN-0652/POST-PN-0652.pdf.

The area of a "*local authority*",[5] other than a county council, may not be split between different Local Nature Recovery Strategies: section 104(4).

6.4   Preparation of Local Nature Recovery Strategies

Section 105 of the Environment Act sets out the process by which Local Nature Recovery Strategies are to be prepared, published, reviewed and re-published. It also provides a power for the Secretary of State to make regulations regarding this process: see section 105(4).

Section 105(1) provides that each Local Nature Recovery Strategy will be prepared and published by a "*responsible authority*".

Section 105(2) provides that the Secretary of State will appoint the responsible authority for each Local Nature Recovery Strategy, and it lists the authorities that may potentially be appointed.

Section 105(3) requires the Local Nature Recovery Strategy to be reviewed and re-published from time to time by the responsible authority. Updates may be periodic or triggered by the Secretary of State publishing an updated National Habitat Map (see below).

The Secretary of State can make regulations to introduce further requirements regarding how Local Nature Recovery Strategies must be prepared and published; both in the first instance and in later versions (see section 105(4)).

Section 105(5) provides a non-exhaustive list of some specific aspects of this process that regulations may provide for. These are:

- provision of information by a local authority that is not the responsible authority;

- agreement of the Local Nature Recovery Strategy by all local authorities within the Local Nature Recovery Strategy area;

- the procedure for reaching agreement and resolving disagreements;

- consultation requirements; and

- timings for reviewing and re-publishing of the Local Nature Recovery Strategy.

6.5   Content of Local Nature Recovery Strategies

Section 106(1) provides that each Local Nature Recovery Strategy must include a "*statement of biodiversity priorities*" for the strategy area and a "*Local Habitat Map*" for the full extent of the area under the plan, either through one or multiple maps.

---

[5]   The bodies included within the definition of "*local authority*" are listed in section 108(2).

Section 106(2) provides that the statement of biodiversity priorities must include:

(a)   a description of the strategy area and its biodiversity;

(b)   a description of the opportunities for recovering or enhancing biodiversity, in terms of habitats and species, in the strategy area;

(c)   the priorities, in terms of habitats and species, for recovering or enhancing biodiversity (taking into account the contribution that recovering or enhancing biodiversity can also make to other environmental benefits); and

(d)   proposals as to potential measures relating to those priorities.

Section 106(3) provides that the Local Habitat Map must include:

(a)   national conservation sites in the strategy area;

(b)   any nature reserves in the strategy area provided under section 21 of the National Parks and Access to the Countryside Act 1949; and

(c)   other areas in the strategy area which in the opinion of the responsible authority:

    (i)   are, or could become, of particular importance for biodiversity; or

    (ii)   are areas where the recovery or enhancement of biodiversity could make a particular contribution to other environmental benefits.

A Local Habitat Map which does not relate to the whole of the strategy area must relate to the area of one or more local authorities within the strategy area: section 106(4).

Section 106(5) provides that the Secretary of State may issue guidance as to information to be included in a Local Nature Recovery Strategy and any other matters to be included in a Local Nature Recovery Strategy. A responsible authority must have regard to the guidance when preparing a Local Nature Recovery Strategy: section 106(6).

Sections 107(5) and 107(6) require the Secretary of State to inform the responsible authority of any areas in the authority's strategy area that the Secretary of State considers could: (a) be of greater importance for biodiversity, or where the recovery or enhancement of biodiversity could contribute to other environmental benefits; and (b) contribute to establishing a network of areas for recovery and enhancement of biodiversity across England as a whole.

Section 107(6) extends the duty on the Secretary of State to provide the responsible authority with information to anything else that the Secretary of State holds that the Secretary of State considers would assist in the preparation of a Local Nature Recovery Strategy.

6.6   The National Habitat Map

For the purpose of assisting responsible authorities in their preparation of Local Nature Recovery Strategies, the Secretary of State must prepare and publish a *"National Habitat Map"* for England: section 107(1).

The concept behind the National Habitat Map is what is sometimes referred to as *"biodiversity opportunity mapping"*. The Government is aware of more than a dozen different examples of biodiversity opportunity maps that have been produced by local authorities or on their behalf such as Surrey Nature Partnership's Biodiversity Opportunity Areas: the basis for realising Surrey's ecological network. It is intended that Local Nature Recovery Strategies will build on and seek to accommodate existing best practice.

The National Habitat Map must, in particular, identify *"national conservation sites"*[6] and other areas that, in the opinion of the Secretary of State, are of particular importance for biodiversity: section 107(2).

6.7   How does it interact with biodiversity net gain?

The Consultation Document states, at pages 94 and 95, that:

> *"The biodiversity metric that will be used for mandatory biodiversity net gain already includes an incentive to deliver habitats in line with Local Nature Recovery Strategies. Delivery of each Local Nature Recovery Strategies* (sic) *will be driven by measures in the Environment Act, including biodiversity net gain."*

---

[6]   Defined in section 108(3) as meaning:

(a) a site of special scientific interest, within the meaning of Part 2 of the Wildlife and Countryside Act 1981;

(b) a national nature reserve declared in accordance with section 35 of that Act;

(c) a Ramsar site, within the meaning of section 37A of that Act;

(d) a marine conservation zone designated under section 116 of the Marine and Coastal Access Act 2009;

(e) a European site, within the meaning of regulation 8 of the Conservation of Habitats and Species Regulations 2017 (S.I. 2017/1012).

Chapter 7

Environmental Impact Assessment And Biodiversity

Whilst it is neither the function of this book nor this chapter to provide an in-depth analysis of the Environmental Impact Assessment process, it is necessary to consider that process so far as it is material to the determination of those planning applications which may impact on biodiversity.

7.1   The Environmental Impact Assessment process

The requirement for the Environmental Impact Assessment of certain projects derives from European law. This is implemented into domestic law by way of the Town and Country Planning (Environmental Impact Assessment) Regulations 2017.

A planning authority must not grant planning permission for "*EIA development*" unless an Environmental Impact Assessment has been carried out in respect of that development. The regulations distinguish between two separate types of "*EIA development*". First, "*Schedule 1 development*", for which Environmental Impact Assessment is mandatory. Secondly, "*Schedule 2 development*", for which Environmental Impact Assessment is required if the project is considered likely to give rise to significant effects on the environment by virtue of factors such as its nature, size or location. If the site is wholly or partly in a "*sensitive area*", Environmental Impact Assessment is normally required regardless of whether the development might be a relatively small one.

It is not, for present purposes, necessary to dwell on "*Schedule 1 developments*". These are, generally, large-scale developments which are unlikely to cross the desk of planning case officers on a regular basis. "*Schedule 2 developments*", however, can present on a regular basis.

"*Schedule 2 development*" means development, other than exempt development, of a description mentioned in column 1 of the table in Schedule 2 where:

(a)   any part of that development is to be carried out in a sensitive area; or

(b)   any applicable threshold or criterion in the corresponding part of column 2 of that table is respectively exceeded or met in relation to that development.

The Schedule sets out tables which denominate the description of relevant developments and applicable thresholds and criteria. For example, Schedule 2 refers to "*urban development projects*" which include the construction of developments of more than 150 dwellings or where the overall area of the development exceeds 5 hectares.

A "*sensitive area*" means any of the following:

(a)   Sites of Special Scientific Interest;

(b)   a National Park;

(c)   the Broads;

(d)   a property appearing on the World Heritage List;[1]

(e)   a Scheduled Monument;

(f)   an Area of Outstanding Natural Beauty; or

(g)   a European site.

As to (g), the listing of "*European Sites*" may, in turn, trigger the need for an assessment under the Habitat Regulations: see Chapter 8.

As noted above, the fact that the proposed project falls within a particular descriptor or threshold is not conclusive as to whether or not the Environmental Impact Assessment process should be engaged. It is necessary to determine whether the development is likely to have a significant effect on the environment. Schedule 3 to the Regulations sets out selection criteria which should be taken into account in assessing significant effects for Schedule 2 development.

It is necessary to stress at the outset that "*Environmental Impact Assessment*" is a process. It proceeds by way of a number of stages which include:

(a)   the preparation of an environmental statement;

(b)   any consultation, publication and notification required by, or by virtue of, those Regulations or any other enactment in respect of EIA development; and

(c)   the steps required under regulation 26.[2] The EIA must identify, describe and assess in an appropriate manner, in light of each individual case, the direct and indirect significant effects of the proposed development on factors which include biodiversity, with particular attention to species and habitats protected under Directive 92/43/EEC and Directive 2009/147/EC.

Part of that process is the document known as an "*environmental statement*". It is the environmental statement (and additions to it) which will be shown on the local planning authority's website as a background document and published in accordance with statutory

---

[1]   A list kept under article 11(2) of the 1972 UNESCO Convention Concerning the Protection of the World Cultural and Natural Heritage.

[2]   Consideration of whether planning permission or subsequent consent should be granted when determining an application or appeal in relation to which an environmental statement has been submitted.

requirements which include the requirement to consult with certain stipulated bodies. An environmental statement is a statement which includes at least:

(a)   a description of the proposed development comprising information on the site, design, size and other relevant features of the development;

(b)   a description of the likely significant effects of the proposed development on the environment;

(c)   a description of any features of the proposed development, or measures envisaged in order to avoid, prevent or reduce and, if possible, offset likely significant adverse effects on the environment;

(d)   a description of the reasonable alternatives studied by the developer, which are relevant to the proposed development and its specific characteristics, and an indication of the main reasons for the option chosen, taking into account the effects of the development on the environment; and

(e)   a non-technical summary of the information referred to in sub-paragraphs (a) to (d).

Schedule 4 to the Regulations sets out particular detailed requirements for the statement.

If a proposed project falls within Schedule 2, the question of whether or not an Environmental Impact Assessment should be carried out is decided by a "*screening*" process. In the first instance, it is the function of the local planning authority to screen the application and consider whether the proposed project may have a significant impact on the environment. The developer is entitled to request a "*screening opinion*" from the local planning authority prior to making the application. Alternatively, the developer might (in order to save time) accept that an Environmental Impact Assessment is appropriate and, thereby, submit an environmental statement along with his application. If the developer simply submits an application without a screening opinion, or without an environmental statement, the local planning authority should produce a screening opinion in any event.

7.2   The scope and content of an environmental statement

A developer may, also, request a "*scoping opinion*" from the local planning authority. The scoping opinion will provide a local planning authority's opinion as to the information to be included in the environmental statement. If the local planning authority fails to provide the opinion, the developer has the ability to apply for "*Scoping Direction*" to the Secretary of State.

It is submitted that the initial scoping process for an environmental statement should include a "*Preliminary Ecological Appraisal*" (PEA) or a "*Phase 1 Habitat Survey*" for the site and its surroundings. This is likely be by reference to either the CIEEM "*Guidelines for Preliminary*

Ecological Appraisal" (2nd edition) or the JNCC's[3] *"Handbook for Phase 1 habitat survey – a technique for environmental audit".*

The CIEEM Guidelines advise that a PEA can also be used to inform scoping for an Environmental Impact Assessment: Para. 1.9. The Guidelines advise:

> *"1.2 Preliminary Ecological Appraisal (PEA) is the term used to describe a rapid assessment of the ecological features present, or potentially present, within a site and its surrounding area (the zone(s) of influence1 in relation to a specific project (usually a proposed development)). A PEA normally comprises a desk study and a walkover survey, the methods for which are further defined in Section 2 of these guidelines.*
>
> *1.3 The key objectives of a PEA are to:*
>
> * *identify the likely ecological constraints associated with a project;*
>
> * *identify any mitigation measures likely to be required, following the 'Mitigation Hierarchy';*
>
> * *identify any additional surveys that may be required to inform an Ecological Impact Assessment (EcIA); and*
>
> * *identify the opportunities offered by a project to deliver ecological enhancement."*

Paragraph 1.2 of the JNCC handbook states:

> *"The aim of Phase 1 survey is to provide, relatively rapidly, a record of the semi-natural vegetation and wildlife habitat over large areas of countryside."*

This is to say, it is a habitat survey and does not involve any assessment of onsite fauna, per:

> *"The habitat classification presented here is based principally on vegetation, augmented by reference to topographic and substrate features, particularly where vegetation is not the dominant component of the habitat."*

It follows that those acting for the developer may need to carry out additional surveys in relation to the preliminary identification of fauna, particularly protected species.

A desktop assessment and records search for scarce, protected and notable species may be carried out. This should identify internationally or nationally designated sites of nature conservation value and non-statutory Sites of Importance for Nature Conservation (SINCs) within 1km/2km of the site.

---

[3]   The Joint Nature Conservation Committee (JNCC).

Surveys may be required in respect of breeding birds, dormice, bats, great crested newts and other significant species of fauna.

7.3   Ecological Impact Assessment

The next step may be an Ecological Impact Assessment (EcIA) as a chapter in the environmental statement. CIEEM has also published "*CD9.10 - Guidelines for Ecological Impact Assessment in the UK and Ireland*", per (page iv):

> "*EcIA is a process of identifying, quantifying and evaluating potential effects of development related or other proposed actions on habitats, species and ecosystems. The findings of an assessment can help competent authorities understand ecological issues when determining applications for consent. EcIA can be used for the appraisal of projects of any scale including the ecological component of Environmental Impact Assessment (EIA). When undertaken as part of an EIA, EcIA is subject to the relevant EIA Regulations.*"

7.4   Securing mitigation measures

If the local planning authority has determined to grant planning permission for an EIA development, then any mitigation measures will, normally, be secured by planning conditions or planning obligations, and these mechanisms are discussed in Chapters 20 and 21 below. There is no reason why these mitigation measures cannot, in appropriate cases, be counted towards Biodiversity Net Gain.

Chapter 8

Habitats Regulations Assessment

8.1   Overview

If the proposed development has the potential to affect certain types of habitat site, the developer might be required to carry out a Habitats Regulations Assessment (HRA). Such an assessment might be required where a nearby area is designated as a *"European site"* or a *"European offshore marine site"*. This process is required by, and regulated by, the Conservation of Habitats and Species Regulations 2017 (S.I. 2017/1012) (the Habitats Regulations), as amended by the Conservation of Habitats and Species (Amendment) (EU Exit) Regulations (S.I. 2019/579).[1] If the proposed plan or project is considered likely to have a significant effect on such a protected habitat site (either individually or in combination with other plans or projects), an *"Appropriate Assessment"* must be carried out. These procedures will, in many cases, overlap with those for assessing and securing Biodiversity Net Gain.

The English Nature Habitats Regulations guidance note[2] provides as follows:

> *"Paragraph 1.1 – If a plan or project is not connected with or necessary for the management of the site and is likely to have a significant effect, the competent authority is required to carry out an Appropriate Assessment to determine whether it will have an adverse effect on site integrity."*

8.2   The Habitats Regulations

Regulation 63(1) of the 2017 regulations provides:

> *"(1) A competent authority, before deciding to undertake, or give any consent, permission or other authorisation for, a plan or project which–*
>
> *(a) is likely to have a significant effect on a European site or a European offshore marine site (either alone or in combination with other plans or projects), and*
>
> *(b) is not directly connected with or necessary to the management of that site,*
>
> *must make an appropriate assessment of the implications of the plan or project for that site in view of that site's conservation objectives."*

A relevant habitat site for these purposes is any site which may be included within the definition of a *"European site"* or a *"European offshore marine site"* in the 2017 Regulations.

---

[1]   See also the Conservation of Offshore Marine Habitats and Species Regulations 2017.

[2]   HRGN No 3 English Nature (November 1999).

By regulation 8(1), a *"European site"* is:

> *(a) a special area of conservation;*
>
> *(b) a site of Community importance which has been placed on the list referred to in the third sub-paragraph of Article 4(2) of the Habitats Directive (list of sites of Community importance) before exit day[3];*
>
> *(c) [...]*
>
> *(d) an area classified before exit day pursuant to Article 4(1) or (2) of the old Wild Birds Directive[4] or the new Wild Birds Directive[5] (classification of special protection areas) or classified after exit day under the retained transposing regulations;[6] or*
>
> *(e) a site which before exit day has been proposed to the European Commission in accordance with Article 4(1) of the Habitats Directive, until such time as -*
>
>> *(i) the site is designated as a special area of conservation under regulation 12 or under a corresponding provision in the other retained transposing regulations; or*
>>
>> *(ii) the appropriate authority gives the appropriate nature conservation body notice of its intention not to designate the site, setting out the reasons for its decision, in accordance with regulation 141A(3).*

A *"European offshore marine site"* means a site within the meaning of regulation 18 of the Conservation of Offshore Marine Habitats and Species Regulations 2017[7], viz:

> *"18. In these Regulations a 'European offshore marine site' means any of the following located in the offshore marine area–*
>
> *(a) a special area of conservation;*

---

[3]   See section 20 of European Union (Withdrawal) Act 2018 as amended by the European Union (Withdrawal) Act 2018 (Exit Day) (Amendment) (No. 3) Regulations 2019 (S.I. 2019/1423), where *"exit day"* means, subject to certain caveats, 31 January 2020 at 11.00 p.m.

[4]   The old *"Wild Birds Directive"* means Council Directive 79/409/EEC on the conservation of wild birds: Regulation 3(1).

[5]   The new *"Wild Birds Directive"* means Directive 2009/147/EC of the European Parliament and of the Council on the conservation of wild birds: Regulation 3(1).

[6]   The *"retained transposing regulations"*, means (i) the Offshore Marine Conservation Regulations 2017 (S.I. 2017/1013); (ii) the Conservation (Natural Habitats, etc.) Regulations (Northern Ireland) 1995 (S.I. 1995/380); (iii) the Conservation (Natural Habitats, &c.) Regulations 1994 (S.I. 1994/2716); and (iv) these Regulations.

[7]   As amended by Conservation of Habitats and Species (Amendment) (EU Exit) Regulations 2019 (S.I. 2019/579).

(b) a site of Community importance which has been placed on the list referred to in the third sub-paragraph of Article 4(2) of the Habitats Directive before exit day;

(c) a site hosting a priority natural habitat type or priority species in respect of which consultation has been initiated under Article 5(1) of the Habitats Directive, during the consultation period mentioned in Article 5(2) or pending a decision of the Council under Article 5(3);

(d) a site classified as a special protection area under regulation 12 or 13; and

(e) a site which, before exit day, was proposed to the European Commission under Article 4(1) of the Habitats Directive, until such time as -

(i) the site is designated as a special area of conservation under regulation 7; or

(ii) the relevant administration gives notice to the appropriate nature conservation body of its intention not to designate the site, setting out the reasons for its decision, in accordance with regulation 86A(3)(b)

Thus, these include designated and candidate Special Areas of Conservation and classified and potential Special Protection Areas, listed and proposed Ramsar sites and any relevant marine sites.

For the purposes of this chapter, these sites will be called, collectively, "*HRA Sites*".

A likely significant effect for these purposes is one which might undermine a site's conservation objectives. The conservation objectives relate to each of the habitats and species for which the site was designated. In practice, the local planning authority will consult Natural England who will provide more detail on this point.[8]

The Ruling of the European Court of Justice in *Waddenzee*[9] provides clarification regarding the term "*likely*" in Regulation 63, namely:

"... In the light, in particular, of the precautionary principle ... such a risk exists if it cannot be excluded on the basis of objective information that the plan or project will have significant effects on the site concerned ... Such an interpretation of the condition to which the assessment of the implications of a plan or project for a specific site is subject, which implies that in case of doubt as to the absence of significant effects such an assessment must be carried out, makes it possible to ensure effectively that plans or

---

[8]   See http://publications.naturalengland.org.uk/category/6490068894089216.

[9]   *National Association for Conservation of the Waddenzee v Secretary of State for Agriculture, Nature Conservation and Fisheries* [2004] EUECJ C-127/02.

> *projects which adversely affect the integrity of the site concerned are not authorised, and thereby contributes to achieving, in accordance with the third recital in the preamble to the Habitats Directive and Article 2(1) thereof, its main aim, namely, ensuring biodiversity through the conservation of natural habitats and of wild fauna and flora..."*

The requirement for objective information at the preliminary examination is not to be equated with a need for scientific knowledge. In *Bagmoor Wind Limited v The Scottish Ministers* [2012] CSIH 93,[10] the Court of Session concluded that *"objective"*, in this context, means information based on clear verifiable fact rather than subjective opinion. Lord Carloway[11] stated that:

> *"The requirement for objective information at the preliminary examination is not to be equated with a need for scientific knowledge. The Court only refers to "the best scientific knowledge" in the context of the appropriate assessment (para [61]). "Objective", in this context, means information based on clear verifiable fact rather than subjective opinion. The ipse dixit of the plan's proposer that a plan involving the use of ground in a SPA will not have any effect will not normally suffice nor will reassurances based on supposition or speculation. If the absence of risk in the plan can only be demonstrated after a detailed investigation, or expert opinion, that is an indicator that a risk exists and the authority must move from preliminary examination to appropriate assessment. If this does occur, however, it is important, if the pitfalls noticed in this case are to be avoided in the future, that the competent authority make the fact that this transition has occurred clear."*

In *Bagmoor Wind*, it was held that the word *"likely"* in the regulation is not to be construed as an expression of probability, in a legal sense, but as a description of the existence of a risk (or possibility). Thus, if the possibility of a significant effect[12] cannot be excluded based on objective information, an Appropriate Assessment will be required. Per Lord Carloway (Para.48):

> *"It is abundantly clear, at least to this court, that the construction and operation of 14 wind turbines, each 110 metres high, in the foraging ground for eagles in a SPA would be 'likely' to have (i.e. that there would be a risk of) a significant effect upon those eagles and hence the conservation objectives of the SPA. Certainly, that prospect could not have been discounted upon a preliminary examination. Accordingly, the court considers that it was inevitable, on these simple facts alone, that an appropriate assessment under regulation 48(1)(a) would have been required."*

---

[10] See also *R (On the application of RSPB) v Natural England* [2019] EWHC 585 (Admin) and *Royal Society for the Protection of Birds v Scottish Ministers* [2016] CSOH 103.

[11] The Opinion of the whole Court was delivered by Lord Carloway.

[12] Presumably more than *de minimus*.

The starting point is for the developer and local planning authority to check whether the proposed development is close to or adjacent to an HRA Site. The test for proximity is whether or not the proposal may be capable of affecting the HRA Site, no matter how distant it may be from the site itself. Developmental impacts may include such matters as recreational disturbance, air quality, road traffic, and water resources. For example, the creation of a large area of impermeable surface may have implications in terms of flooding by way of surface water run-off and this flooding impact might be spread over a considerable area. With windfarm proposals, there might be collision risks for birds: see below.

The Habitats Regulations guidance note provides as follows:[13]

> *"4.6 The following is a list of examples of types of effects which are likely to be significant ...*
>
> • *Causing change to the coherence of the site or to the Natura 2000 series (e.g. presenting a barrier between isolated fragments, or reducing the ability of the site to act as a source of new colonisers);*
>
> • *Causing reduction in the area of habitat or of the site;*
>
> • *Causing direct or indirect change to the physical quality of the environment (including the hydrology) or habitat within the site;*
>
> • *Causing ongoing disturbance to species or habitats for which the site is notified;*
>
> • *Altering community structure (species composition);*
>
> • *Causing direct or indirect damage to the size, characteristics or reproductive ability of populations on the site;*
>
> • *Altering the vulnerability of populations etc to other impacts.*
>
> • *Causing a reduction in the resilience of the feature against external change (for example its ability to respond to extremes of environmental conditions);*
>
> • *Affecting restoration of a feature where this is a conservation objective."*

Regulation 63(5) provides that:

> *"In the light of the conclusions of the assessment, and subject to regulation 64, the competent authority[14] may agree to the plan or project only after having ascertained*

---

[13] HRGN No 3 English Nature (November 1999). For highway schemes, see *Design Manual for Roads and Bridges* (DMRB) Volume 11, LA115.

[14] Defined in Regulation 7.

that it will not adversely affect [sic] *the integrity of the European site or the European offshore marine site (as the case may be)."*

In other words, a scheme which will have such an adverse effect should be refused; however, this is subject to Regulation 64: see below.

The stages of the HRA process are, in summary:

- **Stage 1 – Screening**: To test whether a plan or project (either alone or in combination with other plans) is likely to have a significant effect on an HRA Site.

- **Stage 2 – Appropriate Assessment**: To determine whether the proposal (either alone or in combination with other plans) would pose an unacceptable risk of an adverse effect on the integrity of the HRA Site.

- **Stage 3 – Assessment of alternative solutions**: Where a plan is assessed as having an adverse impact (or risk of this) on the integrity of an HRA Site, to examine alternatives.

- **Stage 4 – Assessment where no alternative solutions remain and where adverse impacts remain**.

8.3   The Screening Assessment

If a proposal may affect an HRA Site, a Screening Assessment might be required. This is an initial review which is intended to filter out those proposals which do not need to be examined in further detail. If the Screening Assessment shows that the proposal is *"likely to have a significant effect"* on an HRA Site, it will be necessary to carry out an Appropriate Assessment. The *"significance test"* is a coarse filter intended to identify which proposed plans and projects require further assessment. The local planning authority should not, when making a screening decision, take account of any proposed mitigation measures. Mitigation is a matter for the Appropriate Assessment itself and not for the screening process.[15] The effect of this is that the screening stage must be undertaken on a preliminary basis, with no regard to any proposed integrated or additional avoidance or reduction measures.

Where the likelihood of significant effects cannot be excluded on the basis of objective information, the competent authority must proceed to carry out an Appropriate Assessment to establish whether the plan or project will affect the integrity of the HRA Site, which can include at that stage consideration of the effectiveness of any proposed avoidance or reduction measures.

---

[15]   See Court of Justice of the European Union Judgment of the Court (Seventh Chamber) of 12 April 2018 – *People Over Wind and Peter Sweetman v Coillte Teoranta* [2018] EUECJ C-323/17.

8.4   The Appropriate Assessment

The Appropriate Assessment should include details of avoidance and mitigation measures, including monitoring. If it is found that there are no adverse impacts to an HRA Site, the proposal will satisfy the regulations. However, if it is found that there may be such adverse impacts, it will be necessary to consider whether there are alternative solutions.

It is important to stress that any proposed mitigation measures should be provided by way of mechanisms which will be enforceable. In practice, one would expect to see those mechanisms incorporated into a section 106 agreement. If they are of a long-term nature, those settling the agreement might need to think in terms of security by way of bonding arrangements, or long-term management by way of bespoke management companies.

8.5   Assessment of alternative solutions

If alternative solutions exist, it might be possible to revisit the proposal.

Again, it might be the case that alternative solutions are secured by way of planning obligations or similar enforcement mechanisms. Ergo, any alternative solution must be deliverable and secured.

8.6   Assessment where no alternative solutions

Otherwise, if there are no deliverable and secured alternative solutions, it might be the case that the proposals fail to satisfy the regulations and should not go ahead unless there are imperative reasons of overriding public interest to do so and, if necessary, compensatory measures can be secured.

Regulation 64 provides:

> *"(1) If the competent authority[16] is satisfied that, there being no alternative solutions, the plan or project must be carried out for imperative reasons of overriding public interest (which, subject to paragraph (2), may be of a social or economic nature), it may agree to the plan or project notwithstanding a negative assessment of the implications for the European site or the European offshore marine site (as the case may be).*
>
> *(2) Where the site concerned hosts a priority natural habitat type or a priority species, the reasons referred to in paragraph (1) must be either–*
>
> *(a) reasons relating to human health, public safety or beneficial consequences of primary importance to the environment; or*

---

[16]   Defined in Regulation 7.

(b) any other reasons which the competent authority, having due regard to the opinion of the appropriate authority,[17] *considers to be imperative reasons of overriding public interest."*

---

[17]   The "*appropriate authority*" means the Secretary of State in relation to England and the Welsh Ministers in relation to Wales (but see modifications of the meaning of that term in regulations 9(4) and 10(12)(a), and modifications of references to that term in regulations 69(1)(b), (3)(c), (5) and (8)(b), 97(6), 110(3)(b) and 112(3) (c)), and any person exercising any function of the Secretary of State or the Welsh Ministers: Regulation 3(1).

Chapter 9

The Biodiversity Metric

9.1 Introduction

Given that the aspects of the Environment Act which are discussed in this book place great emphasis on the protection and enhancement of biodiversity in real-estate development, it might be helpful to provide an overview of the main tool for this exercise; namely, the notion of net gains in biodiversity.

Unless this is to be an aspirational puff, it is necessary to have a system which seeks to provide objective measurements of biodiversity, so that those gains can be assessed and so as to provide tangible targets for those promoting development schemes. Furthermore, it is in the public interest to have objective and transparent decision-making which can be tested by interested third parties. This brings one to the concept of the *"biodiversity metric"*.

9.2 *"You cannot put a number on nature"*

The notion of measurable net gains for biodiversity is, in theory, an attempt to invoke the measurement of that which is inherently immeasurable.[1] It puts one in the position of having to try to measure the immeasurable. However, for planners, the alternative is to sit back and do nothing. It might be the case, and indeed probably will be the case, that the best one can do is to provide an approximation. The chosen instrument for attempting this feat is known as a *"biodiversity metric"*.

The immediate problem is that there are a number of well-established metrics and, also, that some of them are too complicated for use in development control, viz:[2]

> *"12. Perhaps the best known metric system is 'habitat hectares'. This approach was originally developed for use in Victoria, Australia ... and forms the basis for a number of different metrics currently being developed and used....*
>
> *13. The habitat hectares system used in Australia is intensive in terms of the input required to assess the habitat. It requires trained operators to ensure the required levels of consistency. Consultants have to pass an exam before they are allowed to submit assessments ..."*

Thus, it is necessary to use a robust and relatively simple methodology, and the front-runner is the Biodiversity Metric 3.0.

---

[1] For example, does a bee have more value than a wasp, or vice versa? This is not as easy a task as it might at first seem. Or how many wasps equate to one bee or visa versa ? Then, of course, there is the matter of protozoa in unimproved grassland…!

[2] *Biodiversity Offsetting Pilot – Technical Paper: the metric for the biodiversity offsetting pilot in England* (March 2012), published for Defra.

The Metric is intended to use habitat features as a proxy measure for capturing the value and importance of nature within a given parcel of land. Unlike some biodiversity metrics, Biodiversity Metric 3.0 does not include species explicitly, but uses broad habitat categories as a proxy for the biodiversity *"value"* of the species communities that make up different habitats. It does not attempt to weigh the species richness,[3] abundance[4] or diversity[5] of various species on the subject land. It is not a precise measurement of all that exists on the land.

Paragraph 2.2 of the User Guide states that the Metric *"...uses habitats, the places in which species live, as a proxy to describe biodiversity. ...These habitats are converted into 'biodiversity units'. These biodiversity units are the 'currency' of the metric."*

Some might see this as a shortcoming; however, a more sophisticated approach would be impractical in a world constrained by matters of time and money. Also, reasonably held opinions will, properly, differ as to the respective merits of various types of flora and fauna. These points are difficult to resolve in the robust world of real-estate development. Furthermore, one of the arguments in favour of the use of a habitat metric is that the creation of a new or extended habitat should create the environment for its colonisation by the flora and fauna which tend to populate that type of environment, particularly if this colonisation is assisted by man.

Whilst not wishing to be contentious, perhaps the word *"proxy"* means, in reality, a rude subjective approximation. This comment is not intended to be pejorative, because it is better than making no attempt at providing testable objective criteria and transparency of reasoning. It does, however, highlight that the prudent surveyor should be aware that a metric is but one tool in his assessment and its use does not preclude a holistic approach to evaluating the value of a site.

Paragraph 2.3 of the User Guide states that:

> *"2.3 Biodiversity units are calculated using the size of a parcel of habitat and its quality. The metric uses habitat area (measured in hectares) as its core measurement, except for linear habitats (hedgerows and lines of trees and rivers and streams) where habitat length (measured in kilometres) is used."*

The User Guide explains:[6]

---

[3] Species richness is a measure of the number of species present at a site. Sites with more species are considered richer.

[4] Species abundance and density is the total abundance and concentration of individuals present in a selected area.

[5] Species diversity is a measure of how many different types of species are present in communities.

[6] *The Biodiversity Metric 3.0 – auditing and accounting for biodiversity – USER GUIDE* (Natural England Joint Publication JP039), first published 7 July 2021.

"1.8 The units generated by biodiversity metric 3.0, like all biodiversity unit calculations, come with a 'health warning'. The outputs of this metric are not absolute values but provide a proxy for the relative biodiversity worth of a site pre- and post-intervention. The quality and reliability of outputs will depend on the quality of the inputs. This user guide provides advice on how to use the biodiversity unit approach and where and when it is appropriate for use. The metric is not a substitute for expert ecological advice. The metric does not override or undermine any existing planning policy or legislation, including the mitigation hierarchy (see section 1.10 below), which should always be considered as the metric is applied.

1.9 Biodiversity metric 3.0 does not include species explicitly. Instead, it uses habitat types as a proxy for the biodiversity 'value' of the species communities that make up those different habitats. The metric does not change existing levels of species protection and does not replace the processes linked to species protection regimes."

As to the important proxy approach in the Metric, the User Guide states:

"2.20 The metric and its outputs should therefore be interpreted, alongside ecological expertise and common sense, as an element of the evidence that informs plans and decisions. The metric is not a total solution to biodiversity decisions. The metric, for example, helps you work out how much new or restored habitat is needed to compensate for a loss of habitat, but it does not tell you the appropriate composition of plant species to use."

As noted above, the proxy approach in the Metric is not as sophisticated as a metric[7] which seeks to evaluate species. It uses habitat categories as a proxy for biodiversity. Arguably, it would be more accurate to describe it as a *"habitat metric"*[8]. The User Guide defines *"biodiversity"* as:

"1.3 Biodiversity is the term that is used to describe the variety of all life on earth. It includes all species of animals and plants – and everything else that is alive on our planet. Habitats are the places in which species live. ..."

Clearly, the Metric does not seek to cover all these aspects of biodiversity. It follows that the prudent developer will produce a species evaluation to accompany the outputs from the Metric.

The User Guide adds:

---

[7] England has a formal statutory list of flora, fauna and habitats. The England Biodiversity List has been developed pursuant to section 41 of the Natural Environment and Rural Communities Act 2006. This requires the Secretary of State to publish a list of species of flora and fauna and habitats of principal importance for the purpose of conserving biodiversity. The current list was published by Natural England in August 2010: see https://webarchive.nationalarchives.gov.uk/20140712055944/http://www.naturalengland.org.uk/ourwork/conservation/biodiversity/protectandmanage/habsandspeciesimportance.aspx. See also http://publications.naturalengland.org.uk/publication/4958719460769792.

[8] As per the *"habitat hectares"* approach in Australia.

> *"2.18 The metric is a tool that can be used to help inform plans and decisions. It is important, however, to be aware of its limitations and to conduct assessments in accordance with the following principles and rules."*

Despite its limitations, the Metric brings a number of advantages to the development process, including:

- the use of the Metric at an early stage in a scheme should assist in pre-empting objections which might otherwise be raised to it on ecological grounds;

- the Metric is likely to be one of the first things that consultees will consider, or look for, and so the early production of a well-audited output will assist in focusing the discussions at an early stage;

- if executed properly, the outputs from the use of the Metric should provide a transparent and quantifiable basis for pre-application discussions with the local planning authority and thus assist in formulating the design for a scheme.

One of the essential ingredients of any package for the establishment and management of a scheme for biodiversity net gain, whether by way of a section 106 agreement or otherwise, is the provision of an enforcement mechanism. Regardless of the nature of the subject matter, one cannot expect an authority or a Court to enforce that which cannot be measured. A requirement to do something which is characterised by wholly subjective terminology is likely to be unenforceable; however, the use of the Metric to set a measured baseline and then measuring performance against it provides something which can be meaningfully relied upon when it comes to the matter of enforcement.

Furthermore, the use of geographical information systems in combination with biodiversity Metrics is a strong step in the direction of evidence-based planning. Whilst a considerable amount of the input is judgemental, the subjective aspects of those judgements will be plain for all to see.

One of the questions which needs to be considered, when the statutory requirement to provide biodiversity net gain is in force, relates to the weight to be given to the net gain in the *"planning balance"* of something which is provided pursuant to the statutory duty and, then, to any additional net gain above the minimum. Arguably, a developer who provides the statutory minimum is simply complying with the statutory duty which applies to all other developers and, accordingly, he should not be given any particular credit for meeting a statutory obligation. The alternative is that a matter of weight is a matter of weight and it should not make a difference whether this arises from the discharge of statutory duty or not. As a plain matter of fact, the provision of any biodiversity net gain must be a benefit of a scheme for the purposes of the planning balance. Be that as it may, if the developer is providing over and above the statutory minimum, it should be the case that any additional net gain over the minimum is a material consideration which weighs in favour of the grant of planning permission. Another question is the comparative weight to be given to onsite as opposed to offsite net gain. Arguably, the short answer is that this matter of weighting is included within the Metric under the in-built "*spatial risk*" multiplier. However, the Metric does not take account of the benefits of any buffering land between offset sites and nearby urban areas. It should be the case that an offset site which has the advantage of a *cordon sanitaire* between it and an urban area is more desirable than one which abuts an urban area which thereby lends itself to recreational uses or trespass which might be undesirable in establishing or maintaining the relevant habitat.

9.3   The statutory role of the Metric

Those involved in the planning process need to be aware of the statutory and administrative context within which the Metric plays a role.

The outputs from the Metric are expressed as "*Biodiversity Units*" and these units of measurement have been described as the "*currency*" which underpins the biodiversity gain system.[9] The Metric provides a measured method of comparison between, respectively, the impacts of a proposed development on the pre-development onsite biodiversity and the total post-development biodiversity value attributable to the development. The post-development biodiversity value attributable to the development can be onsite or offsite or a combination of the two.

When the provisions of the Environment Act relating to the enhancement of biodiversity through the planning process come into force, most planning permissions granted for the development of land in England will be deemed to have been granted subject to the condition that the development may not be begun unless a Biodiversity Gain Plan has been submitted to and approved by the planning authority.[10]

The Biodiversity Gain Plan must comply with the "*Biodiversity Gain Objective*". In turn, the Biodiversity Gain Objective is met if the "*biodiversity value attributable to the development*" exceeds the pre-development biodiversity value of the onsite habitat by at least the "*relevant percentage*".[11] Clearly, these quantitative objectives can be met only if the relevant factors which are to be taken into account are measured by way of a metric. The Biodiversity Metric is the metric which has been chosen for this task and it has been embedded in the Environment Act itself and, thereby, given statutory weight.

The Act provides that the Biodiversity Metric is to be produced and published by the Secretary of State,[12] who must lay the Biodiversity Metric, and any revised Biodiversity Metric, before Parliament.

---

[9]   The Glossary to the Consultation Document states: "*A biodiversity unit is the 'currency' of the biodiversity metric. A unit represents a combined measure of habitat distinctiveness, area, and condition*". This is not the same thing as a '*biodiversity credit*': see below.

[10]   Paragraph 13 of Schedule 7A to the Town and Country Planning Act 1990 – see Chapters 14 and 15.

[11]   Currently 10%: Paragraph 2(3) of Schedule 7A to the 1990 Act.

[12]   Paragraph 4(2) and (6) of Schedule 7A to the 1990 Act.

The Metric flows through the statutory scheme and provides outputs by way of "*Biodiversity Units*".[13]

The "*biodiversity value attributable to the development*"[14] is the total of:

(a) the post-development biodiversity value of the onsite habitat,

(b) the biodiversity value, in relation to the development, of any registered offsite biodiversity gain allocated to the development, and

(c) the biodiversity value of any Biodiversity Credits purchased for the development.

All of the above mentioned "*values*" will be quantified by reference to Biodiversity Units. The Metric will be used by a developer to provide input into decisions on items (a) and, perhaps, (b); however, the quantification of item (c) should be prescribed by regulations and, thus, should be taken as a given in this calculation.

Turning to Biodiversity Gain Plans,[15] these must specify the following matters:

(a) information about the steps taken or to be taken to minimise the adverse effect of the development on the biodiversity of the onsite habitat and any other habitat;

(b) the pre-development biodiversity value of the onsite habitat;

(c) the post-development biodiversity value of the onsite habitat;

(d) any registered offsite biodiversity gain allocated to the development and the biodiversity value of that gain in relation to the development;

(e) any Biodiversity Credits purchased for the development, and

(f) such other matters as the Secretary of State may by regulations specify.

The Metric can be used to provide input into decisions on matters (a), (b) and (c); however, the quantification of matters (d) and (e) will, presumably, be set by regulations.

Perhaps a rough shorthand way of looking at the matter is that the Metric will probably come into play where the legislation refers to the values of "*habitats*".

---

[13] As will be discussed below, this is something of a misnomer, because the metric provides a measurement of habitats only. A better label would have been "*habitat units*".

[14] Paragraph 2(2) of Schedule 7A to the 1990 Act.

[15] Discussed in Chapter 15.

9.4 Overview

The Biodiversity Metric 3.0 will be discussed below; however, it is a fairly complicated document for those new to the concept, and so it is useful to start with less complicated materials. One such document arises from a pilot study which was carried out in 2012 entitled "*Biodiversity Offsetting Pilots – Guidance for Developers*".[16] This document is part of a short series of similar documents and it is useful to read it by way of introduction.

One of the tables set out in the document provided a simple illustrative example of the way in which that pilot metric operated. The approach was to evaluate the habitat according to certain specified criteria. The ecological features of the site were then evaluated and given a notional weighting. Those weightings were then totalled together to provide a value for the habitat expressed in "*Biodiversity Units*". It was this value which is taken as measured value for the purposes of this exercise.

This can be seen by going through the illustrative example from the study, which is shown below, on a step-by step-basis.

First, it was first necessary to define the site boundaries and then divide the site into appropriate parcels as needed. Parcels are simply distinct portions of each habitat type present. In the example, the habitat is shown as being "*lowland meadow*" and comprises an area of six hectares. Secondly, the "*distinctiveness*" of the habitat was weighted (here on a scale from 1 to 6) and, here, the weighted value is given as 6. Thirdly, the denominator "*condition*" was given a weighting of 2 (again on a scale from 1 to 6 in this example). Finally, the values provided in these columns were totalled to provide 72 "*Biodiversity Units*".

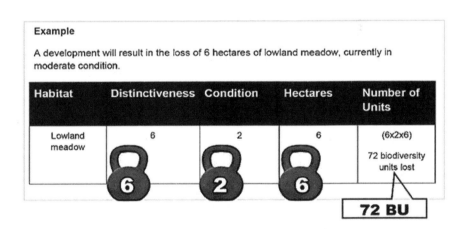

(NB: The added graphics are the author's).

---

[16] *Biodiversity Offsetting Pilots – Guidance for Developers* (March 2012). A joint publication by Natural England and Defra.

9.5 The Biodiversity Metric 2.0

The Biodiversity Metric 2.0 was developed from the 2012 pilot studies and, again, used habitat features as a proxy measure for capturing the value and importance of nature, and came with a free calculation tool designed to simplify and speed up the calculation process. This was replaced in July 2021 with the suite of resources now known as the "*Biodiversity Metric 3.0*". The changes from Version 2.0 to Version 3.0 have been summarised in a document entitled "*Summary of changes from Biodiversity Metric 2.0 to version 3.0*" (Natural England Joint Publication JP039 – July 2021).

9.6 The Biodiversity Metric 3.0

Biodiversity Metric 3.0 is, currently, a system or methodology comprising software programmes (in the form of spreadsheets), an interlinked geographical information system (called "*QGIS*"), and supporting documents. They include the following:

- Biodiversity Metric 3.0 – Calculation Tool (spreadsheet).

- Biodiversity Metric 3.0 – Calculation Tool (spreadsheet) (macro free).

- Biodiversity Metric 3.0 – habitat condition assessment sheets with instructions, (spreadsheet tool).

- Summary of Changes from Biodiversity Metric 2.0 to Metric 3.0.

- Biodiversity Metric 3.0 – User Guide.

- Biodiversity Metric 3.0 – Technical Supplement.

- Biodiversity Metric 3.0 – Short User Guide.

- Biodiversity Metric 3.0 GIS Data Standard, (spreadsheet tool).

- Biodiversity Metric 3.0 GIS Import Tool – Beta Test (spreadsheet tool).

- Biodiversity Metric 3.0 QGIS Template and GIS Import Tool Guidance – Beta Test.

- Biodiversity Metric 3.0 QGIS Template – Beta Test (zip folder).[17]

The Metric is also accompanied by a draft "*Small Sites Metric*", which will be discussed below.

As noted above, the Biodiversity Metric is embedded in the Environment Act.[18] The Metric is defined as:

---

[17]   A folder containing mapping materials to set up the site plan and its characteristics on a pre-populated QGIS template ready for its interface with the Metric.

[18]   Paragraph 4(1) of Schedule 7A to the 1990 Act.

"a document for measuring, for the purposes of this Schedule, the biodiversity value or relative biodiversity value of habitat or habitat enhancement."

This makes it clear that the Metric is a methodology for the measurement of habitats only and does not mention species. The evaluation of impacts on species is a separate exercise.

The problem with the Act is that, as can be seen above, the Metric is not *"a document"* but an interlinked methodology driven by three spreadsheets, an importation tool linking the Metric to the QGIS mapping system, and a number of supporting documents. This leaves open the question of whether the intent behind this statutory provision was to incorporate the whole or part of this suite or just the spreadsheet.[19]

9.7 The importance of mapping

As will be discussed below, the Metric proceeds by reference to three types of habitat; namely, *"area habitats"*, *"rivers"* and *"hedgerows"*. All of these are set out on a base-plan and attributes tool which underpin the application of the Metric. Accordingly, it is important not only that these features are measured but also that a standardised methodology for making and inputting these measurements into the model is established. Hence the published document entitled *"Biodiversity Metric 3.0 QGIS template and import tool USER GUIDE Beta Test"*, first published by Natural England in July 2021, and its accompanying spreadsheet.

The document states:

> *"1.1 A QGIS template, data standard, GIS import tool and this guidance document have been created by FPCR on behalf of Natural England and is intended to be freely distributed as an optional addition to the Biodiversity Metric 3.0."*

As to the purpose of the tool:

> *"1.2 This tool has been designed with the dual purposes of reducing the time required to input data into the Biodiversity Metric, whilst also providing a standardised methodology which produces shareable outputs that track the life cycle of each parcel of land. By utilising a standardised QGIS template, data can be recorded in a format which is consistent with the data requirements to carry out a Biodiversity Metric Calculation. The raw data can then be imported and organised within the import tool before being directly exported to a Biodiversity Metric 3.0 workbook. Additional benefits of this standardised approach include enhanced data validation, automated graphic generation, and a consistent and transparent workflow.*
>
> *1.3 The use of the tool and this standardised approach will allow for easier inter-rogation of data between consultant ecologists, their clients, developers and Local Planning Authorities."*

---

[19] Hence the need for a chapter on statutory interpretation. Arguably, the reality is that neither Parliament nor the Parliamentary draftsman was aware of this point.

This guidance takes account of the use of other approaches by specialists:

> *"1.4 QGIS software has been selected for the freely available template as the most widely used freely available GIS software in the environmental consultancy sector. The GIS import tool is compatible with the QGIS raw data outputs and other GIS software outputs in a compatible format.*
>
> *1.5 Whilst the standardised approach detailed in this guidance provides suitable methodology, it is recognised that practitioners may undertake mapping and initial data compilation utilising alternative workflows and software packages. To this end, a data standard has been supplied which will allow outputs from these approaches to be standardised, providing compatibility with the import tool. This will allow practitioners utilising alternative data creation methodologies to still benefit from the automated import functionality of the import tools."*

If the site has been cleared prior to a planning application and/or the use of the Metric, it will be necessary to see if its pre-development condition can be divined from sources such as aerial photographs, old maps or anecdotal evidence. This could become a difficult issue between applicant and local planning authority and it is unclear where the burden of proof lies. Arguably, it should be with the applicant, because he will be offering the outputs from the operation of the Metric for the approval of the local planning authority. Hence the old precept *"he who asserts must prove"* should operate in this connection.

9.8 The *"key principles"*

The Metric sets out a set of *"key principles"* for its use.[20] These are set out below:[21]

> **Principle 1**: The Metric does not change the protection afforded to biodiversity. Existing levels of protection afforded to protected species and habitats are not changed by use of this or any other Metric. Statutory obligations will still need to be satisfied.
>
> **Principle 2**: Biodiversity Metric calculations can inform decision-making where application of the mitigation hierarchy and good practice principles conclude that compensation for habitat losses is justified.
>
> **Principle 3**: The Metric's Biodiversity Units are only a proxy for biodiversity and should be treated as relative values. While the Metric is underpinned by ecological evidence, the units generated by the Metric are only a proxy for biodiversity and, to be of practical use, it has been kept deliberately simple. The numerical values generated by the Metric represent relative, not absolute, values.

---

[20] See page 16 of the User Guide.

[21] Albeit mildly re-formatted for the purposes of this book.

Principle 4: The Metric focuses on typical habitats and widespread species; important or protected habitats and features should be given broader consideration.

- Protected and locally important species needs are not considered through the Metric; they should be addressed through existing policy and legislation.

- Impacts on protected sites (e.g. SSSIs) and irreplaceable habitats are not adequately measured by the Metric. They will require separate consideration which must comply with existing national and local policy and legislation. Data relating to these can be entered into the Metric, so as to give an indicative picture of the biodiversity value of the habitats present on a site, but this should be supported by bespoke advice.

Principle 5: The Metric design aims to encourage enhancement, not transformation, of the natural environment. Proper consideration should be given to the habitats being lost in favour of higher-scoring habitats, and whether the retention of less distinctive but well-established habitats may sometimes be a better option for local biodiversity. Habitat created to compensate for loss of natural or semi-natural habitat should be of the same broad habitat type (e.g. new woodland to replace lost woodland), unless there is a good ecological reason to do otherwise (e.g. to restore a heathland habitat that was converted to woodland for timber in the past).

Principle 6: The Metric is designed to inform decisions, not to override expert opinion. Management interventions should be guided by appropriate expert ecological advice and not just the Biodiversity Unit outputs of the Metric. Ecological principles still need to be applied to ensure that what is being proposed is realistic and deliverable based on local conditions (such as geology, hydrology and nutrient levels) and the complexity of future management requirements.

Principle 7: Compensation habitats should seek, where practical, to be local to the impact. They should aim to replicate the characteristics of the habitats that have been lost, taking account of the structure and species composition that give habitats their local distinctiveness. Where possible, compensation habitats should contribute towards nature recovery in England by creating *"more, bigger, better and joined up"* areas for biodiversity.

Principle 8: The Metric does not enforce a mandatory minimum 1:1 habitat size ratio for losses and compensation, but consideration should be given to maintaining habitat extent and habitat parcels of sufficient size for ecological function. A difference can occur because of a difference in quality between the habitat impacted and the compensation provided. For example, if a habitat of low distinctiveness is impacted and is compensated for by the creation of habitat of higher distinctiveness or better condition, the area needed to compensate for losses can potentially be less than the area impacted. However, consideration should be given to whether reducing the area or length of habitat provided as compensation is an appropriate outcome.

The Metric operates on the assumption that, if one gets the habitat right, the species will follow.

9.9 The *"six key rules"*

The Metric sets out six key rules for its use[22] as follows:[23]

Rule 1: Where the Metric is used to measure change, Biodiversity Units need to be calculated to show, respectively, values prior to the intervention and for post-intervention for all parcels of land/linear features affected.

Rule 2: Compensation for habitat losses can be provided by creating new habitats, or by restoring or enhancing existing habitats. Measures to enhance existing habitats must provide a significant and demonstrable uplift in distinctiveness and/or condition to record additional Biodiversity Units.

Rule 3: "*Trading down*" must be avoided. Losses of habitat are to be compensated for on a "*like for like*" or "*like for better*" basis. New or restored habitats should aim to achieve a higher distinctiveness and/or condition than those lost. Losses of irreplaceable or very high distinctiveness habitat cannot adequately be accounted for through the Metric.

Rule 4: Biodiversity unit values generated by Biodiversity Metric 3.0 are unique to this metric and cannot be compared to unit outputs from version 2.0, the original Defra metric or any other biodiversity metric. Furthermore, the three types of Biodiversity Unit generated by this metric (for area, hedgerow and river habitats) are unique and cannot be summed.

Rule 5: It is not the area/length of habitat created that determines whether ecological equivalence or better has been achieved but the net change in Biodiversity Units. Risks associated with creating or enhancing habitats mean that it may be necessary to create or enhance a larger area of habitat than that lost, to fully compensate for impacts on biodiversity.

Rule 6: Deviations from the published methodology of Biodiversity Metric 3.0 need to be ecologically justified and agreed with relevant decision makers. While the methodology is expected to be suitable in the majority

---

[22] See page 17 of the User Guide. Slightly amended in this narrative.

[23] Albeit mildly re-formatted for the purposes of this book.

of circumstances, it is recognised that there may be exceptions. Any local or project-specific adaptations of the metric must be transparent and fully justified.

9.10 The four key steps to using Biodiversity Metric 3.0[24]

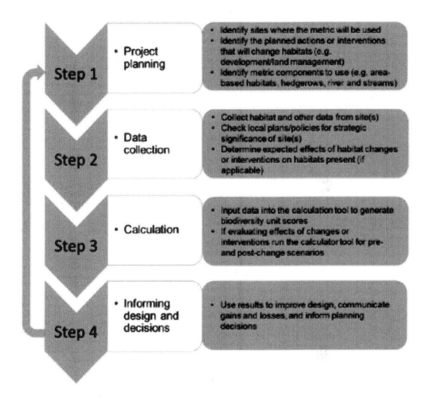

Step 1 • Project planning
- Identify sites where the metric will be used
- Identify the planned actions or interventions that will change habitats (e.g. development/land management)
- Identify metric components to use (e.g. area-based habitats, hedgerows, river and streams)

Step 2 • Data collection
- Collect habitat and other data from site(s)
- Check local plans/policies for strategic significance of site(s)
- Determine expected effects of habitat changes or interventions on habitats present (if applicable)

Step 3 • Calculation
- Input data into the calculation tool to generate biodiversity unit scores
- If evaluating effects of changes or interventions run the calculator tool for pre- and post-change scenarios

Step 4 • Informing design and decisions
- Use results to improve design, communicate gains and losses, and inform planning decisions

9.11 The *"pre-intervention"* biodiversity calculation

The assessment of pre-intervention quality comprises three components:[25]

- **Distinctiveness** – A score based on the type of habitat present (e.g. modified grassland has a "*Low*" distinctiveness score, and lowland meadows are "*Very High*").

- **Condition** – A score based on the biodiversity value of the habitat relative to others of the same type. This is determined by condition criteria set out in the technical supplement.

---

[24] See page 14 of the User Guide.
[25] See page 10 of the User Guide.

- **Strategic significance** – A score based on whether the location of the development and/or offsite work or the habitats present/created have been identified as significant for nature.

The Metric's spreadsheet operates by applying a score to each of these elements. It then performs a calculation which takes the size of each habitat parcel with each of these *"quality"* scores to produce a number that represents the *"biodiversity unit value"* of each habitat parcel. The initial calculation represents the *"baseline"* or *"pre-intervention"* value in Biodiversity Units.

PRE-intervention biodiversity calculation (the baseline)

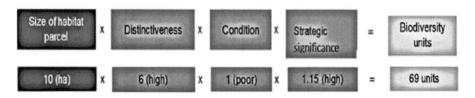

9.12 The *"post-intervention"* biodiversity calculation

The calculation is then repeated for the post-intervention (either development or land management change) scenario. This calculation should include any measures to retain existing habitats and create or enhance habitats to generate additional Biodiversity Units. This gives the user a *"post-intervention"* Biodiversity Unit score.

At this point, because the Metric is measuring predicted changes rather than existing habitats, additional factors to account for the risks associated with creating, restoring or enhancing habitats are also considered.[26] The three risks incorporated into the Metric are:

- **Difficulty of creating or restoring a habitat** – a pre-assigned score based on how difficult the habitat type is to create and restore/enhance.

- **Temporal risk** – *"time to target"* condition. A pre-assigned score based on how long the habitat site takes to establish and reach a target condition.

- **Spatial risk** – the score based on distance between the site of habitat loss and the site where the creation/enhancement is provided.

---

[26] See page 11 of the User Guide.

The risk associated with the delivery of biodiversity creation or enhancement is due to uncertainty in the effectiveness of management techniques used to restore or create habitat. The level of risk differs between habitat types because of ecological factors and due to the availability of techniques or know-how to create habitats in a realistic time-frame. Uncertainty in achieving the target outcome for each habitat is addressed by a habitat-specific *"difficulty"* multiplier based on available science and expert opinion.

Temporal risk relates to the delivery of compensation where there may be a mismatch in the timing of the impact and compensation, i.e. the difference in time between the negative impact on biodiversity and the compensation reaching the required quality. This results in lower levels of biodiversity for that period of time. The time taken for habitats to mature means that there will almost inevitably be a time lag and, where this does occur, a risk multiplier is applied.

As to *"spatial risk"*(aka *"offsite risk multiplier"*), there are both ecological and social reasons for compensatory habitat to be provided close to where losses occur. There is a risk of the compensation being delivered at a distance from the impact site. Where this is the case, the spacial risk multiplier is applied.

POST-intervention biodiversity calculation (for newly created or enhanced habitats)

89

9.13 The net change in unit value

The predicted[27] value of the habitats in Biodiversity Units "*post-intervention*" score is then deducted from the "*baseline*" pre-intervention unit score to give a net change unit value.

If the project has explicit Biodiversity Unit requirements, the Metric can be used to calculate the numbers of units that the design is predicted to deliver. The design can be revised to improve the number of Biodiversity Units obtained. The Metric can be used to measure offsite compensation where this is required. The processes for measuring onsite and offsite changes and compensation are very similar. The Biodiversity Unit values of the offsite habitats are calculated for the "*pre-intervention*" and "*post-intervention*" stages. The "*pre-intervention*" units are then subtracted from the "*post-intervention*" units to work out how many Biodiversity Units will result from that habitat change.

If it is possible to arrive at a value for a site (expressed in terms of Biodiversity Units), it is possible to go on and consider the concept of Biodiversity Credits.

It might be the case that there is no nearby site available at the appropriate time to act as the receptor site for any habitat offset. One alternative is for the developer to provide the monetary wherewithal for the creation of biodiversity gain, and then for the developer to leave it to an appropriate body to use that money to achieve that objective. The calculation of this funding can be expressed in monetary terms, so as to cover the price of purchasing land which will deliver the required Biodiversity Units or in terms of "*Biodiversity Credits*" (see Chapter 13).

It follows, from the numerical nature of the Metric, that it is possible to use it to calculate the measurable biodiversity net gain (the "*relevant percentage*")[28] which is sought from the development scheme.

9.14 Boundary manipulation

The Consultation Document[29] provides a definition of "*habitat*". This must, for integration into the planning process, be translated into identified boundaries and areas (presumably by way of QGIS) and then inserted into, or identified by, the relevant planning documents (i.e. conditions/planning obligations). The obvious problem is that the developer might try to split the overall development site into separate small parcels to take advantage of the *de minimis* exemption or to isolate the redevelopment of buildings and habitats so as to maintain the "*zero*" net gain which would be attributable to the development of them. The discussion of this point, therefore, turns on whether or not the "*development*" is the totality

---

[27] The fact that this will be a predication cannot be overlooked when it comes to securing the delivery of the net gain at some point in the future. Hence the need to consider mechanisms such as planning obligations and the like in order to provide for long-term management arrangements.

[28] See Chapters 14 and 15 below for an explanation.

[29] This chapter makes frequent reference to the "*Consultation Document.*" This is the Defra document entitled "*Consultation on Biodiversity Net Gain Regulations and Implementation*" (January 2022). The consultation started on 16 March 2022 and closed on 4 April 2022.

of these individual parcels of land or whether regulations will provide for the aggregation of small associated parcels by way of their cumulative impacts.

The current short answer might be that there is nothing to stop a local planning authority from taking the view that the separate applications are so bound up with each other that they demand a bespoke approach which looks at the cumulative impact of the applications when taken together. Most local planning authorities will be astute for the developer who is trying to pull the wool over their eyes by way of dis-aggregating an otherwise single development scheme.

9.15   Linear habitats

The Metric incorporates similar but separate calculations for linear habitats that require a different method of measurement, and there are two broad categories of linear habitats:

*   hedgerows and lines of trees; and

*   rivers and streams.

These supplementary modules of the Metric are calculated differently and have their own discrete Biodiversity Unit types. These features will, if present, feed into the model.

9.16   Urban trees

The Metric calculation tool includes a sub-category called the *"urban tree helper"*, viz:

Urban tree helper		
Tree size	**Tree number**	**Area**
Small		**0.0000**
Medium		**0.0000**
Large		**0.0000**
Total	**0.00**	**0.0000**

9.17   The Small Sites Metric

Defra intends to take forward the option of a simplified Biodiversity Metric for developments on small sites: page 36 of Consultation Document. However, it does not consider that a lower percentage gain would be appropriate for small development.

The phrase *"small sites"* is not defined in the glossary to the Consultation Document;[30] therefore, it would appear that Defra has yet to settle a final definition. The front-runner would appear to be:

> *"Sites of fewer than 10 [dwellinghouses]*[31] *or an area of less than 0.5 hectares for other types of development (unless priority or protected habitats are present)."*

Guidance for small sites is given in the joint publication entitled *"Small Sites Metric Calculation Tool: User Guide – Beta Test".*[32] Per page 5:

> *"The [Small Sites Metric (aka "SSM")] is very similar to the main Biodiversity Metric 3.0 for larger development, but it simplifies the process and can be undertaken by a competent person for the habitats involved (which may be the project managers and architects on many sites)."*

The guidance states that the Small Sites Metric can only be used when both of these criteria are met:[33]

Criterion 1

- For a residential development: where the number of dwellings to be provided is between one and nine inclusive on a site having an area of less than one hectare or, where the number of dwellings to be provided is not known, there is a site area of less than 0.5 hectares.

- For all other development types: where the site area is less than 0.5 hectares or 5,000 square metres.

Criterion 2

There is no Priority Habitat[34] within the development area (excluding hedgerows and arable margins).

The Small Sites Metric must not be used for assessing biodiversity outside the development area. Any habitat creation or enhancement outside the site area must be assessed using Biodiversity Metric 3.0.

---

[30] Albeit *"minor development"* is defined as: (i) for residential: where the number of dwellings to be provided is between one and nine inclusive on a site having an area of less than one hectare or, where the number of dwellings to be provided is not known, a site area of less than 0.5 hectares; and (ii) for non-residential: where the floor space to be created is less than 1,000 square metres OR where the site area is less than one hectare.

[31] Page 36. Ibid footnote 30: *"This threshold would be defined in terms of "dwellinghouses" rather than "residential units" for consistency with the Town and Country Planning (Development Management Procedure) (England) Order 2015."*

[32] Natural England Joint Publication JP040. First published July 2021.

[33] Ibid Page 4.

[34] Also called *"Habitats of Principal Importance"*. A list and definition for these habitats can be found at UK BAP Priority Habitats | JNCC - Adviser to Government on Nature Conservation.

If the above criteria are met, the Small Sites Metric can be used. If this is not the case, the site should be scored using the Biodiversity Metric 3.0.

Chapter 10

Local Biodiversity Reports

10.1   Introduction

It is necessary, before delving down into this particular topic, to digress into the background to it.

This has to do with the Natural Environment and Rural Communities Act 2006; and, in particular, section 40(1) of the 2006 Act, which provides as follows:

> *"a public authority must, in exercising its functions, have regard, so far as is consistent with the proper exercise of those functions, to the purpose of conserving biodiversity."*

This provision is, plainly, a material consideration in the determination of planning applications.

New section 40(A1) of the 2006 Act now pursues the *"general biodiversity objective"*. The *"general biodiversity objective"* is the conservation and enhancement of biodiversity in England through the exercise of functions in relation to England.

The local authority will be required to produce a Biodiversity Report. The report must show that the general biodiversity objective has been met. In seeking to discharge its duties, the local authority must provide and adopt policies which pursue the general biodiversity objective. It is not clear whether it is intended that those policies will relate to site-specific applications. Also, it is unclear whether there are any robust site-specific enforcement mechanisms.

10.2   General duty to conserve and enhance biodiversity

In its 2016 iteration, section 40(1) provided that a public authority must, in exercising its functions, have regard, so far as is consistent with the proper exercise of those functions, to the purpose of conserving biodiversity. For these purposes, *"public authority"* included a local planning authority: section 40(4). By section 40(3), the phrase *"conserving biodiversity"* included, in relation to a living organism or type of habitat, restoring or enhancing a population or habitat.

Section 102(1) now provides that section 40 of the Natural Environment and Rural Communities Act 2006 is amended so that section 40(1) is replaced.

As to the *"general biodiversity objective"*, section 40(1) now reads:

> *"A public authority which has any functions exercisable in relation to England must from time to time consider what action the authority can properly take, consistently with the proper exercise of its functions, to further the general biodiversity objective."*

New section 40(A1) provides:

> *"For the purposes of this section 'the general biodiversity objective' is the conservation and enhancement of biodiversity in England through the exercise of functions in relation to England."*

A new section 40(3) now provides that:

> *"(3) The action which may be taken by the authority to further the general biodiversity objective includes, in particular, action taken for the purpose* (sic) *of -*
>
> *(a) conserving, restoring or otherwise enhancing a population of a particular species, and*
>
> *(b) conserving, restoring or otherwise enhancing a particular type of habitat."*

The reference to "*a population of a particular species*" might be slightly confusing to the trained ecologist, because the accepted classifications list four distinct tiers of organisational complexity, of which "*population*" is but one.

Section 40(1A) now provides that, "*after that consideration*"[1], the authority must (unless it concludes that there is no new action it can properly take):

> *"(a) determine such policies and specific objectives as it considers appropriate for taking action to further the general biodiversity objective, and*
>
> *(b) take such action as it considers appropriate, in the light of those policies and objectives, to further that objective."*

A determination required by subsection (1A)(a) must be made as soon as practicable after the completion of the consideration to which it relates: section 40(1E).

New section 40(1B) provides that:

> *"The requirements of subsection (1A)(a) may be satisfied (to any extent) by revising any existing policies and specific objectives for taking action to further the general biodiversity objective."*

Arguably, this seems to water down the original section 40 because it does not appear to suggest that the furtherance of the general biodiversity objective may be taken into account as a material consideration in site-specific decision-making. This appears to be so when one considers that the requirements of section 40(1A)(a) may be satisfied by revising any

---

[1]   Presumably the consideration by the authority of the matters in section 40(1).

existing policies and specific objectives for taking action to further the general biodiversity objective: section 40(1B). However, section 40(1F) then goes on to say that nothing in section 40 prevents the authority from determining or revising policies and specific objectives at any time or taking action to further the general biodiversity objective at any time. It might, thus, be the case that a person seeking to introduce the general biodiversity objective into the decision-making process can seek to do so by reference to this proviso.

By new section 40(1C), the first consideration required by section 40(1) must be completed by the authority within the period of one year beginning with the day on which section 102 of the Environment Act came into force. Any subsequent consideration required by subsection (1) must be completed no more than five years after the completion of the authority's previous consideration: section 40(1D).

A new section 40(2A) provides that, in complying with section 40(1) and (1A), the authority must in particular have regard to any relevant local nature recovery strategy and any relevant species conservation strategy or protected site strategy prepared by Natural England.

The Secretary of State must issue guidance to local planning authorities as to how they are to comply with their duty under section 40(2A)(a): section 40(2B).

10.3   Biodiversity reports

A new section 40A provides that a public authority to which this section applies (*"the authority"*) must publish *"biodiversity reports"*.

By section 40A(3), a biodiversity report must contain:

> *"(a) a summary of the action which the authority has taken over the period covered by the report for the purpose of complying with its duties under section 40(1) and (1A),*
>
> *(b) a summary of the authority's plans for complying with those duties over the period of five years following the period covered by the report,*
>
> *(c) any quantitative data required to be included in the report by regulations under subsection (8)(b), and*
>
> *(d) any other information that the authority considers it appropriate to include in the report."*

By section 40A(4), if the authority is a local planning authority, its biodiversity report must also contain:

> *"(a) a summary of the action taken by the authority in carrying out its functions under Schedule 7A to the Town and Country Planning Act 1990 (biodiversity gain as condition of planning permission) over the period covered by the report,*

(b) information about any biodiversity gains resulting or expected to result from biodi-versity gain plans approved by the authority during that period, and

(c) a summary of the authority's plans for carrying out those functions over the five year period following the period covered by the report."

A biodiversity report must specify the period covered by the report, and must be published within the period of 12 weeks following the last day of that period: see section 40A(5).

The authority's first biodiversity report must cover a period chosen by the authority which is no longer than three years, and begins with the day on which the authority first becomes subject to the duty under subsection (2): section 40A(6).

A subsequent biodiversity report made by the authority must cover a period chosen by the authority which is no longer than five years, and begins with the day after the last day of the period covered by its most recent biodiversity report: section 40A(7).

The Secretary of State may by regulations provide for specified public authorities, or public authorities of a specified description, to be designated authorities for the purposes of this section and require biodiversity reports to include specified quantitative data relating to biodiversity in any area of land in England in relation to which the authority exercises any functions: section 40A(8).

Chapter 11

Conservation Covenant Agreements

11.1 Introduction

Conservation Covenant Agreements are voluntary agreements between a landowner and a *"responsible body"* (see below) providing positive or restrictive obligations to fulfil a conservation objective in respect of his land. They may bind not only the landowner but also subsequent landowners.

The Law Commission[1] recommended the adoption of a scheme based on Conservation Covenants in 2014 and it found its way into the Environment Act.

This new legislation was deemed necessary to overcome the ancient constraints of property law, which made the securing of continuing obligations at common law either impractical or impossible. It is only possible to bind freehold land (the *"servient tenement"*) in the long-term, and against a successor in title, if the covenant is negative and it benefits nearby land (the *"dominant tenement"*) and the only person with the ability to enforce it is the owner of the dominant tenement. Neither the public nor any public body have any input into this purely voluntary property arrangement. Importantly, this private property law principle applies only to negative obligations (i.e. a promise not to do something), and not to positive obligations (i.e. a promise to do something). Due to the doctrine of *"privity of contract"*, positive obligations are binding in contract only and do not *"run with the land"* to bind persons who were not parties to the contract.

Those familiar with the history of section 106 agreements will know that they evolved to overcome these common law constraints and *"run with the land"* by virtue of the provisions of the Town and Country Planning Act 1990. The creation of the Conservation Covenant Agreement is a similar statutory intervention.

11.2 Formation of Conservation Covenant Agreements

By section 117(1), a *"Conservation Covenant Agreement"* is an agreement between a landowner and a *"responsible body"* where:

> *"(a) the agreement contains provision (sic) which–*
>
> *(i) is of a 'qualifying kind',*
>
> *(ii) has a 'conservation purpose', and*
>
> *(iii) is intended by the parties to be for the public good,*

---

[1]   The Law Commission - (LAW COM No 349) – *"CONSERVATION COVENANTS"* – 23 June 2014.

(b) it appears from the agreement that the parties intend to create a Conservation Covenant, and

(c) the agreement is executed as a deed by the parties."²

By section 117(2), a provision of a *"qualifying kind"* is a provision:

"(a) requiring the landowner–

(i) to do, or not to do, something on land in England specified in the provision in relation to which the landowner holds a *'qualifying estate'* specified in the agreement for the purposes of the provision, or

(ii) to allow the responsible body to do something on such land, or

(b) requiring the responsible body to do something on such land."

By section 117(3), a provision has a *"conservation purpose"* if its purpose is:

(a) "to conserve³ the natural environment of land or the natural resources of land,

(b) to conserve land as a place of archaeological, architectural, artistic, cultural or historic interest, or

(c) to conserve the setting of land with a natural environment or natural resources or which is a place of archaeological, architectural, artistic, cultural or historic interest."

By section 117(4), a *"qualifying estate"* means:

"(a) an estate in fee simple absolute in possession (i.e. a freehold), or

(b) a term of years absolute (i.e. a leasehold) granted for a term of more than seven years from the date of the grant and in the case of which some part of the period for which the term of years was granted remains unexpired."

A *"responsible body"* is the Secretary of State or a body designated by the Secretary of State (referred to in this Part as *"designated bodies"*): section 119(1).

---

² The requirement as to execution as a deed was added at the *"ping-pong"* stage in Parliament on the thesis that it imports some magic in terms of enforceability!

³ By section 119(9),*"conservation"* means conservation of–

(a) the natural environment or natural resources of land,

(b) places of archaeological, architectural, artistic, cultural or historic interest, or

(c) the setting of land with a natural environment or natural resources or which is a place of archaeological, architectural, artistic, cultural or historic interest.

The Secretary of State may, on the application of a local authority or other body, designate it as a responsible body but may only designate a *"Local Authority"*[4] if satisfied that it is suitable to be a responsible body: section 119(3).

The Secretary of State may only designate a body that is not a local authority if satisfied that it is suitable to be a responsible body and:

> *"(a) in the case of a public body or a charity,*[5] *at least some of its main purposes or functions relate to conservation, or*

> *(b) in any other case, at least some of the body's main activities relate to conservation."*[6]

11.3 Duration of obligation under Conservation Covenant

An obligation under a Conservation Covenant has effect for the *"default period"*, unless the covenant provides for a shorter period. The *"default period"* is:

> *(a) if the qualifying estate in relation to the obligation is freehold, a period of indefinite duration, and*

> *(b) if the qualifying estate in relation to the obligation is a leasehold, the remainder of the period for which the lease was granted.*

11.4 Benefit and burden of obligation of landowner

An obligation under a Conservation Covenant is owed by a landowner to the responsible body under the Conservation Covenant: section 122(1).

An obligation of the landowner under a Conservation Covenant binds the landowner under the covenant, and any person who becomes a *"successor"* of the landowner under the covenant: section 122(2).

For these purposes, a *"successor"* (in relation to the landowner under the covenant) means a person who holds, in respect of any of the land to which the obligation relates, the *"qualifying estate"* (see above) or an estate in land derived (whether immediately or otherwise) from the qualifying estate after the creation of the covenant: section 122(3).

By section 122(4), an obligation of the landowner under a Conservation Covenant ceases to bind the landowner under the covenant, or a person who becomes a successor of that landowner, in respect of:

---

[4]   A *"local authority"* means–

(a) a county or district council in England; (b) a London borough council; (c) the Common Council of the City of London; or (d) the Council of the Isles of Scilly: section 119(9).

[5]   A *"charity"* means a charity registered under the Charities Act 2011 or an exempt charity (within the meaning of that Act): section 119(9).

[6]   Sections 119(4) and 119(5).

"(a) land which ceases to be land to which the obligation relates,

(b) in the case of the landowner under the covenant, land in relation to which the landowner ceases to be the holder of the qualifying estate, or

(c) in the case of a successor, land in relation to which the successor ceases to be the holder of the qualifying estate or of the estate derived from the qualifying estate, as the case may be."

By section 122(5), a successor is not bound if:

"(a) the obligation in the Covenant is positive and the person becomes a successor by virtue of holding a lease granted for a term of seven years or less from the date of the grant,

(b) the Conservation Covenant was not registered in the local land charges register at the time when the successor acquired the estate in land concerned, or

(c) the successor's immediate predecessor in title was not bound by the obligation in respect of the land to which the successor's interest relates."

11.5   Benefit of obligation of responsible body

An obligation of the responsible body under a Conservation Covenant is owed to the landowner under the covenant, and to any person who becomes a successor of the landowner under the covenant.

For these purposes, *"successor"* (in relation to the landowner under the covenant) means a person who holds, in respect of any of the land to which the obligation relates the qualifying estate, or an estate in land derived (whether immediately or otherwise) from the qualifying estate after the creation of the covenant: section 123(2).

By section 123(3), an obligation of the responsible body under a Conservation Covenant ceases to be owed to the landowner under the covenant, or to a person who becomes a successor of that landowner, in respect of:

"(a) land which ceases to be land to which the obligation relates,

(b) in the case of the landowner under the covenant, land in relation to which the landowner ceases to be the holder of the qualifying estate, or

(c) in the case of a successor, land in relation to which the successor ceases to be the holder of the qualifying estate or of the estate derived from the qualifying estate, as the case may be."

11.6 Breach and enforcement

A person bound by a negative obligation under a Conservation Covenant breaches the obligation by doing something which it prohibits, or permits or suffers another person to do such a thing: section 124(1). A person bound by a positive obligation under a Conservation Covenant breaches the obligation if it is not performed: section 124(2).

By section 125(1), in proceedings for the enforcement of an obligation under a Conservation Covenant, the available remedies are:

(a)   specific performance;

(b)   injunction;

(c)   damages; and

(d)   order for payment of an amount due under the obligation.

As to the remedy of damages, contract principles will apply to the settlement of any award, and a Court may award exemplary damages in such circumstances as it thinks fit: section 125(3) and 125(4).

On an application for a remedy, a Court must, in considering what remedy is appropriate, take into account any public interest in the performance of the obligation concerned: section 125(2).

11.7 Discharge of obligations

The parties to a Conservation Covenant may discharge it by agreement. If the local planning authority is not the responsible body, then this discharge provision might cause them to place little confidence in such a covenant, when seeking to secure a long-term biodiversity scheme. By comparison, a planning obligation would give them greater control over the delivery and implementation of the scheme.

The responsible body and a person who holds the qualifying estate in respect of any of the land to which a Conservation Covenant relates, or a person who is a successor of the landowner, may agree to discharge from the obligation any of the land in respect of which the person holds that estate: sections 127(1) and 127(2).

A person to whom an obligation of the responsible body under a Conservation Covenant is owed by virtue of the person holding an estate in land may, by agreement with the responsible body, discharge the obligation, so far as owed in relation to that estate, in respect of any of the land in respect of which the person is entitled to the benefit of the obligation: section 128(1).

If the parties cannot agree to discharge the covenant, the matter can be referred to the Upper Tribunal pursuant to Schedule 18 to the Act.

The Upper Tribunal may, on the application of a person bound by, or entitled to the benefit of, an obligation under a Conservation Covenant by virtue of being the holder of an estate in land, by order discharge the obligation in respect of any of the land to which it relates: paragraph 1 of Schedule 18.

The Upper Tribunal may, on the application of the responsible body under a Conservation Covenant, by order discharge an obligation under the covenant in respect of any of the land to which it relates: paragraph 2 of Schedule 18.

In exercising its powers to discharge, the Upper Tribunal must have regard to a list of considerations set out in paragraphs 3(2) to 3(4) of Schedule 18.

11.8   Modification of Conservation Covenants

The parties to a Conservation Covenant may modify it by agreement. Again, one has to ask whether this power to modify would deter a local planning authority, which is not the responsible body from reliance on a Conservation Covenant to secure a scheme.

By section 129(1), a person bound by, or entitled to the benefit of, an obligation under a Conservation Covenant may, by agreement with the responsible body under the covenant, modify the obligation in its application to any of the land in respect of which the person is bound by, or entitled to the benefit of, it. This power does not include power to make a change which, had it been included in the original agreement, would have prevented the provision of the agreement that gave rise to the obligation being a provision in relation to which the conditions in section 117(1) were met: section 129(2).

If the parties cannot agree a modification, the matter can be referred to the Upper Tribunal pursuant to Schedule 18 to the Act.

The Upper Tribunal may, on the application of a person bound by, or entitled to the benefit of, an obligation under a Conservation Covenant by virtue of being the holder of an estate in land, by order modify the obligation in respect of any of the land to which it relates: paragraph 6(1) of Schedule 18.

The Upper Tribunal may, on the application of the responsible body under a Conservation Covenant, by order modify an obligation under the covenant in respect of any of the land to which it relates: paragraph 6(1) of Schedule 18.

This power does not include power to make a change to an obligation which, had it been included in the original agreement, would have prevented the provision of the agreement which gave rise to the obligation being a provision in relation to which the conditions in section 117(1)(a) were met: paragraph 8 of Schedule 18.

In exercising its powers to modify, the Upper Tribunal must have regard to a list of considerations set out in paragraph 9(2) to 9(3) of Schedule 18.

11.9   Examples of Conservation Covenants

The Law Commission report[7] provided some useful examples of how Conservation Covenants may be used:

Protecting woodland over the generations[8]

Example: The owner of an extensive family estate, much of which is forested and used by the public for hiking, intends to leave the land to her children. She wants to ensure that the forest is maintained and that public access continues, but she is not sure that her children – or future generations – would share those priorities.

Selling heritage property[9]

Example: A heritage group has invested funds in buying and restoring a Tudor house. The organisation wishes to sell the property, but wants to ensure that the work it has undertaken, and the heritage value of the property, is preserved.

Philanthropic uses[10]

Example: A landowner has inherited extensive moorland which includes a crag much used by rock climbers. The landowner intends to leave the land to his children, but wants to ensure that the moorland is properly looked after and that the public continue to have access to the crag.

Heritage and community assets[11]

Example: A farmer, who is also a keen amateur archaeologist, permits a local archaeo-logical society to undertake a dig on his land. The society has found artefacts, which both the farmer and the society want to remain in the land.

For conservation organisations, as an alternative to purchase[12]

Example: A wildlife charity identifies a plot of land as containing the habitat of a native bird species. It makes a financial offer to the landowner in return for the land being maintained as a habitat; the landowner agrees.

---

[7]   See above.

[8]   Ibid para 1.5.

[9]   Ibid para 1.6.

[10]   Ibid para 2.7.

[11]   Ibid para 2.11.

[12]   Ibid para 2.12.

For conservation organisations wishing to dispose of property[13]

Example: A heritage group has invested funds in buying and restoring a Victorian house. The organisation wishes to sell the land but ensure that the work it has undertaken, and the heritage value of the property, are preserved.

Payment for eco-system services and agri-environment schemes[14]

Example: A landowner's decision to remove an area of woodland upstream of a river which passes near homes has contributed to localised flooding. After negotiations, the landowner agrees to adopt different land management practices, restoring and maintaining the woodland in return for a yearly payment.

11.10   Conservation Covenant Agreements and planning

The consultation paper which preceded the Law Commission Report described two aspects of offsetting in the planning system. These were then described in the Law Commission Report:[15]

(1)   A landowner/developer applies for planning permission to undertake development. That development will cause environmental harm, which will need to be compensated. The tools for enabling the developer to commit money or resources to offsetting the environmental harm, and thereby to increase the likelihood that planning permission will be granted, already exist in planning legislation.

(2)   Obligations on an offset site need to be created. This means that the owner of the offset site – whether the developer or, more likely, a different owner – needs to agree to carry out certain activities to develop or maintain the site's environmental value, and to refrain from undertaking certain activities to maintain that value.

As to (2), the Report states: "*It is here that we envisaged a conservation covenant could be used: to secure permanent and binding obligations on an offset site.*"

It is here that difficulties arise, because the conventional planning mechanism would be a section 106 obligation binding the receptor site. To put it bluntly, "*why reinvent the wheel?*".

The Law Commission Report stated:

"*2.34 Prior to publication of the Consultation Paper, some stakeholders – in particular the Environment Bank, as discussed above – told us that conservation covenants would,*

---

[13]   Ibid para 2.16.

[14]   Ibid para 2.19.

[15]   Ibid para 2.32.

in their view, be a better way of securing an offset site, owing to perceived difficulties with the existing tools available."

An experienced planning lawyer might ask whether these *"perceived difficulties with the existing tools"* are soundly based.

Whilst a *"Grampian"* type (*"pre-commencement"*) condition may act to embargo the commencement of a development, it will not normally be effective in connection with the management of receptor sites. This leaves section 106 agreements, and it is difficult to see why they do not meet the requirements of the Environment Act in an efficient and effective way. The expressed preferences of the Environmental Bank are noted; however, it is fair to ask whether the authors of their consultation response at any practical experience of settling planning obligations.

11.11   Section 106 agreements versus Conservation Covenant Agreements
The Law Commission Report stated:

"2.37 Consultees confirmed that section 106 planning obligations and planning conditions could be used in offsetting; so could chains of covenants. A section 106 planning obligation was the instrument most frequently referred to. Some consultees also had experience or knowledge of the use of planning conditions. The Environment Bank, which is currently involved in the Defra pilot, indicated its preference for compulsorily-renewed and registered personal covenants."

The problems mentioned by consultees were:

•   Ensuring offsetting obligations are permanent.

•   Modification and discharge.

•   Management and enforcement.

•   Cross-boundary issues.

•   The cost of putting legal mechanisms in place.

These points are discussed below.

The Law Commission Report acknowledged that:[16]

"A section 106 planning obligation can be used to require a developer to make a monetary contribution to the cost of offsetting. The local authority can then use that

---

[16]   Ibid. Page 18, footnote 29.

> contribution to create or maintain an offset site and may pool a number of contributions into one site."

11.12   Ensuring offsetting obligations are permanent
The Law Commission Report stated:

> *"2.42 Where the loss of biodiversity is permanent, compensatory measures must also be permanent. Hence, the obligation to create and maintain an offset site should be able to run in perpetuity (as well as binding any future owner of the site), or at least for a lengthy period. Consultees indicated that although section 106 planning obligations can be for an unlimited period, they are normally created for a period of between 10 and 30 years. The Woodland Trust said "the time period is too short for many habitats or species to develop sustainable communities and there is little or no protection if, at some later date, someone wants to propose the compensation land as a development site."*

It is difficult to follow the argument that there are problems with the duration of section 106 agreements, because they can endure in perpetuity where the case demands it (for example, a SUDS scheme, management scheme or a perpetual restriction against an undesirable land use). If they are *"normally"*[17] created for a period of between 10 and 30 years, then this is, presumably, because this was appropriate to the case in point.

The Law Commission Report continued:

> *"2.43 The ability to make a conservation covenant perpetual, and binding on future landowners, provides the long-term security needed for offsetting. This could be combined with a short-term, renewable management agreement to deal with matters of detail and funding."*

All of these points can be covered by planning obligations. Furthermore, the section 106 agreement can include *"a short-term, renewable management agreement to deal with matters of detail and funding"* without the need for a separate side agreement.

11.13   Modification and discharge
The Law Commission Report stated:

> *"2.44 Consultees were concerned that section 106 planning obligations can be modified or discharged. This is done in one of two ways. First, if five years have passed since the section 106 agreement was entered into, the landowner may apply to the local authority for modification or discharge (with an appeal to the Secretary of State). Secondly, if five years have not elapsed since the agreement was entered into, then it may be modified or discharged by agreement between the landowner and local authority. Consultees thought that local authorities are under pressure to discharge or modify section 106*

---

[17]   This is purely anecdotal and unsupported by any empirical evidence.

planning obligations that are halting development. This is regarded as unsatisfactory for a biodiversity offsetting site, where obligations should have a level of permanent protection from modification or discharge."

The Law Commission Report dealt with this point:

"2.45 Our recommendations provide ways in which a conservation covenant can be discharged or modified by agreement between the parties. In either case, where agreement cannot be reached, the parties could also seek approval for modification or discharge from the Lands Chamber of the Upper Tribunal. So conservation covenants may not limit the possibility for modification and discharge to the extent that some consultees desire. However, this is something which could be addressed by making special provision for offsetting schemes."

11.14   Management and enforcement
The Law Commission Report stated:

"2.46 The lack of protection for the long-term management and enforcement of an offset site under the existing mechanisms is a key concern: consultation responses referred to it, and it was also raised during stakeholder meetings that we attended. So, for example, UKELA and the Land Trust were concerned about a lack of robustness in planning mechanisms and Link referred to "an absence of adequate long-term monitoring and enforcement measures" in relation to section 106 planning obligations."

2.47 It was thought that the bespoke regime for enforcement in a scheme of conservation covenants would provide a better mechanism for handling breaches of obligations than the existing tools. This is particularly the case after an extended period of time."

It is difficult to follow these objections because the planning obligation system provides a raft of enforcement mechanisms, viz:

* The section 106 agreement is enforceable *per se* against the original parties and their successors in title.

* Section 106(5) provides that a restriction or requirement imposed under a planning obligation is enforceable by injunction. This remedy has been observed by the Courts.[18]

* Section 106(6) provides that, without prejudice to section 106(5), if there is a breach of a requirement in a planning obligation to carry out any operations in, on, under or over the land to which the obligation relates, the authority by whom the obligation is enforceable may enter the land and carry out the operations and recover from

---

[18]   See *Waltham Forest LBC v Oakmesh Limited et al* [2009] EWHC 1688 (Ch) and *Newham LBC v Ali* [2014] EWCA Civ 676.

the person or persons against whom the obligation is enforceable[19] any expenses reasonably incurred by them in doing so.

Indeed, it remains to be seen whether the enforcement mechanisms for Conservation Covenant Agreements will be equal to these provisions.

11.15   Cross-boundary issues

The Law Commission Report stated:

> *"2.48 In some cases a developer might own both the development site and an offset site, but the latter may be in a different local authority's area. A section 106 agreement can only be entered into with the local authority for the area where the relevant land is situated, and accordingly there may be difficulties in this situation. The difficulties are not insurmountable – for example two different local authorities could enter into separate 106 obligations (one relating to the funding from the developer and the granting of planning permission, the other to secure performance of obligations on the offset site). However, the solutions are by no means simple or problem-free."*

On the contrary, planning practitioners will be familiar with section 106 agreements where the parties include more than one council. For example, a county council which is the education authority or local highway authority will often be a party in addition to the local planning authority. Furthermore, cross-boundary planning applications are not unusual and local planning authorities are normally familiar with them.

11.16   The cost of putting legal mechanisms in place

The Law Commission Report stated:

> *"2.50 Natural England noted that section 106 planning obligations are bespoke, and are formulated and agreed at the very end of the planning decision process. By comparison, conservation covenants might offer reduced costs resulting from simpler legal processes and lower legal fees to set up and secure land for offsetting purposes. ...*
>
> *2.51 At this stage it is difficult to say with certainty whether conservation covenants would be a cheaper way to protect an offset site than the negotiation and drafting of a section 106 planning obligation. ..."*

This criticism is not founded on any empirical evidence and, therefore, it is difficult to assess objectively. However, it is important to note that, if a planning application is supported by a section 106 agreement, the agreement will normally cover a range of matters, of which offset would be one. Accordingly, the costs of settling the offsetting obligations will be absorbed in the overall costs of settling the global section 106 agreement. By contrast, it will be the Conservation Covenant Agreement which will be thus *"bespoke"*.

---

[19]   This will include successors in title.

Whilst it is true to say that the Conservation Covenant Agreement might be seen as a valuable additional tool for the planning profession, it is untried and it is not entirely clear that it confers any advantage over the conventional section 106 agreement in any event.

11.17   Common practical problems

Those settling section 106 agreements and Conservation Covenant Agreements will have to face the same time-honoured problems in relation to ensuring the long-term viability of their agreements. It is one thing to draft an agreement which binds a developer or landowner to an enduring commitment, but it is another to ensure that this commitment is actually delivered. For example, the owner or developer could become insolvent. Both draftsmen will have to decide how they tackle this problem and, presumably, both will be looking to mechanisms such as bonds, guarantees or escrow accounts. If the mechanism is by way of a management company, it will be necessary to examine how this company will be set up, financed and managed.

Chapter 12

The Biodiversity Gain Site Register

12.1   Introduction

For offsite gains to be included in a development's Biodiversity Gain Plan, they must be registered on the Biodiversity Gain Site Register and the registered gains allocated to the specific development in question.

12.2   The Biodiversity Gain Site Register

Section 100(1) of the Environment Act provides that the Secretary of State may by regulations make provision for a *"Biodiversity Gain Site Register"*.

By section 100(2), a *"Biodiversity Gain Site"* is land where:

> *"(a) a person is required under a Conservation Covenant or planning obligation to carry out works for the purpose of habitat enhancement,*
>
> *(b) that* [sic][1] *or another person is required to maintain the enhancement for at least 30 years after the completion of those works,*[2] *and*
>
> *(c) for the purposes of Schedule 7A to the Town and Country Planning Act 1990 the enhancement is made available to be allocated (conditionally or unconditionally, and whether for consideration or otherwise) in accordance with the terms of the covenant or obligation to one or more developments for which planning permission is granted.*[3]*"*

Regulations must provide for the information in the register to be accessible to members of the public: section 100(3).

By section 100(4):

> *"Regulations under this section may in particular make provision about:*[4]
>
> *(a) the person who is to establish and maintain the Biodiversity Gain Site register;*
>
> *(b) circumstances in which land is or is not eligible to be registered;*

---

[1]   Presumably the developer or person bound by a Conservation Covenant.

[2]   Regulations may amend this period so as to provide a different period of at least 30 years: section 100(7).

[3]   In this section, *"development"*, *"habitat enhancement"*, *"planning obligation"* and *"planning permission"* have the same meanings as in Schedule 7A to the Town and Country Planning Act 1990: see section 100(11) and Schedule 14, para.12.

[4]   Who may be the Secretary of State, Natural England or another person.

(c) applications to register land in the register;

(d) the information to be recorded in relation to any land that is registered;

(e) amendments to the register;

(f) removal of land from the register;

(g) fees payable in respect of any application under the regulations."

By section 100(5) and (6), regulations may include:

- who is entitled to apply to register land in the Biodiversity Gain Site Register;

- the procedure to be followed in making an application;

- the information to be provided in respect of an application;

- how an application is to be determined;

- appeals against the rejection of an application;

- financial penalties for the supply of false or misleading information in connection with an application;

- the location and area of the land;

- the works to be carried out on the land and the habitat enhancement to be achieved by them;

- information about the habitat of the land before the commencement of those works;

- the person who applied to register the land and (if different) the person by whom the requirement to carry out the works or maintain the habitat enhancement is enforceable;

- any development to which any of the habitat enhancement has been allocated; and

- the biodiversity value[5] of any such habitat enhancement in relation to any such development.

---

[5] For the purposes of Schedule 7A to the Town and Country Planning Act 1990 or Schedule 2A to the Planning Act 2008.

Chapter 13

Biodiversity Credits

13.1   Background

If the object of the exercise is to ensure that there is no net loss of Biodiversity Units, then one is probably thinking in terms of some form of replacement habitat outside of the site – that is to say, habitat *"offset"*. It is natural to assume that this offset can be provided by way of one site; however, the notion of *"Biodiversity Credits"* provides for a more sophisticated approach. It might be the case that there is no nearby site available at the appropriate time to act as the receptor site for this offset.

One alternative is for the developer to provide the monetary wherewithal for the creation of biodiversity gain and then for the developer to leave it to an appropriate body to use that money to achieve that objective.[1]

The Environment Act provides that the Secretary of State may make arrangements under which a developer may purchase *"Biodiversity Credits"* from him for the purpose of meeting the *"Biodiversity Gain Objective"*.[2]

One of the advantages of Biodiversity Credits is that the use of them can help to move forward developments which are otherwise in difficulty when it comes to the provision of either onsite or offsite net gain. The purchase of credits by a developer can ensure that his scheme does not fall into the doldrums as a result of difficulties in connection with the provision of land for net gain.

There is also a considerable advantage in the use of Biodiversity Credits in that the accumulated funding provided by them can be used to assemble large habitat areas as opposed to developers providing fragmented and smaller areas. For example, arguably, the larger the area, the more robust it will be, particularly insofar as it should be possible to provide buffers around it to prevent the ingress of undesirable activities. It might be the case that a small area in close proximity to an urban area will be used for the walking of dogs and other recreational activities which might be antithetical to the purposes of the establishment of the intended habitat. The assembly of a larger habitat area should make it more robust in this regard.

The Defra consultation document entitled *"Consultation on Biodiversity Net Gain Regulations and Implementation"* (January 2022) states that the Government will undertake a credit price review to confirm how the price for Biodiversity Credits will be set, and an initial credit price will be published in advance of Biodiversity Net Gain becoming mandatory.

---

[1]   See Chapters 9 and 16.

[2]   See Chapters 14 and 15.

The Consultation Document states (page 76):

"We will be intentionally uncompetitive with the biodiversity unit market, and we aim to minimise the use of statutory biodiversity credits and phase them out at the earliest opportunity, once the biodiversity unit market has matured and we are confident that there is no longer a need for them."

This quotation throws up some significant points. First, that *"Biodiversity Credits"* and *"Biodiversity Units"* are different things. For the purposes of the *"biodiversity unit market"*, Biodiversity Units are treated as commodities to be bought and sold in an open market: see Chapter 16. By contrast, Biodiversity Credits are purchased from the Secretary of State by developers and then applied to the works mentioned in section 101(6): see below. Secondly, it is important to note that the Government sees the credit system as being temporary only, pending the creation of a market in Biodiversity Units. The Consultation Document states (page 76):

"However, the market analysis published alongside this consultation highlighted a significant risk that the sale of statutory biodiversity credits by the UK Government could undermine the establishment of the market. ...

The proposals set out in this consultation seek to mitigate that risk and ensure that the sale of statutory biodiversity credits and investment of associated revenues is undertaken in a way that supports, and does not conflict with, the establishment of a functioning market for biodiversity units."

13.2 Biodiversity credits

Section 101(1) of the Environment Act provides that the Secretary of State may make arrangements under which a person who is entitled to carry out the development of any land may purchase a credit from the Secretary of State for the purpose of meeting the Biodiversity Gain Objective referred to in Schedule 7A to the Town and Country Planning Act 1990 or Schedule 2A to the Planning Act 2008. A credit is to be regarded for the purposes of that Schedule as having such biodiversity value as is determined under the arrangements: section 101(2). It follows that there is, not necessarily, any correspondence between the unit value of Biodiversity Credits and Biodiversity Units. That is to say, one Biodiversity Credit will not necessarily equate to one Biodiversity Unit.

By section 101(3), the arrangements may in particular include arrangements relating to:

"(a) applications to purchase credits;

(b) the amount payable in respect of a credit of a given value;

(c) proof of purchase;

(d) reimbursement for credits purchased for development which is not carried out."

Item (d) is very important because proposed schemes do not always materialise on the ground. This, therefore, allows for the reimbursement of those credits which were purchased in anticipation of the scheme going ahead.

In determining the amount payable under the arrangements for a credit of a given value, the Secretary of State must have regard to the need to determine an amount which does not discourage the registration of land in the Biodiversity Gain Sites Register: section 101(4).

By section 101(6), the Secretary of State may use payments received under arrangements under this section for the following purposes only, viz:

(a) carrying out works,[3] or securing the carrying out of works, for the purpose of habitat enhancement[4] on land in England;

(b) purchasing interests in land in England with a view to carrying out works, or securing the carrying out of works, for that purpose;

(c) operating or administering the arrangements.

The Secretary of State must publish information about the arrangements, including in particular the amount payable for credits: section 101(5).

---

[3] The references to "*works*" do not include works which the Secretary of State is required to carry out apart from this section by virtue of any enactment: section 101(7).

[4] Within the meaning of Schedule 7A of the Town and Country Planning Act 1990.

Chapter 14

The Biodiversity Gain Condition

14.1   Summary

The Environment Act contain provisions[1] relating to biodiversity gain[2] as a condition of planning permission.[3]

When it comes into force,[4] the condition will be that the development may not be begun unless:

(a) a *"Biodiversity Gain Plan"*[5] has been submitted to the planning authority; and

(b) the planning authority has approved the plan.

The Biodiversity Gain Plan must comply with the *"Biodiversity Gain Objective"*. The Biodiversity Gain Objective is met if the biodiversity value attributable to the development exceeds the pre-development biodiversity value of the onsite habitat by at least the *"relevant percentage"*. This provision takes one to evaluating the biodiversity habitat values of the development, both pre-development and post-development, by reference to the Biodiversity Metric.[6]

The *"relevant percentage"* is, initially, set as an uplift of 10% against the pre-development biodiversity value of the relevant site (aka the *"baseline"*), as measured by using the Metric. However, the Secretary of State may change the relevant percentage by regulations. This would suggest that the Secretary of State has the ability to set different percentages for different types of site or development.

14.2   What are the benefits of biodiversity gain assessments?

The benefits of biodiversity gain assessments to landowners, developers, local authorities and interested parties can be summarised as follows:

---

[1]   See section 98 and Schedule 14.

[2]   The phrase *"biodiversity net gain"* is said to be interchangeable with *"biodiversity gain"*. The Glossary to the Consultation Document states: *"The term 'biodiversity gain' can be used interchangeably with 'biodiversity net gain' or can be used to mean the enhancements or gains which are delivered as part of meeting an overall biodiversity net gain objective"*.

[3]   References to the grant of planning permission include the deemed grant of planning permission: paragraph 12(3) of new Schedule 7A to the 1990 Act.

[4]   The trigger date for the condition is currently anticipated to be two years after the Act gained Royal Assent – about November 2023.

[5]   See Chapter 15.

[6]   Note that the current Biodiversity Metric 3.0 is undergoing a review at the time of writing and will probably be changed by 2023.

- Clearer expectations around ecological factors within proposed developments.

- Reducing the risk of ecological objections to a proposal.

- Levelling the *"playing field"* between developers and developers (and landowners and landowners) by applying a common and measurable methodology.

- Greater transparency for stakeholders.

- Developers can anticipate costs early.

- Wider social and economic benefits.

- Joined-up conservation efforts.

14.3   The Biodiversity Gain Condition

The Environment Act inserts new section 90A and new Schedule 7A into the Town and Country Planning Act 1990.[7] New Schedule 7A makes provision for grants of planning permission in England to be subject to a condition to secure that the *"Biodiversity Gain Objective"* is met: paragraph 1(1).

By Paragraph 13 of Schedule 7A, every planning permission granted for the development of land in England shall be deemed to have been granted subject to the condition that the development may not be begun unless:

(a)   a *"Biodiversity Gain Plan"*[8] has been submitted to the planning authority; and

(b)   the planning authority has approved the plan.

This is a *"pre-commencement condition"* (aka a *"Grampian"* type condition) and is subject to a complicated set of rules, the application of which may include that any works which have, purportedly, been carried out subject to the permission are unauthorised development and could be candidates for enforcement action requiring their removal: see Chapter 20.

Given that Schedule 7A has been imported into the 1990 Act, it must, *mutatis mutandis*, take up the definitions in that Act and (by way of a reminder) this includes the definition of *"development"* in section 55(1). This means the carrying out of building, engineering, mining or other operations in, on, over or under land, or the making of any material change in the use of any buildings or other land. The phrase *"building operations"* includes the demolition of buildings, rebuilding, structural alterations of or additions to buildings, and other operations normally undertaken by a person carrying on business as a builder: section 55(1A).

---

[7]   Section 98 and Schedule 14.

[8]   See Chapter 15 below.

By section 336 of the 1990 Act, *"planning permission"* means permission under Part III of the 1990 Act, or section 293A, but does not include *"permission in principle"*.

This should mean, also, that the exceptions which take certain actions outside the definition of *"development"* (and are set out in section 55(2) of the 1990 Act) should apply. These include:

- The carrying out (for the maintenance, improvement or other alteration of any building) of works which affect only the interior of the building, or do not materially affect the external appearance of the building: section 55(2)(a);

- The carrying out (on land within the boundaries of a road by a highway authority) of any works required for the maintenance or improvement of the road but, in the case of any such works which are not exclusively for the maintenance of the road, not including any works which may have significant adverse effects on the environment: section 55(2)(b);

- In the case of buildings or other land which are used for a purpose of any class specified in an order made by the Secretary of State under this section, the use of the buildings or other land or, subject to the provisions of the order, of any part of the buildings or the other land, for any other purpose of the same class: section 55(2)(f);

- The demolition of any description of building specified in a direction given by the Secretary of State to local planning authorities generally or to a particular local planning authority: section 55(2)(g).

Section 55(2)(b) (works required for the maintenance or improvement of a road) is important, because it has the effect of subsuming any roadworks which may have significant adverse effects on the environment within the definition of *"development"*; and this will, of course, include effects on ecology. Ergo, proposals to carry out such works in a manner which may have an adverse effect on ecology should be subject to some form of screening or triage to assess whether those effects might be significant adverse effects.

Section 55(2)(f) is taken up by the Town and Country Planning (Use Classes) Order 1987.

The reference to material change of use in section 55(1) means that a planning permission for such a change of use, which is granted after the trigger-date for new Schedule 7A, will be deemed to be subject to the statutory biodiversity net gain condition and the requirement to show a net gain of not less than 10% over the pre-development baseline. This may prove to be challenging in cases where the onsite space for any enhancement is very limited and may mean that the developer will be forced to find some offsite mitigation or to buy some Biodiversity Credits.[9]

---

[9]   One option for the developer in a constrained urban area is to explore a *"green roof system"* which should not only provide ecological benefits but also have additional benefits such as improvements in rainwater management. As an aside, there my wife's question about asserted *"grassed"* roofs: *"Who's going to mow them?"*.

14.4   Exceptions and modifications to the Biodiversity Gain Condition
Paragraph 17(1) of Schedule 7A to the 1990 Act provides that paragraph 13 (the deemed biodiversity net gain condition) does not apply in relation to:

> *"(a) development for which planning permission is granted -*
>
> *i) by a development order, or*
>
> *ii) under Section 293A (urgent Crown development), or*
>
> *(b) development of such other description as the Secretary of State may by regulations specify."*

The reference to a *"development order"* should, therefore, exclude permitted development pursuant to the Town and Country Planning (General Permitted Development) (England) Order 2015 from the operation of the statutory condition.

Paragraph 18(1) of Schedule 7A allows for modifications for onsite *"irreplaceable habitats"*.

The Secretary of State may, by regulations, make provision to modify or exclude the application of Schedule 7A in relation to any development for which planning permission is granted where the onsite habitat is *"irreplaceable habitat"* (to be defined in the regulations): paragraph 18(1).

The regulations must require, in relation to any such development, the making of arrangements for the purpose of minimising the adverse effect of the development on the biodiversity of the onsite habitat: paragraph 18(2).

The regulations may confer powers and duties, including powers and duties in relation to the giving of guidance, on Natural England: paragraph 18(3). Presumably, this advice will be a material planning consideration in the determination of applications for planning permission.

The Consultation Document sets out three topic areas in this connection, viz:

*   proposed exemptions;

*   possible exemptions; and

*   developments which are not proposed to be subject to any exemptions.

So far as proposed exemptions are concerned, these fall under three headings; namely:

*   *"de minimis"* developments;

- householder developments; and

- material changes of use.

"*De minimis*" developments are, in short, development proposals for very small areas of land and the Consultation Document is examining parcel sizes between 10m² and 50m² and looking for proposals for any other threshold: page 22. This gives rise to concerns about boundary manipulation by the artificial sub-division of the site into a number of parcels, each of which falls within the "*de minimis*" category. The Consultation Document does, to some extent, acknowledge this problem, and states that the "*de minimis*" threshold will apply to the sum of all habitat types within the development site, not the size of the development site as a whole. But it does not go on to consider the artificial separation of a development into discrete parcels.

Householder works are proposed to be exempt because, again, they are likely to be very small in scale.

It is also proposed that material changes of use will be exempt due to the notion that a typical material change of use will not involve physical changes that would result in habitat losses (page 23):

> "*We are, however, interested to hear whether there are change of use applications that could have a significant impact on biodiversity and how these might be defined.*"

It is easy to produce examples which are not fanciful. For example, a material change of use from an agricultural field to a site for the stationing of caravans could have a significant impact on the diversity of the site by the introduction, or intensification, of human activity. This is particularly problematic, given that many caravan sites are located in holiday "*hotspots*", and often in close proximity to areas of high ecological value. Furthermore, if a caravan site is granted a site licence under the Caravan Sites Acts, permitted development rights come into play and the site operator is entitled to carry out such works as are necessary to comply with the site licence without the need for further planning permission. This may include the construction of onsite roadways, hard standings etc which may, in turn, impact not only directly upon onsite biota, but also have an indirect offsite impact due to noise, lighting, changes in surface water run-off etc. It is, therefore, conceivable that, regardless of the statutory condition created in the Environment Act, many local planning authorities will need to impose bespoke conditions and requirements on a site-by-site basis. Arguably, the same considerations could apply in relation to proposals for the construction of golf courses and, no doubt, many other types of development where the overarching proposal is for a material change of use and the onsite engineering actions could, otherwise , then be used for colourable boundary manipulation and so fall within the "*de minimis*" exemption.

Defra are also considering whether to make exemptions for the creation of biodiversity gain sites and self-build and custom housebuilding.

The above narrative in connection with material change of use applies, *mutatis mutandis*, to proposed biodiversity gain sites. The first question to be answered in relation to proposals to create a biodiversity gain site is whether the proposal needs planning permission in any event. This might be by way of a material change of use, but is questionable whether a site which is left to nature falls within the 1990 Act. In many cases, the proposal will not involve "*development*" within the meaning of section 55 of the Town and Country Planning Act 1990; however, in some cases, it might be necessary to carry out onsite groundworks in order to provide appropriate site features such as ponds. These features might be "*engineering operations*" for the purposes of the 1990 Act and, therefore, need planning permission. The Consultation Document states that, in order to avoid creating a loophole, it is proposed that the exemption would apply to projects which only enhance biodiversity for the purposes of net gain. Clearly, the pursuit of such an objective can be secured, by the local planning authority, by the imposition of appropriate conditions or the execution of a planning obligation.

Self-build and custom-build developments might be exempt on the basis that they are said to be cost-sensitive and small-scale. Those drafting the Consultation Documents feel that self-build developments are often particularly ambitious in wider sustainability terms, such as climate change mitigation.[10]

Turning to those matters which are not being put forward for exemption in the Consultation Document, they are brownfield sites, temporary planning permissions, and developments for which permitted development rights are not applicable due to their location in conservation areas or natural parks.

Dealing first with brownfield sites. There is a definition in the Glossary to the Consultation Document:

> "*Brownfield land: Land which is or was occupied by a permanent structure including the curtilage of the developed land (although it should not be assumed that the whole of the curtilage should be developed) and any associated fixed surface infrastructure. This excludes: land that is or was last occupied by agricultural or forestry buildings; land that has been developed for minerals extraction or waste disposal by landfill, where provision for restoration has been made through development management procedures; land in built-up areas such as residential gardens, parks, recreation grounds and allotments; and land that was previously developed but where the remains of the permanent structure or fixed surface structure have blended into the landscape.*"

The argument appears to be that exempting brownfield sites would provide little real benefit and would add unnecessary complication. It goes on to say that, if brownfield development is by way of buildings and structures only, it would be "*zero*" in terms of biodiversity net gain and also might be subject to the "*de minimis*" exemption. This characterisation is not

---

[10]   Although it is not clear whether this notion is based on any empirical survey.

founded on any disclosed empirical evidence and begs the question of whether it is correct. Another problem with this analysis is that it does not take account of the fact that many brownfield sites are contaminated and, therefore, the overall economic viability assessment for the development will have to take account of the costs of the remediation or mitigation of these pollutants. This adds additional pressure to the bottom line of the viability assessment, and it could be the case that, if the costs of providing biodiversity net gain are added to the spreadsheet, some otherwise acceptable developments will not go forward because they are not financially viable. Unfortunately, the Consultation Document does not propose to introduce any degree of flexibility in relation to viability. It is difficult to understand the rationale behind this approach.

The Consultation Document does not propose to exempt temporary planning permissions because, it is said, they should cause short-term impacts on biodiversity which may be restored quickly. It is arguable that this assertion is incorrect. It depends upon the facts of each particular case, and, as such, should be assessed on a site-by-site basis. There could be many temporary developments which have long-term impacts on the biodiversity of the area within which they are carried out. Be that as it may, the Consultation Document goes on to say that the Biodiversity Metric allows for temporary losses to be disregarded when the original baseline habitat will be restored to the same or better condition within two years of the loss.

Finally, it is not proposed to exempt developments to which permitted development rights are not applicable due to their locations in conservation areas, areas of outstanding natural beauty or national parks. It is said that such developments will be small-scale and so may usually take advantage of other exemptions and process easements, such as the Small Sites Metric.

14.5 The *"Biodiversity Gain Objective"*
The *"Biodiversity Gain Objective"* is set out in Schedule 7A to the 1990 Act .

The Biodiversity Gain Objective is met in relation to development for which planning permission is granted if the *"biodiversity value attributable to the development"* exceeds the pre-development biodiversity value of the onsite habitat by at least the *"relevant percentage"*: paragraph 2(1) of Schedule 7A.

By paragraph 2(2) of Schedule 7A, the *"biodiversity value attributable to the development"* is the total of:

"(a) the post-development biodiversity value of the onsite habitat,

(b) the biodiversity value, in relation to the development, of any registered offsite biodiversity gain allocated to the development, and

(c) the biodiversity value of any biodiversity credits purchased for the development."

The "*relevant percentage*" set out in the 1990 Act is a measured uplift of at least 10% over the pre-development baseline; however, the Secretary of State may, by regulations, change the "*relevant percentage*": paragraph 2(3) and (4) of Schedule 7A.

The Consultation Document states that it remains the Government's intention to continue to allow higher percentage targets to be set by planning authorities at a local or site level (Page 54):

> "*Any higher target should be made clear at an early stage in the planning or development process and careful consideration should be given to the feasibility and achievability of any requirements above 10%, which can have significant impacts on the costs of developing a site.*"

The reference to "*significant impacts on the costs of developing a site*" is very important because the pursuit of a commercially unrealistic target by a local planning authority may have the effect of stultifying otherwise beneficial development: see the discussion of viability considerations in Chapter 19.

The Consultation Document goes on to propose that onsite biodiversity gains should be secured for delivery within 12 months of the development being commenced or, where not possible, before occupation. It is not clear why this 12-month period has been chosen, and this proposal is problematic where a scheme is being delivered in phases. Nor is it clear why occupation has been mentioned as a trigger. The proposal seems to be driven by considerations which do not appear to encompass these difficult points (page 54):

> "*A clear timeframe for delivery should be reflected in any planning conditions, obligations or covenants which secure onsite gains. Any longer delay in creation must be reflected in the biodiversity metric calculation, meaning that a lower number of biodiversity units is generated. This will mean that long delays to the delivery of habitats would require more enhancement to be done, usually at greater cost.*"

The mechanism is that a Biodiversity Gain Plan[11] must be submitted to the planning authority and approved by it, and the function of the Plan is to show that the Biodiversity Gain Objective will be met by the completion of the permitted development.

These are complicated provisions and so it is necessary to approach them in stages.

14.6   The Biodiversity Metric

The provisions of this and succeeding paragraphs can be met only by the application of a biodiversity metric which provides data to evaluate the pre-development and the post-development biodiversity value of the site and, to some extent, of any proposed compensation

---

[11]   See Chapter 15.

by way of offset land. This is, currently, the Defra Biodiversity Metric 3.0: see the discussion of the Metric in Chapter 9.

The Consultation Document proposes that one of the considerations which must be to the satisfaction of a local planning authority before it approves a Biodiversity Gain Plan is the receipt of a *"completed Biodiversity Metric (submitted as the completed calculator document, not a 'snapshot' or summary) show* [sic] *a measurable net gain of at least 10% across all unit types"*.[12] Thus it might be the case that, if Defra is aware of this anomaly, it will promote regulations which seek to rectify it.

The Biodiversity Metric is to be produced and published by the Secretary of State: paragraph 4(2) of Schedule 7A. Unusually for a *"document"* (sic) of this type, the Secretary of State must lay the Biodiversity Metric, and any revised Biodiversity Metric, before Parliament: paragraph 4(6) of Schedule 7A.[13]

14.7   Pre-development onsite biodiversity value
In relation to any development for which planning permission is granted, the pre-development biodiversity value of the onsite[14] habitat is the biodiversity value of the onsite habitat on the *"relevant date"* as calculated by the Biodiversity Metric: paragraph 5(1) of Schedule 7A to the 1990 Act.

By paragraph 5(2), the *"relevant date"* is:

(a)   in a case in which planning permission is granted on application, the date of the application, and

(b)   in any other case, the date on which the planning permission is granted.

Arguably, paragraph 5(2)(a) above might be problematic for the simple reason that any site evaluation is likely to have been completed long before the date that permission is granted and, therefore, may be well out of date when the permission is issued. This is particularly the case where (as in most cases) a planning obligation must be settled following a committee resolution to grant permission. Paragraph 5(2)(b) might be relevant where the permission is granted on appeal, but this depends on whether a permission granted on appeal can be said to be a planning permission granted on application. It might be the case that the Planning Inspectorate might require up-dated ecological assessments notwithstanding the legislative position and, again, it might be that this is a matter for regulations.

---

[12]   Page 53 - See Chapter 15 below.

[13]   It is not clear how one lays a spreadsheet before Parliament.

[14]   The phrase *"onsite habitat"* means *"habitat on the land to which the planning permission relates"*: paragraph 12(1) of Schedule 7A to the 1990 Act.

Paragraph 5(3) goes on to provide that the person submitting the Biodiversity Gain Plan for approval and the planning authority may agree that the relevant date is to be a date earlier than that specified in paragraph 5(2)(a) or (b).[15] This may come into play where a developer has provided a significant uplift in the biodiversity value of his site before making the application and the parties agree that it would be unfair to use this already enhanced condition as a baseline.

The mandatory condition applies to planning permissions and not reserved matters approvals. It will often be the case that applications are granted in outline and then followed by reserved matters approvals, because the layout of the scheme will not be clear until the reserved matters are considered. This would suggest that the prudent local planning authority might, by way of "*Rochdale*" type conditions, set out the overall net gain targets for the scheme as a whole at the outline stage: see discussion in Chapters 20 and 23.

Applications pursuant to section 73 of the 1990 Act pose a particular problem. It is important to note that, whilst an application pursuant to section 73 is often called an application to "*vary*" a planning condition, it results in the grant of a new planning permission. The new permission will be subject to the statutory net gain condition; but this means that any planning obligation which is tied to, or triggered by, the original permission must be refreshed or varied so as to apply to the new section 73 permission. Otherwise, the arrangements previously secured by the original permission might be lost, and this could include arrangements which provided security for the delivery of biodiversity net gain: see discussion of conditions in Chapters 20 and 22.

Where planning permission is granted in respect of land which is registered in the Biodiversity Gain Site Register, under section 100 of the Environment Act, the pre-development biodiversity value of the land is the total of:

(a)   the biodiversity value of the onsite habitat on the relevant date, and

(b)   to the extent that it is not included within that value, the biodiversity value of the habitat enhancement[16] which is, on that date, recorded in the Register as habitat enhancement to be achieved on the land.

The habitat value for (a) will be quantified by way of the Biodiversity Metric.

As to (b), the somewhat circular definition for "*habitat enhancement*" is given as meaning the "*enhancement of the biodiversity of habitat*": paragraph 12 of Schedule 7A. However, it is optimistic to suggest (if this is what is intended) that the Environment Act attempts to tackle

---

[15]   But not a date which is before the day on which Schedule 7A comes into force in relation to the development.

[16]   The somewhat circular definition being "'*Habitat enhancement*' means '*enhancement of the biodiversity of habitat*': paragraph 12(2) of Schedule 7A to the 1990 Act. Also, it is optimistic to suggest (if this is what is intended) that the Environment Act attempts to tackle the impossible task of quantifying improvements to "*biodiversity*" *per se*.

the impossible task of quantifying improvements to "*biodiversity*" *per se* in any remotely measurable form. The biota of any given habitat is too complex. In truth, the proposals in the Consultation Document appear to be that the Register Operator will award Biodiversity Units by applying eligibility criteria which include that:

> "*For a site to be considered eligible for inclusion on the register it must meet the following proposed criteria:*
>
> *... it is subject to a conservation covenant or a planning obligation that will require* **habitat enhancement***: ... is measured using the biodiversity metric against a baseline metric assessment (the baseline being its pre-enhancement state unless activities on the land have reduced its biodiversity value since 30 January 2020, in which case it becomes the pre-reduction biodiversity value). ...* " (Emphasis added).[17]

Given that the Biodiversity Metric is invoked to generate Biodiversity Units, this appears to be a habitat improvement only, as opposed to a developer's promise to provide benefits to selected species. Ergo, this is not the enhancement of the "*biodiversity of habitat*", but of the habitat itself.

There is always the danger that an unscrupulous person will deliberately degrade his site to depreciate its biodiversity value, thereby providing him with an artificially lowered, and advantageous, baseline. Accordingly, paragraph 6 of Schedule 7A to the 1990 Act makes provision for the case where a person carries on activities on land on or after 30 January 2020 otherwise than in accordance with a planning permission, or any other permission of a kind specified by the Secretary of State by regulations, and as a result of the activities the biodiversity value of the onsite habitat is lower on the relevant date than it would otherwise have been. If so, the pre-development biodiversity value of the onsite habitat is to be taken to be its biodiversity value immediately before the carrying on of these activities. The problem here, of course, is the evidential one; namely, how one goes about determining the condition of the site before the acts of degradation took place. No doubt, old photographs, aerial photographs and anecdotal evidence will all provide important sources of information.

It is, also, necessary to consider the "*biodiversity attributable to the development*" and this is discussed above.

14.8 Post-development onsite biodiversity value

In relation to any development for which planning permission is granted, the "*post-development biodiversity value*" of the onsite habitat is the projected value of the habitat as at the time the development is completed: paragraph 8(1) of Schedule 7A to the 1990 Act.

---

[17] Pages 64 to 65.

By paragraph 8(2), the anticipated onsite *"post-development biodiversity value"* is to be calculated by taking the onsite *"pre-development biodiversity value"* and:

(a)   if at the time the development is completed the development will, taken as a whole, have increased the biodiversity value of the onsite habitat, adding the amount of that increase, or

(b)   if at the time the development is completed the development will, taken as a whole, have decreased the biodiversity value of the onsite habitat, subtracting the amount of that decrease.

The phrase *"the development will, taken as a whole"* begs a number of questions. For example, what is the *"whole"* in relation to an outline planning permission or a scheme which is to be delivered in phases? The short answer is that the matter might be clarified by regulations, but some points are discussed in Chapter 23.

Applying the methodology in the Biodiversity Metric, the biodiversity value relevant to the development is by way of mutually exclusive classes relating to area-based habitats, linear features (hedgerows) and riverine features.

The notion of a date when *"the development is completed"* is a very amorphous one, because this may be many years into the future. The mere fact that a development is up and running does not mean that it is *"complete"*. For example, if the development of a contaminated site includes some form of onsite remediation, this may not be complete for many years.[18] This is why lawyers tend to draft documents by reference to *"substantial completion"*.

Paragraph 9 of Schedule 7A is an exception which applies in relation to any development for which planning permission is granted and:

(a)   the person submitting the Biodiversity Gain Plan for approval[19] proposes to carry out works in the course of the development that increase the biodiversity value of the onsite habitat, and

(b)   the planning authority considers that the increase is significant in relation to the pre-development biodiversity value.

The increase in biodiversity value is then to be taken into account in calculating the post-development biodiversity value of the onsite habitat only if the planning authority is satisfied

---

[18]   Indeed, a road scheme is normally open to traffic before the final touches are put to it by reference to any faults detected during the *"maintenance period"*: see Tom Graham, *A Practical Guide to Planning, Highways and Development* (Bath Publishing, 2019).

[19]   The reference to the *"person submitting the Biodiversity Gain Plan for approval"* is a strange one and, taken literally, would fix that duty on that person notwithstanding that, with many schemes, the person making the application might not be the one who carries out the development.

that any habitat enhancement resulting from the works will, by virtue of a condition subject to which the planning permission is granted, a planning obligation,[20] or a Conservation Covenant,[21] be maintained for at least 30 years after the development is completed. This, of course, begs the same question of when the development is "*completed*". There is, also, the question of how such a long-term commitment can be secured: see Chapters 20 and 21 below.

The Secretary of State may, by regulations, substitute for the above 30-year period a different period of at least 30 years: paragraph 9(4) of Schedule 7A.

The Consultation Document states[22] that, while there is not an explicit requirement to legally secure other less significant onsite enhancements (such as amenity planting areas or individual street trees), Defra would also expect suitable management arrangements to be made for these in landscaping plans, as is already normal practice, and it will clarify this in guidance.

14.9 Registered offsite biodiversity gains
By paragraph 10(1) of Schedule 7A to the 1990 Act, a "*registered offsite biodiversity gain*" means any habitat enhancement, where:

(a)   the enhancement is required to be carried out under a Conservation Covenant or planning obligation, and

(b)   the enhancement is recorded in the Biodiversity Gain Site register.[23]

The biodiversity value of registered offsite biodiversity gain is measured, under the Biodiversity Metric, in relation to development to which it is allocated: paragraph 10(3) of Schedule 7A.

References to the allocation of registered offsite biodiversity gain are to its allocation in accordance with the terms of the Conservation Covenant or planning obligation: paragraph 10(2) of Schedule 7A.

---

[20]   A "*planning obligation*" is a "*unilateral undertaking*" or "*section 106 agreement*" pursuant to section 106 of the Town and Country Planning Act 1990.

[21]   See Chapter 11 for Conservation Covenant Agreements.

[22]   Page 53, Footnote 37.

[23]   The "*Biodiversity Gain Site Register*" is discussed in Chapter 12.

Chapter 15

Biodiversity Gain Plans

15.1   Biodiversity Gain Plans

A "*Biodiversity Gain Plan*" is a plan which relates to development for which planning permission[1] is granted.

The Plan relates to measurable net gains and it must be navigated by applying the methodology in the Biodiversity Metric. As noted above, the biodiversity value relevant to the development is by way of mutually exclusive classes relating to, respectively, area-based habitats, linear features (hedgerows) and riverine features. Also as noted above, the metric is a document for the measurement of habitats only and does not mention species.

The Plan must specify the following matters:

(a)   information about the steps taken, or to be taken, to minimise the adverse effect of the development on the biodiversity of the onsite habitat and any other habitat;

(b)   the pre-development biodiversity value of the onsite habitat;

(c)   the post-development biodiversity value of the onsite habitat;

(d)   any registered offsite biodiversity gain allocated to the development; and the biodiversity value of that gain in relation to the development;

(e)   any Biodiversity Credits purchased for the development;[2] and

(f)   such other matters as the Secretary of State may by regulations specify.[3]

Matter (a) is predicated on the basis that the relevant development will incur habitat damage and has regard to the mitigation hierarchy. Level 1 is that of avoidance; namely, where possible habitat damage should be avoided. Clearly, matter (a) is triggered when the avoidance is not possible. Ergo, it applies in the second stage of the hierarchy; namely, where possible habitat damage and loss should be minimised.

In terms of the mitigation hierarchy, matters (d) and (e) go beyond minimisation and, arguably, beyond remediation. They, therefore, fall into the "*last resort*" of the mitigation

---

[1]   References to the grant of planning permission include the deemed grant of planning permission: paragraph 13(3) of Schedule 7A to the 1990 Act. For "*deemed grant of planning permission*" see section 100(11) of the Environment Act and Schedule 7A to the 1990 Act.

[2]   See Chapter 13 above for "*biodiversity credits*".

[3]   See paragraph 14(1) and (2) of Schedule 7A to the 1990 Act.

hierarchy; namely, damaged or lost habitat should be compensated for. This is to say, consideration must be given to biodiversity offsetting, either by reference to an offset site or by way of the purchase of Biodiversity Credits.

There is the question of whether the offset site must be identified in the Plan and this, arguably, is a matter for an interaction between the Plan and any planning obligation. In principle, it seems that there is no reason why a planning obligation should be subject to a *"Grampian"* type clause which places a bar on certain stages of a development unless and until an offset site which delivers the requisite quantum of Biodiversity Units has been identified and secured. Indeed, the notion of Biodiversity Units as being the *"currency"* of the Biodiversity Metric would seem to encourage just such flexibility in approach.[4]

If one focuses on (d), one can see that reference is made to registered offsite biodiversity gain. This takes one to the Biodiversity Gain Site Register and *"biodiversity gain sites"*. A *"biodiversity gain site"* includes land where *"a person is required under a Conservation Covenant or planning obligation to carry out works for the purpose of habitat enhancement"*: section 100(2). If one draws this into the context provided by the planning process, then, in the normal course of events, the planning permission would not be granted until the relevant planning obligation has been executed. Likewise, one would anticipate this to be the case where the biodiversity objective is to be secured by way of a Conservation Covenant Agreement. This would suggest that (depending on staffing levels within the planning authority) the heads of terms for these matters are best settled long before the statutory condition is triggered by the grant of a planning permission and before the Biodiversity Gain Plan is completed. If the Biodiversity Gain Plan turns, in part, on a planning obligation or Conservation Covenant for its enforcement then, logically, it is appropriate to have those matters removed from the scope at the outset.

One, therefore, should have an iterative process. Whilst a grant of the planning permission will incorporate the statutory biodiversity net gain condition, the Biodiversity Gain Plan will rely, for its effective enforcement, on a pre-existing planning obligation or Conservation Covenant.

The Secretary of State may by regulations make provision about:

> *"(a) any other matters to be included in a Biodiversity Gain Plan;*
>
> *(b) the form of a Biodiversity Gain Plan;*
>
> *(c) the procedure to be followed in relation to the submission of a Biodiversity Gain Plan (including the time by which a plan must be submitted); and*

---

[4] The Glossary to the 2022 Consultation Document states: *"A biodiversity unit is the 'currency' of the biodiversity metric. A unit represents a combined measure of habitat distinctiveness, area, and condition"*.

(d) persons who may or must submit a Biodiversity Gain Plan."[5]

The Consultation Document gives an indication of the way in which the Government might approach the Plan.

Annex B to the Consultation Document now includes a proposed draft template for Biodiversity Gain Plans. Defra aims to produce a more concise version of the Biodiversity Gain Plan template for developments using the Small Sites Metric and a different template for outline development applications. It remains to be seen how these proposed templates will interact with planning obligations for development sites.

15.2 Core biodiversity gain information

In terms of procedure, the Consultation Document proposes that certain *"core biodiversity gain information"* must be provided with the application for planning permission: page 52. This information will not be as comprehensive as a complete Biodiversity Gain Plan (which will not be required at this stage), in recognition of certain circumstances where details of landscaping are not fully developed or where the details of a Biodiversity Gain Plan are contingent on other matters, such as site investigation works. It is proposed that there will be additional biodiversity gain information requirements for applications for outline planning permissions and permissions for phased developments.

The proposed core biodiversity gain information may include:

- the pre-development biodiversity value;

- steps taken to minimise adverse biodiversity impacts;

- the proposed approach to enhancing biodiversity onsite; and

- any proposed offsite biodiversity enhancements (including the use of Biodiversity Credits) that have been planned or arranged for the development.

15.3 Submission of Biodiversity Gain Plans

As to the submission of Biodiversity Gain Plans, the Consultation Document proposes that applicants may submit their Plans:

- With their planning applications or before permission is determined; in this case (assuming permission is granted and the Plan is approved) the net gain condition will be immediately discharged and development can commence.

- Alternatively, after planning permission is granted, but before the commencement of development.

---

[5] Paragraph 15 of Schedule 7A to the 1990 Act.

The biodiversity gain information would usually form part of the relevant Biodiversity Gain Plan.

In practice, one would anticipate that the prudent developer will have provided drafts of their Biodiversity Gain Plan and any associated planning obligation as part of their application documents, so that these can be taken into account in the balancing exercise which will be applied by the local planning authority in coming to its decision.

15.4　Approval of a Biodiversity Gain Plan

By Schedule 7A to the 1990 Act,[6] a planning authority to which a Biodiversity Gain Plan is submitted must approve the plan if, and only if, it is satisfied as to the following matters:

(a)　that the pre-development biodiversity value of the onsite habitat is as specified in the plan;

(b)　that the post-development biodiversity value of the onsite habitat is at least the value specified in the plan;

(c)　that, in a case where any registered offsite biodiversity gain is specified in the plan as allocated to the development—

　　(i)　the registered offsite biodiversity gain is so allocated (and, if the allocation is conditional, that any conditions attaching to the allocation have been met or will be met by the time the development begins); and

　　(ii)　the registered offsite biodiversity gain has the biodiversity value specified in the plan in relation to the development;

(d)　that any Biodiversity Credits specified in the plan as purchased for the development have been so purchased;

(e)　that the Biodiversity Gain Objective is met; and

(f)　any other matters specified in the plan under paragraph 14(2)(f).[7]

The Secretary of State may make regulations as to:

(a)　the procedure which a planning authority is to follow in determining whether to approve a Biodiversity Gain Plan;

(b)　factors which may or must be taken into account in making such a determination; and

---

[6]　See paragraph 15(1) and (2) of Schedule 7A to the 1990 Act.

[7]　As to the reference to paragraph 14(2)(f), this is a reference back to the matters to be included in a Biodiversity Gain Plan which include matters which are stipulated by the Secretary of State.

(c)   appeals relating to such a determination.

The Consultation Document foreshadows those regulations, in stating that the local planning authority will approve a Biodiversity Gain Plan once it is satisfied that:

- the Plan and completed Biodiversity Metric (submitted as the completed calculator document, not a "*snapshot*" or summary) show a measurable net gain of at least 10% across all unit types (area-based and, where relevant, linear, and riverine habitats), having regard to policy on matters such as "*additionality*" (see below);

- the information (including pre-development and post-development biodiversity values) presented in the Biodiversity Gain Plan is complete and meets the statutory requirements; and

- any claimed gains (both onsite and offsite) are appropriately secured and allocated, including the point in the development process that these gains are to be delivered and a proportionate description of how enhancements will be managed and monitored.

15.5   Dual functionality

It should be relatively self-evident that, if a parcel of land within the development serves as both a "*green*" or "*sustainability*" use and has value in terms of biodiversity, it should be included as part of the biodiversity net gain calculation – for example, Sustainable Urban Drainage Systems ("*SUDS*") and Suitable Alternative Natural Greenspace ("*SANG*").

The Consultation Document proposes that any onsite measure delivered as part of a development[8] may be counted towards biodiversity net gain, provided that the Biodiversity Metric recognises the uplift in biodiversity value. This includes measures delivered to comply with a statutory obligation or policy (such as green infrastructure, SUDS, or nutrient mitigation). It goes on to say that mitigation and compensation measures for protected species may be counted towards a biodiversity net gain calculation but should not make up all of a development's biodiversity net gain. At least 10% of the gain should be delivered through separate activities which are not required to mitigate and compensate for protected species impacts.

SUDS may include floodplains or reservoir ponds which are subject to infrequent inundation only. Some species will be tolerant of these conditions. SANGs might be acceptable; however, given the function of SANGs, this might be a problem with access by the public because, of course, SANGs are not provided for the purposes of providing ecological enhancements but are buffers in relation to the sensitive sites. Accordingly, it might be the case that a SANG can be included in the biodiversity net calculation, albeit subject to some form of discount. There is a limit to this duality of function approach where the green spaces put forward by a developer are small and fragmented – for example, roadside margins and other vegetation within a road scheme.

---

[8]   Unless that part of the development site is a designated feature within a statutory protected site or irreplaceable habitat.

All of this seems relatively straightforward; however, the Consultation Document seems to subsume this under the somewhat amorphous phrase *"additionality"*.

15.6   *"Additionality"*

The term *"additionality"* is defined in the Glossary to the Consultation Document by the somewhat cryptic: *"The characteristic of an intervention denoting a real increase in social value that would not have occurred in the absence of the intervention being appraised"*.[9] So far as the term is used in the Document is concerned, this seems to allude to *"the extent to which enhancements undertaken in response to wider policies, legislation and markets can be counted towards a development's biodiversity net gain calculation"* (page 71).

None of this is particularly clear and one is left to wonder what planning officers and councillors will make of the expression.

In a 2012 discussion paper entitled *"What is Additionality? – Part 1: A long standing problem"*, Michael Gillenwater said:

> *"Unfortunately, and despite years of debate within the environmental policy community, there is no commonly held precise understanding of what additionality means or how to best implement it."*[10]

This topic is, very much, a moot one, but it is arguable that a rough translation might be that a proposed action is *"additional"* if it is different to the baseline of the matter in examination. The question in this context is, thus, the extent to which any enhancements arising from such *"additionality"* can be prayed in aid in calculating Biodiversity Units. Given that those units are habitat units, the potential for adding *"a real increase in social value"* would seem to be somewhat limited.[11]

Perhaps in a manner which more closely accords with the notion of *"additionality"*, the document proposes that this principle will also apply to mitigation measures proposed to address offsite impacts on protected sites.[12]

The notion also seems to come into play where a developer can exceed the statutory requirements for biodiversity net gain on their site, and any relevant targets for biodiversity net gain or green infrastructure required by local planning policy. This appears to be tied into the proposals relating to a market for Biodiversity Units. Defra indicates that it is minded to allow developers to use or sell the *"excess"* Biodiversity Units as offsite gains for another development. However, it needs to be borne in mind that, where a developer is proposing

---

[9]   Based on *"The Green Book"* (2018). See now *The Green Book* (2020) (publishing.service.gov.uk).

[10]   https://ghginstitute.org/2012/01/25/how-do-you-explain-additionality/.

[11]   Unless the parameters of the Biodiversity Metric are heavily amended in the future!

[12]   For example, SANGs, habitat creation to reduce nutrient pollution, or a line of trees to prevent light pollution into a protected site.

more than their statutory requirement for biodiversity net gain, it might not be an "*excess*" in the context of their scheme. They may be looking to provide additional benefits for a scheme which might have shortcomings in other areas, e.g. problems in delivering affordable housing.

It is further stated that enhancements may not usually be counted if they are already being taken to fulfil a form of statutory obligation (for example, improving a designated feature of a Site of Special Scientific Interest into a favourable condition).[13] Presumably, the underlying logic is that, otherwise, there would be a double counting of the same enhancement measures.

15.7   Exemptions and modifications

Paragraph 17 of Schedule 7A to the 1990 Act sets out a number of exemptions to the above requirements. They include development order land, Crown development and "*development of such other description as the Secretary of State may specify*".

Paragraph 19 allows the Secretary of State to modify these requirements in connection with:

(a)   the grant of outline planning permission, where the reservation of matters for subsequent approval has the effect of requiring or permitting development to proceed in phases; or

(b)   the grant of any kind of planning permission, where the grant is subject to conditions (whether requiring the subsequent approval of any matters or otherwise) having that effect.

By paragraph 20(1), the Secretary of State may, by regulations, modify or exclude the application of these requirements in relation to development for which planning permission is granted under section 73A of the 1990 Act or by an order under section 102 of the 1990 Act. The regulations may either disapply paragraph 13 (see above) or provide that the planning permission will be subject to other conditions related to meeting the Biodiversity Gain Objective: paragraph 20(2). By paragraph 20(3), these conditions may include:

(a)   habitat enhancement on the land to which the planning permission relates;

(b)   the allocation of registered offsite biodiversity gain to any development for which the planning permission is granted;

(c)   the purchase of Biodiversity Credits for any such development.

Section 73A is, in the main, aimed at developers who have "*jumped the gun*" and started their schemes without the benefit of planning permission. In many cases, the local planning

---

[13]   An exception to this is discussed in the consultation for the coastal and estuarine environment.

authority will be minded to grant a retrospective approval, and so this additional provision is designed to ensure that the errant developer does not, thereby, gain an advantage by avoiding the statutory biodiversity net gain condition. The position in relation to section 73A is discussed in Chapter 24.

Exemptions will also include permitted development, householder applications, brownfield sites that meet specific criteria, and certain small residential schemes.

15.8   Modifications for irreplaceable habitats

The Secretary of State may make regulations modifying these provisions in relation to any development where the onsite habitat is *"irreplaceable habitat"* (to be defined in regulations). The regulations must require the making of arrangements to minimise the adverse effects of the development on the biodiversity of the onsite habitat.

It is helpful to revert to the National Planning Policy Framework at this point. Paragraph 180(c) of the Framework states that development resulting in the loss or deterioration of irreplaceable habitats (such as ancient woodland, ancient or veteran trees, blanket bog, limestone pavement, sand dunes, salt marsh and lowland fen[14]) should be refused, unless there are wholly exceptional reasons and a suitable compensation strategy exists. This is an application of the *"last resort"* level in the mitigation hierarchy.

The Consultation Document states that the Government intends to use secondary legislation to remove development, or component parts of development, on irreplaceable habitats from the scope of the requirement for 10% biodiversity net gain. When a development results in losses of both irreplaceable and non-irreplaceable habitat, the biodiversity net gain requirement will still apply to any affected non-irreplaceable habitat. The area of irreplaceable habitat, and the bespoke compensation agreed for this area, should be omitted from the main Biodiversity Metric calculation for the development. When exempted from mandatory biodiversity net gain, development, or parts of development proposals, on irreplaceable habitats would still require bespoke compensation to be agreed with the relevant decision maker.

The Consultation Document proposes that any developer putting forward development on irreplaceable habitat would still be required to submit, for the planning authority's information, a version of a Biodiversity Gain Plan providing information about irreplaceable habitats present before and after development (which may be recorded using the Biodiversity Metric) and the steps taken to minimise adverse effects on these habitats.

The regulations may confer powers and duties, including in relation to the giving of guidance, on Natural England. This would suggest that the guidance issued by Natural England will carry considerable weight in planning decisions.

---

[14]   See the National Planning Policy Framework and the Conservation of Habitats and Species Regulations 2017.

15.9   Appeals
Appeals will be determined through the existing planning appeal process.

15.10   Variations to an approved Biodiversity Gain Plan?
There are some obvious questions to be asked of the statutory condition; namely, whether it allows for post-permission variations to an approved Biodiversity Gain Plan as a scheme evolves, and how the provisions of the conditions may be enforced in practice? There is no clear-cut answer to either question.

The Environment Act does not mention the all-too-common situation where the details of a scheme evolve over time, with the result that the baseline changes, or where there have been changes in evaluation or mitigation techniques.

One way of dealing with running changes might be in the wording of the condition itself. Many permissions have, over the years, been granted subject to conditions which allow for minor variations to the matters prescribed by them by agreement with the local planning authority. For example:

> *"The development may not be begun unless:*
>
> *(a) a Biodiversity Gain Plan has been submitted to the planning authority; and*
>
> *(b) the planning authority has approved the plan*
>
> **and the Biodiversity Gain Plan may be varied from time to time as agreed in writing by the local planning authority."**

The emphasised words are now known as "*tail-pieces*" and have been found to be objectionable. Whether such a "*tail-piece*" will invalidate a condition depends on its substantive effect: see discussion of *R (Midcounties Co-operative Ltd) v Wyre Forest DC* [2009] EWHC 964 (Admin) below.

15.11   Is the statutory condition enough by itself?
Whilst this might look like a straightforward linear progression from one bullet point to another in the Environment Act, it is suggested that the position is more sophisticated than this. It is necessary to consider these discrete matters in an holistic fashion and think in terms of an iterative interplay between them. For example, it is not possible to come to a realistic conclusion about the content of the Biodiversity Gain Plan unless one has some proposals for actually enforcing it in practice. Furthermore, it is necessary to consider how the production of a Biodiversity Gain Plan will fit in with the process leading from planning application to planning permission. To put it another way, it is unrealistic to engage in the exercise of producing a Biodiversity Gain Plan without having regard to the context within which it will be used and its own intrinsic limitations within that context.

The condition is that the development may not be begun unless:

(a)   a Biodiversity Gain Plan has been submitted to the planning authority; and

(b)   the planning authority has approved the plan.

Those versed in the drafting of planning conditions will see an omission immediately; namely, that there is no provision for the implementation or enforcement of the requirements of the Biodiversity Gain Plan. The condition is, thus, discharged by the approval of the Plan and no more. Accordingly, the prudent draftsman would, at the least, add wording which relates to the implementation of the Plan, for example:

> *"The development may not be begun unless:*
>
> *(a) a Biodiversity Gain Plan has been submitted to the planning authority and*
>
> *(b) the planning authority has approved the plan*
>
> *and the provisions of the approved Biodiversity Gain Plan shall thereafter be carried out and complied with."*

So, does such an amendment cover the problem? This depends, in turn, on whether the Biodiversity Gain Plan has been drafted with a degree of precision which allows for the objective and measurable assessment of its requirements and the developer's compliance with them.

Arguably, this may be the weakest link. The following is taken from a Biodiversity Management Plan for a large housing development, and had to do with "*Native Hedgerow & Retention of Boundary Trees*":

> **"Remedial actions**
> *Beat up hedgerow as necessary, manage understory."*

This type of wording might be acceptable in some places, but it cannot lend itself to a legally enforceable obligation because it is too imprecise. There is no measure of what is to be deemed "*necessary*" in connection with beating up hedgerow, and likewise for the vague "*manage understory*". Nor is there any mechanism whereby a dispute over whether these imprecise (at least to a lawyer) terms have been complied with can be resolved by an independent expert.

To take a requirement for monitoring from the same page:

> *"Year 2 & 5 Ecologist survey to record relative cover values according to objective 1, 2 & 3.*

Output
ECoW[15] report, to be submitted to the LPA by no later than the end of year 3 and 5 respectively."

The obvious question relates to the consequences of an adverse "*ECoW report*". There is no mechanism which ensures that the outputs recorded in the report must be approved by the LPA or that, in the absence of approval, a remediation or default mechanism is triggered.

The Secretary of State may, by regulations, specify the form of a Biodiversity Gain Plan and any other matters to be included in one (see above). The above-mentioned problems might, to some extent, be mitigated by the provision of a mandatory template which contains "*boilerplate*" terms covering such matters as dispute resolution and default mechanisms. If this does not come to pass, the local planning authority might well decide that the statutory condition is not enough and that it should be supplemented by a planning obligation pursuant to section 106 of the 1990 Act.

---

[15] Ecological Clerk of Works.

Chapter 16

Habitat banks and trading biodiversity units

16.1   Habitat banks

Habitat banks will be areas of land which have been ring fenced for the creation or enhancement of habitats for such flora and fauna as may be of value in terms of biodiversity net gain.

One of the advantages of the use of a pre-existing habitat bank is that, one would anticipate, it will have been in use as such before developers start purchasing parts of it. This prior wilding should add value to the site because it should eliminate or mitigate some of the risk which goes with the adoption of other land for offset where habitats have yet to be established. Ergo, habitat banks can reduce the risk of failure where they are already up and running.

The document entitled *"Consultation on Biodiversity Net Gain Regulations and Implementation"*[1] encourages habitat banking, saying that it can help to smooth out supply and demand by completing the necessary works to establish the habitat in advance and *"banking"* the resulting units, so they are available for sale when needed by developers: page 61. This approach is anticipated to enable delivery of larger, more strategic sites for nature.

It goes on to say that a habitat bank would need to be able to record and provide suitable monitoring information to demonstrate that the initial works to create or enhance the habitat had been completed by a given date if *"they"* (sic)[2] wish to take advantage of the *"advanced creation"* function in the Biodiversity Metric.[3] When Biodiversity Units are sold to a developer, the associated parcel of land within the habitat bank would need to be secured by a legal agreement and registered prior to approval of the Biodiversity Gain Plan for the associated development: page 62.

The proposed regulations would not require the whole land area within a habitat bank to be secured by a legal agreement for the minimum 30-year period prior to the first sale of units to a developer; however, when Biodiversity Units are sold to a developer, the associated parcel(s) of land within the habitat bank would need to be secured by a legal agreement and registered prior to approval of the developer's Biodiversity Gain Plan.

As is always the case with this type of arrangement, the local planning authority must be astute to avoid making an agreement with the proverbial *"man of straw"*. Accordingly, it might be necessary to look into collateral securities such as bonding arrangements. Also, there is a purely practical question of valuing the parcels of land in terms of Biodiversity

---

[1]   Published on behalf of the Department for Environment, Food and Rural Affairs in January 2022.

[2]   Presumably the developer.

[3]   See Natural England (July 2021) Biodiversity Metric 3.0 – User Guide www.gov.uk/guidance/biodiversity-metric-calculate-the-biodiversity-net-gain-of-a-project-or-development.

Units. Unless the proprietor of the habitat bank has recently applied the Biodiversity Metric to those parcels which will be tied to the proposed development, it will be necessary to provide a local planning authority with an up-to-date Metric spreadsheet for the Biodiversity Gain Plan.

The Consultation Document proposes that habitat created or enhanced after 30 January 2020 will be eligible for registration, and sale of the associated biodiversity gains permitted, provided it meets specified criteria. Habitat created or enhanced before this date will not be eligible: page 62.

16.2   Pointers from SANG land

The acronym *"SANG"* means *"Suitable Alternative Natural Greenspace"*. Its origins lie in the protection of Special Protection Areas (SPAs). In 2005 an EU Directive imposed restrictions on new developments in close proximity to Special Protection Areas, where ground nesting birds are prominent. The SPAs are normally surrounded by buffer zones which inhibit development which may harm them. Development outwith these zones, but close to an SPA, may be allowed provided that mitigation is provided by way of the provision of SANG or a monetary contribution towards the purchase and maintenance of it.

The most notable example is the Thames Basin Heaths Special Protection Area which covers over 8,000 hectares within Berkshire, Hampshire and Surrey.[4] It has a 5-7 km buffer zone around it. The SPA is designated for breeding populations of Dartford warbler, nightjar and woodlark, which are protected species .

The notion has, however, been extended beyond the SPAs and can be found to be used in less particular situations, where sensitive areas may be threatened or diminished by development proposals. Be that as it may, the employment of the SANG characterisation has provided practices and information which are readily transferrable to offset sites for biodiversity gains. These examples are explored in the chapters on planning conditions and planning obligations, but it is worth pausing to consider the commercial aspects of the SANG initiative.

Those familiar with compulsory purchase will also be familiar with the concept politely known as *"marriage value"* (aka, less politely, *"ransom value"*). This arises where an area of land gains additional value due to its association with more lucrative commercial development. The very familiar example is where an access to a development site must cross land owned by someone other than the developer (aka a *"ransom strip"*) and the development cannot go ahead, or is rendered difficult, unless this land is secured by the developer.

The commercial reality is that, unless a developer owns the SANG land itself, he will have to purchase it. Unless the owner of the proposed SANG land is helpfully altruistic, he will be seeking a price which would represent the value of that land to the developer. This will

---

[4]   See Guildford Borough Council's *"Thames Basin Heaths Special Protection Area Avoidance Strategy 2017 - Supplementary Planning Document"* (Factually updated October 2021).

neither be the agricultural value of the land nor the value of the land as a country park. That is to say, it will be a realistic commercial value, having regard to the contribution which the proposed SANG land brings to the overall commercial viability of the scheme. One can, readily, see the parallel with biodiversity offset sites. There is no particular reason why the owner of such a site would sell it for less than its realistic commercial value.

Not only this, but one of the commercial by-products of the SANG initiative is that some investors are purchasing land purely in order to resell it as SANG land. Clearly, those investors will be seeking the best commercial return on their investments. Again, one can readily see the parallel with biodiversity offset sites.

Perhaps the short point to be made here is that it would be extremely disingenuous to pretend that the purchase of land for biodiversity offsetting somehow escapes the normal commercial realities of property transactions.

16.3 Trading Biodiversity Units

The Consultation Document sets out proposals for the buying and selling of Biodiversity Units,[5] viz:

> *"Any landowners or managers will be able to create or enhance habitat for the purpose of selling biodiversity units, provided that they are able to meet the requirements of the policy, including additionality and register eligibility requirements, and demonstrate no significant adverse impacts on protected and priority habitats."*

Whilst the document describes Biodiversity Units as a *"currency"*, there is an argument that a market approach is one step too far along the road to the monetisation of nature.

By way of a slight deviation from the script, it is difficult to see how one could form an objective valuation system for the various, and varying, elements of a biota, which is not anthropomorphic or ethnocentric. For example, the widely used notion of *"natural capital"* relates to economic assessments and not valuing biodiversity for its own sake. Indeed, some have sought to express the value of *"ecological services"* in monetary terms; for example, the Government's erstwhile Natural Capital Committee.[6] The NCC's definition was:

> *"Natural capital refers to the elements of nature that produce value or benefits to people (directly and indirectly), such as the stock of forests, rivers, land, minerals and oceans, as well as the natural processes and functions that underpin their operation." (NCC 2013)*

This somewhat venal notion is not without its detractors. The Guardian journalist, George Monbiot, had this to say in 2014:

---

[5] Page 58 - Note: this is not the same thing as buying and selling Biodiversity Credits; they are different things.
[6] See *Towards a Framework for Defining and Measuring Changes in Natural Capital*, Working Paper, 1 March 2014 (Natural Capital Committee).

> *"They are trying to compare things which cannot be directly compared. The result is the kind of nonsense to be found in the Natural Capital Committee's latest report, published a couple of weeks ago. The Natural Capital Committee was set up by this Government, supposedly in pursuit of better means of protecting the natural world.*
>
> *It claimed, for example, that if freshwater ecosystems in this country were better protected, the additional aesthetic value arising from that protection would be £700 million. That's the aesthetic value: in other words, what it looks like. We will value the increment in what it looks like at £700 million. It said that if grassland and sites of special scientific interest were better protected, their wildlife value would increase by £40 million. The value of their wildlife – like the chalk hill blues and the dog violets that live on protected grasslands – would be enhanced by £40 million.*
>
> *These figures, ladies and gentlemen, are marmalade. They are finely shredded, boiled to a pulp, heavily sweetened and still indigestible. In other words, they are total gibberish."[7]*

Be that as it is may, the proposal is that suppliers of Biodiversity Units will be able to sell to developers anywhere in England, provided that the use of those units is appropriate for the development in question and the distance between the development and the offsite habitat is properly accounted for in the Biodiversity Metric. The Consultation Document goes on to say (page 59):

> *"If a developer is able to exceed the statutory requirements for biodiversity net gain on a given development site, and any relevant targets for biodiversity net gain or green infrastructure required by local planning policy, we are minded to allow them to use or sell the excess biodiversity units as offsite gains for another development."*

The document states that it expects the price for Biodiversity Units to be agreed between buyers and sellers, and for them to ensure that it is sufficient to cover the costs of creating or enhancing the habitat and maintaining it for a minimum of 30 years. Again, there must be a concern that the seller will be seeking a *"ransom value"*. Ergo, it remains to be seen whether these proposals will be commercially viable in real life.

Again, as noted above in connection with habitat banks, in this it is necessary to consider how any such arrangement is going to be secured for the purposes of the planning process. Given that the vendor of the Biodiversity Units is unlikely to be connected to the development site, it follows that a condition would be inappropriate. Thus, this somewhat remote

---

[7] *Put a price on nature? We must stop this neoliberal road to ruin* - George Monbiot's SPERI Annual Lecture, hosted by the Sheffield Political Economy Research Institute at the University of Sheffield – 2014. Not to be accused of sitting on the fence, he also said: *"All we require now is for the Cabinet Office to give us a price for love and a true value for society and we will have a single figure for the meaning of life. I know what you're thinking: it's 42. But Deep Thought failed to anticipate the advent of Strictly Come Dancing, which has depreciated the will to live ... It is complete rubbish, and surely anyone can see it's complete rubbish. Not only is it complete rubbish, it is unimprovable rubbish. It's just not possible to have meaningful figures for benefits which cannot in any sensible way be measured in financial terms"*. Deep Thought was, of course, the computer in *The Hitchhiker's Guide to the Galaxy!*

party will have to provide long-term security by way of either a Conservation Covenant or a planning obligation and, again, there is a question of whether or not the vendor is a "*man of straw*".

16.4   The practical question

The more pertinent question, for both developers and local planning authorities, is whether this somewhat ideational approach is simply too complicated for an already over-complicated planning process.

Furthermore, one is left to wonder how councillors and members of the public will respond to a scheme which relies on the trading of metaphysical Biodiversity Units as opaque simulacra to meet its targets. Some may have an ideological objections to the apparent monetisation of biodiversity in any event. They might well adopt George Monbiot's:

> "*It's just not possible to have meaningful figures for benefits which cannot in any sensible way be measured in financial terms*".

Chapter 17

Securing And Delivering Biodiversity Net Gain

"Be water, my friend." (Bruce Lee)

Governmental and quasi-Governmental bodies and persons are quick to state that their proposed mechanisms will be managed and monitored by bodies such as local planning authorities. However, it is important to have regard to a matter mentioned elsewhere in this book; namely, the matter of staff resources.

In the document entitled *"Biodiversity in the UK: bloom or bust? – First Report of Session 2021–22" (the "Commons Audit Report")*, the Environmental Audit Committee of the House of Commons raised concerns about the abilities of local authorities to secure and deliver biodiversity net gain:

> *"186. CIEEM[1] also raised doubts over enforcement mechanisms and the will of the construction sector to realise net gain:*
>
> > *'Within the construction sector, there is little, if any, appetite to monitor successes of biodiversity mitigation (if actually delivered) due to a lack of enforcement. Baseline data collected pre-planning is generally not placed in the public domain so whilst there is a volume of data collected in locations and environments ... this is not made available in a timeframe that could enable more efficient use, benefitting biodiversity and understanding outcomes.'*
>
> *187. A lack of compliance monitoring, non-implementation of mitigation measures, and a failure to consider the cumulative effect of small losses of biodiversity at the landscape level have been highlighted as further challenges to implementing net gain. For example, a 2013 study found that only 30% of mitigation measures are implemented, and hardly any monitoring commitments are made."*

The key is for developer, landowner and local authority to be fluid and to adjust their approach to a proposed scheme on a site-specific basis. Whilst a well-rehearsed routine might inform an approach, it will, in most cases, have to be adjusted on a case-by-case basis, particularly with complex schemes.

The Defra Consultation Document has promised that templates will be provided for Conservation Covenants, Biodiversity Gain Plans etc, but it might be the case that these proposals will introduce an unwanted inflexibility to the process. As lawyers often say, templates are good servants but bad masters.

---

[1] Chartered Institute of Ecology and Environmental Management.

The following chapters set out a variety of possible approaches to these problems, but they are not intended to be rigid: "*Be water, my friend.*"

Chapter 18

Management Plans

18.1　Construction Works Plans

It is important to remember that ecological impacts are likely to arise as soon as work starts on site, whether by way of direct physical impact on habitats or the indirect effects of noise, activity and lighting on both onsite and offsite species. It follows that consideration needs to be given to how those impacts will be managed, and one appropriate mechanism for doing so is by way of a discrete Biodiversity Construction Works Plan. This requirement could be embedded in planning conditions or, preferably, a section 106 agreement and should, it is suggested, contain, at the least, controls over the construction and use of the following elements:

- access tracks;

- settlement ponds and drainage;

- soil storage bunds;

- storage yards;

- welfare cabins/offices; and

- temporary car parks.

These controls should set out areas to be avoided, and relate to both activities within the site and, so far as it may be affected, sensitive nearby land.

It is also worth bearing in mind that Class A, Part 4 of Schedule 2 to the Town and Country Planning (General Permitted Development) (England) Order 2015 (S.I. 2015/596) (aka "*GPDO*") allows the provision on land of buildings, moveable structures, works, plant or machinery required temporarily in connection with and for the duration of operations being or to be carried out on, in, under or over that land or on land adjoining that land. The prudent local planning authority might give consideration as to whether this permitted development right should be disabled in favour of a bespoke arrangement in a section 106 agreement. For example, there are certain ambiguities in the way in which this provision is drafted. The "*duration of operations*" could be more closely defined in a bespoke document. Likewise, the reference to "*land adjoining that land*" might need to be narrowed down so as to define the said adjoining land on a drawing and characterised depending on its proximity to sensitive habitats.

The management plan should include details of how long these facilities or works will be in place and should also include a methodology for the removal of them when they are no longer needed and then making good the site to a prescribed standard. As is oft repeated in this book,[1] it is necessary to not only provide for these cessation mechanisms on paper, but also by reference to the financial realities of the situation. Again, one has to think in terms of securities such as bonding arrangements.

If the developer is relying on the Part 4 permitted development rights mentioned above, it is worth remembering that paragraph A.2 provides the condition that development is permitted by Class A subject to the conditions that, when the operations have been carried out:

(a)   any building, structure, works, plant or machinery permitted by Class A is removed; and

(b)   any adjoining land on which development permitted by Class A has been carried out is, as soon as reasonably practicable, reinstated to its condition before that development was carried out.

It might be that this removal and reinstatement provision is deemed to be inadequate insofar as the phrase *"as soon as reasonably practicable"* is concerned (particularly with a phased development) and as to the condition in which the land should be left once a temporary use has ceased. Again, the prudent local planning authority might feel that these matters should be addressed by way of a section 106 agreement which takes account of the matters mentioned above.

---

[1]   Because they are so often neglected in practice.

Chapter 19

Financial Viability

19.1 Introduction

It is a simple fact of life that financial viability underpins almost all development schemes and it follows that it is important to have regard to viability when considering the importation of biodiversity net gain requirements during the planning process. This is not least because the developer and the local planning authority might have to make hard choices between matters which are desirable in terms of biodiversity and other desirable matters, such as affordable housing. These choices are driven by concerns which include the economic viability of the project in question.

The following chapters discuss the securing and delivery of biodiversity net gain; but a seemingly deep and earnest discussion of planning conditions and planning obligations et cetera is pointless if the developer cannot afford to implement them and, simply, walks away from the development with a few uncomplimentary words about the local planning authority. Ergo, to be credible, the navigation of this process must entail an iterative approach which has regard to the financial realities of the scheme in question.

19.2 The zero-sum problem and financial viability

Those who have studied economics might be familiar with the expression "*zero-sum*". This expression seems to have derived from game theory and seeks to represent a situation where there is a fixed "*pot*" throughout and the gains or losses of each participant are exactly balanced by the gains and losses of other participants with the result that, when all gains and losses are totalled up, they amount to a zero change to the size of the original pot itself. The values within the pot are simply redistributed. One way of imagining this is by way of the proverbial pie which can be cut into any number of slices, albeit that the total volume of the pie remains the same throughout, notwithstanding the varying distribution of shares in it between those who have the pleasure of eating it.

The translation of this concept into economic theory is, thus, discernible. If the total sum of money on the table in a particular game is fixed, there will be winners and losers; however, this will be by way of a redistribution of the fixed total sum within the initial pot. The simple fact of the matter is that, when it comes to land development projects, one is often dealing with a zero-sum game.

This is to say that a particular development project will yield a particular financial outcome;[1] and, for all practical purposes, it is the main measurement of the fixed pot of money which is on the table. It is from this pot that all costs of bringing forward the project must be

---

[1] Perhaps the total revenues deriving from all house sales in a residential scheme.

drawn. There is no other money in the game. If the total costs of the projected project will exceed the anticipated financial income, the project is not viable.

This excursion into economics and game theory is not, therefore, an academic one. If a local planning authority is seeking certain adjustments or benefits in a scheme, they will cost money and the money must be found from a redistribution of the finite resources which are available within the financial model for the scheme. Unless there is some form of external Government support, this is an exercise in the redistribution of costs within a closed zero-sum model. In a nutshell, one has to rob Peter to pay Paul!

The business model for almost all property development schemes is a negative cash flow one, in the sense that large financial investments must be made before any income starts to flow into the site.[2] And, with a residential scheme, a housebuilder does not normally start realising a significant revenue stream until the first dwelling is sold.

Thus, if the members of the planning committee take the view that the developer should provide certain provisions within a scheme, they should also recognise that the money for doing so might be taken from other planning benefits within the scheme, such as affordable housing.

The alternative is that the cash flow implications of their approach might find its way into the financial viability appraisal for the scheme. This, in turn, might lead the developer to turn to the local planning authority and say that he cannot afford to provide all of the planning benefits which the authority might otherwise be seeking, such as affordable housing.

In an extreme case (perhaps where the site is compromised by contamination), a developer who is faced with the proposition that he must front-load his scheme to an unacceptable degree might, simply, walk away from the site on the basis that his money is better spent elsewhere, or his proposed venture capital partner might decide that it is not worth the risk.

Thus, the pursuit of planning benefits within a scheme must be an iterative process which takes account of the financial viability assessment for the scheme. It is pointless asking for a benefit when the developer will, palpably, not be able to afford it. Furthermore, this iterative process must take into account the cash flow model for most development schemes; this is to say, a model which will normally be heavily reliant on negative cash flow for a significant part of the early stages of the development process. For example, a housebuilder might not start making money until he actually starts to sell houses. This could be some significant period of time from the date of commencement of the development, during which the developer is having to finance construction operations etc out of capital. This means that, in terms of the cash flow model for a typical residential development, the loading of the

---

[2]   Those involved in finance call this a *"high burn rate"*, and it is a warning sign where the entrepreneur is *"burning"* working capital and cash reserves at a high rate with a slow or negative inward cash flow. The projected burn rate should, with property development, be shown in the economic viability assessment for the scheme.

costs of benefits onto the early stages of a scheme by the local planning authority is going to be unnecessarily detrimental when, in practice, it might be possible to defer those costs until a later stage, preferably when houses are being sold and income is flowing into the financial model.

Having discussed what might be described as the *"meta-narrative"*, it is now possible to go on and think about how this might be reflected in day-to-day development control transactions.

Take, for example, the situation where a large residential scheme is in front of members for approval. Both members and officers seem to be happy with the scheme; however, Councillor Brown suddenly proposes an additional planning condition. He suggests that all of the houses within the development should be provided with charging points for electric vehicles. All members agree that this sounds eminently sensible and so the application is approved subject to this additional condition. There is, however, a significant problem in this scenario; namely, that no member has taken the trouble to consider how much these electric vehicle charging points are going to cost. They have not given any consideration to the impact that these additional costs may have upon the cash flow model for the scheme in question. Not only are these in the overall costs of the scheme; they will also have a significant impact on the cash flow model. They will, of course, need to be picked up during the construction process. If so, it is not simply the costs of providing these charging points but also the notional cost of financing those construction costs until such time as they can be met out of the income flowing from the scheme. It might be doing Councillor Brown a disservice, but it is doubtful whether he re-ran the economic viability assessment for the scheme before venturing to propose his additional condition. Put another way, if one supposes that the additional cost of a charging point will be £300 per dwelling, and it is proposed that the scheme will deliver 100 houses, then the overall costs will be £30,000. If one adds financing charges for this developer, the hypothetical final cost could be in the order of perhaps £35,000.[3] Given that the scheme is a zero-sum model, this money must come from somewhere within the scheme. Unless the developer releases some of their anticipated profit,[4] money must be drawn from elsewhere. It might be the case that the developer then reverts saying that they cannot, now, provide all the affordable housing they initially promised – that the budget for affordable housing must be trimmed by £35,000. The ultimate question for Councillor Brown, in reality, might come down to whether or not he prefers affordable housing to electric vehicle charging points.[5]

This was a simple example. If one moves on to biodiversity net gain, the sums of money involved or the costs of opportunities lost could be very considerable. It should follow that the parties need to consider the viability aspects of these considerations early on in discussions about the scheme, in the hope that this will obviate later misunderstandings or

---

[3]   On analysis one sometimes finds that the loan costs to the developer are very high, to the extent that many are surprised when provided with a real-life worked example.

[4]   In which case, they might just walk away and put their money into a less troublesome investment.

[5]   In passing, it is worth asking whether Councillor Brown has exposed the council to the threat of an adverse costs award in the event that the developer lodges an appeal.

disputes when the details of the scheme become apparent. There is little point in members approving an illustrative masterplan which shows considerable green areas[6] when the costs of delivering and maintaining those areas has not been considered between officers and developers. If the developer is saying that their application is an outline application, and that it would be premature to enter into such discussions, then, perhaps, the answer is that they have chosen the wrong vehicle for their promotion of this part of the scheme.

There is also the question of whether a local planning authority should seek to front-load a phased scheme so as to reduce the risks that latter phases might not come forward or might be delayed.

It is, therefore, suggested that one of the considerations which needs to flow through the minds of those within local planning authorities at the outset is whether proposed benefits are financially viable and, if so, whether the realisation of those benefits will be at the expense of other benefits.

---

[6] It seems to be almost axiomatic within the development industry that illustrative masterplans must show as much green as can be fitted into them.

Chapter 20

Planning Conditions

20.1 Legal constraints

Section 70(1) of the Town and Country Planning Act 1990 provides that a local planning authority may grant a planning permission unconditionally or "*subject to such conditions as they think fit*".

This power is not as wide as the literal words of the section might suggest. The Courts have held, on numerous occasions, that local planning authorities must observe certain legal principles in imposing conditions.

In *Newbury DC v Secretary of State* [1981] A.C. 578, the House of Lords identified these principles as follows:

- a condition must be imposed for a "*planning purpose*" only and not for any ulterior motive;

- the condition must fairly and reasonably relate to the development permitted by the planning permission; and

- the condition shall not be so unreasonable that no reasonable planning authority could have imposed it.

20.2 Conditions seeking financial contributions

It might seem to be that a local authority which seeks a financial contribution by way of a condition is acting laudably if that money is going to be used to benefit the public. However, executive bodies (which includes local planning authorities) cannot obtain money from the public unless authorised to do so by Parliament. No pecuniary burden can be imposed upon the public, except under clear and distinct legal authority.

In *R v Bowman* (1897) 1 Q.B. 663 it was held that justices who were charged with issuing liquor licences were acting unlawfully in requiring applicants to make payments for public purposes; namely, that the applicant should pay £1,000 in reduction of the rates.[1]

These principles were affirmed by the House of Lords in *Total Network SL v Commissioners of Customs and Excise* [2008] UKHL 19.

---

[1]   See also *Leeds City Council v Spencer* [1999] 5 WLUK 61, [1999] E.H.L.R. 394 and (1999) 1 L.G.L.R. 917.

If a local planning authority is seeking a financial contribution from a developer, the best course is to consider whether the use of an agreement under section 106 of the 1990 Act might be possible: see below.

20.3   Conditions interfering with land ownership

The Courts have tended to lean against conditions which interfere with rights of land ownership, particularly when a condition has the effect of expropriating land without the compensation which would otherwise be payable. This is important because it precludes the use of a condition to secure the transfer of land for the purposes of biodiversity.

The leading case is *Hall & Co Ltd v Shoreham-by-Sea UDC* [1964] 1 W.L.R. 240. There, the plaintiffs obtained planning permission to develop land for industrial purposes. The main road was overloaded with traffic and, in the interests of highway safety, the local planning authority granted permission subject to conditions which included that the plaintiffs *"shall construct an ancillary road over the entire frontage of the site at their own expense and as and when required by the local planning authority, and shall give right of passage over it to and from such ancillary roads as may be constructed on adjoining land"* and that *"the new access shall be temporary for a period of five years initially but the local planning authority will not enforce its closure until the ancillary roads ... have been constructed and alter¬native access to the main road is available"*. In quashing the conditions, Willmer LJ stated:

> *"I turn now to consider what I regard as the main point in the case, namely, the contention that conditions 3 and 4 are ultra vires. It is contended that the effect of these conditions is to require the plaintiffs not only to build the ancillary road on their own land, but to give right of passage over it to other persons to an extent that will virtually amount to dedicating it to the public, and all this without acquiring any right to recover any compensation whatsoever. This is said to amount to a violation of the plaintiffs' fundamental rights of ownership which goes far beyond anything authorised by the statute.*

> *... Under the conditions now sought to be imposed, on the other hand, the plaintiffs must construct the ancillary road as and when they may be required to do so over the whole of their frontage entirely at their own expense. ... The defendants would thus obtain the benefit of having the road constructed for them at the plaintiffs' expense, on the plaintiffs' land, and without the necessity for paying any compensation in respect, thereof. ... In these circumstances, although I have much sympathy with the object sought to be achieved by the defendants, I am satisfied that conditions 3 and 4 are so unreasonable that they must he held to be ultra vires."* [2]

In *M J Shanley Ltd (in Liquidation) v Secretary of State* [1982] J.P.L. 380, a condition requiring the developer to provide 40 acres of open space for public use was invalid; similarly, a

---

[2]   See now *DB Symmetry Ltd v Swindon BC* [2020] EWCA Civ 1331.

condition that a developer provide land for, and then donate it for, public parking spaces: *Westminster Renslade Ltd v Secretary of State for the Environment* [1983] J.P.L. 454.

If a local planning authority is seeking this type of arrangement from a developer, then, again, the best course is to consider whether the use of an agreement under section 106 of the 1990 Act might be possible: see below.

20.4   Drafting problems

The following example is taken from a real-life planning condition. It might, at first brush, appear to be relatively uncontentious; however, it might be the case that it is, in reality, somewhat more problematic:

> *"The development shall be undertaken in complete accordance with recommendations set out in Section 6 of the Great Crested Newt Survey prepared by [*****] dated [*****] 2016, Section 4 of the Badger Survey Report prepared by [*****] dated [*****] 2016, Section 5 of the Reptile Survey prepared by [*****] dated [*****] 2016, Sections 8.3 and 8.5 of the Ecological Appraisal prepared by [*****] dated [*****] 2016."*

The first point is that the condition provides that the development should be undertaken in accordance with a number of reports. It is highly unlikely that the authors of those reports would have drafted them with a view to providing prescriptive formulae. They will often have been drafted without legalistic precision. Furthermore, it is always possible that there might be conflicts between the various requirements of these diverse reports, with no way to reconcile them. For example, the timeline in respect of one biodiversity topic might interfere with or prejudice activities being carried out for another biodiversity topic. Or they might, in the absence of an overall critical path analysis, simply be out of sequence with other aspects of the development scheme as a whole. Accordingly, it might be the case that the condition is not enforceable in practical terms.

The second problem is that no development of any size will proceed in a *"once and for all"* fashion. In all probability, there will be some degree of phasing involved. It follows that any condition which seeks to introduce any biodiversity measures during the course of the development should have regard to matters of timing. This is, of course, particularly so when the initial planning permission is an outline planning permission and the particulars of each phase will emerge during the course of reserved matters approvals.

Accordingly, it is arguable that the better course is not to provide a condition which seeks to promote a simple *"once and for all"* requirement but, instead, allows for some degree of sophistication, including the provision of a timetable. For example:

> *"No part of the development shall be commenced unless and until a scheme for ecological mitigation (the 'Mitigation Scheme') has been submitted to and approved by the local planning authority. The Mitigation Scheme shall incorporate the recommendations set out in Section 6 of the Great Crested Newt Survey prepared by [*****] dated [*****]*

> *2016, Section 4 of the Badger Survey Report prepared by [*****] dated [*****]*
> *2016, Section 5 of the Reptile Survey prepared by [*****] dated [*****] 2016,*
> *Sections 8.3 and 8.5 of the Ecological Appraisal prepared by [*****] dated [*****]*
> *2016 and shall include a timetable for its implementation. The development shall be*
> *carried out in accordance with the timetable and provisions of the Mitigation Scheme."*

There is, however, an unfortunate limitation on the way in which this type of scheme condition can be deployed, and this results from uncertainty created by recent caselaw.

It might seem to be sensible, and indeed would be sensible, if the condition provided for variations to the approved scheme from time to time. There might be numerous reasons why the approved scheme does not fit with the way in which the development is emerging onsite. For example, it might be that previously unknown ground conditions have emerged as the works have progressed. It might be the case that the economic viability assessment for the scheme must, then, be revisited and the scheme altered as a result. This is not unusual and may mean that certain *"benefits"* must be trimmed or removed. Accordingly, it might seem appropriate to add the following words to the end of the conditions, so as to allow for future variations:

> *"Provided that variations to the approved mitigation scheme may, from time to time,*
> *be approved in writing by the local planning authority."*

These additional words are now known as *"tail-pieces"* and have been found to be objectionable. Whether such a *"tail-piece"* will invalidate a condition depends on its substantive effect.

The leading case is *R (Midcounties Co-operative Ltd) v Wyre Forest DC* [2009] EWHC 964 (Admin). There, two such conditions were challenged; one was held to be defective and the other was not.

One (*'Condition 6'*) imposed limits on the retail floorspace of a new superstore and continued *"unless otherwise agreed in writing with the Local Planning Authority"*. Ouseley J held that the effect of the tail-piece was to enable development to take place:

> *"[70] ... which could be very different in scale or impact from that applied for, assessed or*
> *permitted, and it enables it to be created by means wholly outside any statutory process."*

The second condition identified the drawings in accordance with which the development was to be carried out. It added: *"unless other minor variations are agreed in writing after the date of this permission and before implementation with the Local Planning Authority"*. Ouseley J stated:

> *"[79] I do not regard this tail-piece as unlawful. Its clear scope is to enable 'minor*
> *variations' to an obligation otherwise to develop 'in strict accordance' with plans and*
> *drawings. Both those parts of the condition operate to limit the flexibility which the*
> *tailpiece provides."*

In the event, Ouseley J held that he could excise the offending tail-piece from the Condition 6 so as to leave the balance (and the permission) intact.

In *R (On the application of Warley) v Wealden DC* [2011] EWHC 2083 (Admin), permission was granted for lighting at a tennis court subject to a condition which provided that the tennis court should not be operated outside prescribed times *"without the prior consent in writing of the Local Planning Authority"*. Mr Rabinder Singh QC (as he then was), sitting as a deputy High Court Judge, concluded that these words were inappropriate and severed them from the permission.

Regardless of whether such conditions can be saved by severance, the lesson to be learned is not to use such tail-pieces. There can be no certainty that a tail-piece which appears to be inoffensive might be severed by a judge who takes a different view.

It is essential, in drafting conditions, to think about the practical realities of enforcing them. In many cases, a condition which might seem relatively straightforward on its face might prove to be either unenforceable in law or an embarrassment in practice.

To give an example:

> *"The landscaping and tree and shrub planting hereby approved shall be implemented in accordance with the following plans and details [...] All planting, seeding or turfing comprised in the approved details of landscaping shall be carried out in the first planting season following the occupation of the dwelling(s)."*

This might seem like a relatively straightforward and innocuous landscaping condition; however, it has been attached to a planning permission for residential development. If some of the planting falls within the residential curtilages of properties which are going to be sold on to individual owner occupiers, it will be those individuals who must discharge the condition, if at all. The developer will have sold on and, therefore, relinquished control over those areas of land. There is no point in seeking to enforce against the developer because, of course, he no longer has the ability to discharge the condition. The local planning authority is then placed in the invidious position of having to decide whether it is going to enforce against individual owner occupiers. In many cases, the authority will decline to do so because of the political ramifications which would then ensue.

Furthermore, one must have regard to the old legal maxim about never taking a bond from a *"man of straw"*. It is one thing to impose a condition which requires an impecunious developer to carry out a scheme, but it is another thing to seek to enforce it when he has gone into liquidation. As noted above, it is not open to the local planning authority to require a payment of money by way of a condition, and so the provision of a financial security is not an option.

20.5   British Standard for model planning conditions

BS42020:2013[3] provides a suite of standard or model planning conditions and planning informatives which can be readily adapted on a case-by-case basis. However, as will be noted below, care has to be taken with the detailed wording of these precedents – which is, sometimes, problematic. One has to play *"devil's advocate"* and ask what a defence lawyer might argue when faced with a putative breach of an imprecise provision. Sometimes, the drafting of these models might make his job easier. It is prudent to apply the notion of *"defined inputs, measurable outputs"* to each and every part of a draft condition before committing to it.

Whilst this chapter explores the application of BS42020 to planning conditions, it is noted that it will be invoked in the following chapter, in connection with planning obligations, and so the comments made here will be appropriate when one comes to that chapter.

Model D.2.1 relates to *"Biodiversity method statements"*. The explanation for the condition states that such a condition can be used to secure detailed specification(s) for a wide range of biodiversity avoidance (sic), mitigation, compensation and enhancement measures.

Paragraph D.2.2 goes on to say that method statements are suited to the delivery of a range of biodiversity conservation measures, including provision for:

(a)   activities relating to conservation good practice:

(1)   creation of new wildlife features, e.g. bespoke bat roosts/caves/structures, erection of bird boxes in buildings/structures, otter holts, badger setts, barn owl boxes and ponds;

(2)   creation, restoration and enhancement of semi-natural habitats;

(3)   tree, hedgerow, shrub and wildflower planting/establishment;

(4)   habitat removal and reinstatement/replacement;

(5)   shaping new landforms associated with habitat creation, e.g. pond construction;

(6)   bat crossings over or under new roads;

(7)   provision and control of access and environmental interpretation facilities, e.g. bird hides, paths, fences, bridges, stiles, gates and signs/information boards;

(b)   activities relating to construction:

---

[3]   British Standard BS42020:2013, Annex D (informative) – *Standard or model planning conditions and planning 'informatives'.*

(1)   species rescue and translocation, e.g. reptiles and amphibians;

(2)   roof stripping or the full or partial demolition of buildings;

(3)   habitat salvage and translocation, e.g. hedgerows;

(4)   temporary management of existing habitats during construction;

(5)   temporary shelters during construction for vulnerable species, e.g. barn owl boxes;

(6)   alternative routes required for otters to cross roads during any construction works restricting access to a stream;

(7)   soil handling, movement and management.

As to (b) above, Method Statements might also be appropriate to secure specific biodiversity measures during construction; however, paragraph D.2.1 advises that, in complex cases, it might be more appropriate to secure these through a Construction Environmental Management Plan. Model D.4.1 provides for Construction Environmental Management Plans ("*CEMP Biodiversity*"):

> *"No development shall take place (including demolition, ground works, vegetation clearance) until a construction environmental management plan (CEMP: Biodiversity) has been submitted to and approved in writing by the local planning authority. The CEMP (Biodiversity) shall include the following:*
>
> *a) Risk assessment of potentially damaging construction activities.*
>
> *b) Identification of 'biodiversity protection zones'.*
>
> *c) Practical measures (both physical measures and sensitive working practices) to avoid or reduce impacts during construction (may be provided as a set of method statements).*
>
> *d) The location and timing of sensitive works to avoid harm to biodiversity features.*
>
> *e) The times during construction when specialist ecologists need to be present on site to oversee works.*
>
> *f) Responsible persons and lines of communication.*
>
> *g) The role and responsibilities on site of an ecological clerk of works (ECoW) or similarly competent person.*
>
> *h) Use of protective fences, exclusion barriers and warning signs.*

The approved CEMP shall be adhered to and implemented throughout the construction period strictly in accordance with the approved details, unless otherwise agreed in writing by the local planning authority."

An *"Ecological Clerk of Works (ECoW)"* is defined in the glossary as being a person who has the ecological qualifications, training, skills and relevant experience to undertake appropriate monitoring and to provide specialist advice to development site personnel on necessary working practices required to (i) safeguard ecological features on site, and (ii) aid compliance with any consents and relevant wildlife legislation related to the works.

The model uses the phrase *"specialist ecologists"* and appears to be inconsistent with Model D.3.2, which uses the phrase *"a competent ecologist"* and the glossary, which provides a definition of a *"professional ecologist"* as being a person who has, through relevant education, training or experience, gained recognised qualifications and expertise in the field of ecology and environmental management. One is left to wonder why this phrase was not adopted or whether a *"specialist ecologist"* is intended to mean something different. The problem is compounded because, whilst the glossary provides a definition of *"professional ecologist"*, the phrase is not put to operative use in any of the model conditions or the narrative.[4]

Model D.4.5 refers to Landscape and Ecological Management Plans (LEMPs):[5]

A landscape and ecological management plan (LEMP) shall be submitted to, and be approved in writing by, the local planning authority prior [... to the commencement or occupation ...] of the development [or specified phase of development]. The content of the LEMP shall include the following:

a) Description and evaluation of features to be managed.

b) Ecological trends and constraints on site that might influence management.

c) Aims and objectives of management.

d) Appropriate management options for achieving aims and objectives.

e) Prescriptions for management actions.

f) Preparation of a work schedule (including an annual work plan capable of being rolled forward over a five-year period).

g) Details of the body or organisation responsible for implementation of the plan.

---

[4]   One is left to wonder at the standard of proof reading! A lawyer would, or should, check that cross-references and definitions sit properly in a legal document as part of the final draft.

[5]   Also referred to as a *"Habitat or Biodiversity Management Plans"*.

h) Ongoing monitoring and remedial measures.

The LEMP shall also include details of the legal and funding mechanism(s) by which the long-term implementation of the plan will be secured by the developer with the management body(ies) responsible for its delivery. The plan shall also set out (where the results from monitoring show that conservation aims and objectives of the LEMP are not being met) how contingencies and/or remedial action will be identified, agreed and implemented so that the development still delivers the fully functioning biodiversity objectives of the originally approved scheme. The approved plan will be implemented in accordance with the approved details."

It would be helpful if the mantra *"defined inputs, measurable outputs"* is applied to this central condition in order to assist in the application and enforcement of it.

First, the phrase *"A landscape and ecological management plan (LEMP) shall be submitted to, and be approved in writing by, the local planning authority prior [... to the commencement or occupation ...] of the development ..."* is unclear in terms of enforcement. The notion is, presumably, to replicate the *"Grampian"* formula and so it is, perhaps, best to do so with clarity; for example: *"No part of the development shall be [commenced] [occupied] unless and until the LEMP has been submitted to and approved in writing by the local planning authority"*.

Secondly, the LEMP now provides an opportunity to import objectivity by making reference to hard targets which are based on the Biodiversity Metric.[6] For example, sub-paragraph (c) refers to aims and objectives of management and it would be possible to add a reference to the metric, viz:

*"(c) aims and objectives of **management which will (without limitation) include the provision of 15% biodiversity net gain within the Site as calculated by the Biodiversity Metric 3.0.**"* (Emphasis added).

Model D.3.2.1 provides for the protection of breeding birds during construction:

"No removal of hedgerows, trees or shrubs [... consider also brambles, ivy and other climbing plants if appropriate ...] [... or works to or demolition of buildings or structures that may be used by breeding birds ...] shall take place between 1st March and 31st August inclusive, unless a competent ecologist has undertaken a careful, detailed check of vegetation for active birds' nests immediately before the vegetation is cleared and provided written confirmation that no birds will be harmed and/or that there are appropriate measures in place to protect nesting bird interest on site. Any such written confirmation should be submitted to the local planning authority."

---

[6] BS42020 was, of course, drafted whilst the Biodiversity Metric was in draft form only.

Unfortunately, the terminology used is far from perfect. The phrase *"a competent ecologist"* is subjective and, instead, reference should be made to an appropriate professional qualification, probably a chartered ecologist. Arguably, one might be assisted by the given definition of a *"competent person"* in the glossary as being a person who has the qualifications, training, skills and experience relevant to the task being undertaken, but the point is far from clear. A similar point arises again in connection with Model D.4.1: see above.

Likewise, a *"careful, detailed check"* is not only subjective but confusing and, indeed, otiose. The ecologist is required to provide a written report and it is to be presumed that this will be prepared to usual professional standards. Finally, there is no provision for the approval of the report by the local planning authority's own ecologist, and so this requirement should be added.

Model D.3.5 provides for a lighting design strategy for light-sensitive biodiversity. Many species active at night (bats, badgers and otters) are sensitive to light pollution. The introduction of artificial light might mean that such species can be disturbed and/or discouraged from using their breeding and resting places, established flyways or foraging areas, viz:

> *"Prior to occupation, a 'lighting design strategy for biodiversity' for [... specify buildings, features or areas to be lit ...] shall be submitted to and approved in writing by the local planning authority. The strategy shall:*
>
> *a) identify those areas/features on site that are particularly sensitive for [... insert species...] and that are likely to cause disturbance in or around their breeding sites and resting places or along important routes used to access key areas of their territory, for example, for foraging; and*
>
> *b) show how and where external lighting will be installed (through the provision of appropriate lighting contour plans and technical specifications) so that it can be clearly demonstrated that areas to be lit will not disturb or prevent the above species using their territory or having access to their breeding sites and resting places.*
>
> *All external lighting shall be installed in accordance with the specifications and locations set out in the strategy, and these shall be maintained thereafter in accordance with the strategy. Under no circumstances should any other external lighting be installed without prior consent from the local planning authority."*

The phrase *"prior to occupation"* should, it is suggested, be extended to a particular part of the development, perhaps first occupation of a residential development or the like. It might be the case that the phrase *"under no circumstances should any other external lighting be installed without prior consent from the local planning authority"* would be construed as an illegitimate *'tail-piece"* and so should be avoided.

The difficulty here is that one wonders why this strategy would be left to a condition and not settled as part of the process leading to the grant of the permission. Be that as it may, it is important to note that any proposed estate roads will, in all probability, be procured via a highways agreement pursuant to section 38 of the Highways Act 1980 and therefore it is important that the local highway authority agrees the lighting strategy, so far as it affects proposed street lights. Otherwise, there might be a conflict between the condition and the section 38 agreement.

20.6   Conditions or planning obligations?

It is not unlawful to have a planning obligation which secures matters which could have been secured by planning conditions: *Good v Epping Forest DC* [1994] J.P.L. 372. Planning obligations are, traditionally, used to secure benefits which cannot be secured by way of conditions; but there is often an overlap between conditions and planning obligations with complex schemes. However, it might be unwise to split the matter of securing complex mechanisms between them and there are a number of reasons behind this observation. First, that of navigating (i.e. making sense of) two disparate documents. Secondly, the enforcement mechanisms for, respectively, planning obligations and planning conditions are very different. Thirdly, the respective appeal, discharge and modification mechanisms are different.

It may be the case that, with a particular scheme, planning obligations (especially planning agreements) offer considerable advantages over conditions. A planning obligation can:

- include complex bonding/guarantee arrangements by way of security for performance;

- include expert determination/arbitration clauses;

- provide for the payment of money; and

- include obligations entered into by third parties, e.g. mortgagees.

It is worth considering a worked example at this point. A condition might provide:

> *"No part of the development shall commence unless a Biodiversity Management Plan incorporating the recommendations in the [****] report has been submitted to and approved by the local planning authority."*

This condition might, on the surface, appear to be perfectly unexceptional. However, there are a number of hidden problems.

First, one needs to consider a situation where there is a dispute between the parties as to the detailed content of the biodiversity management plan. It might become necessary to resolve a dispute; however, with a condition, the dispute resolution mechanism available to the parties would (unless they can agree a mediation approach) be by way of an appeal to the Planning Inspectorate. Needless to say, this will take a considerable period of time. However, if the requirement is, instead, provided by way of a planning obligation, the obligation should include a standard dispute resolution mechanism – hopefully by way of provisions requiring that disputes be resolved by an independent expert in accordance with a specified timetable.

Secondly, it is not enough to consider the condition in isolation. It might be the case that the planning obligation for the scheme includes requirements relating to biodiversity but that they are intermingled with provisions relating to Sustainable Urban Drainage Systems (SUDS), the provision of public open space, the provision of Suitable Alternative Natural Greenspace (SANG) or the like. Accordingly, one might find that the matters mentioned in the condition are best drawn into the planning obligation so as to ensure an integrated approach between these elements.

Chapter 21

Planning Obligations

21.1   Introduction

At the outset, it is appropriate to refresh one's memory as to the general principles relating to in relation to planning obligations because they will be one of the principal mechanisms whereby biodiversity net gain is secured in practice. The efficacy of the planning obligation approach will turn, very heavily, on the felicitous application of these general principles. Unfortunately, it is the author's experience that planning obligations are often drafted without reference to the statutory framework within which they sit, with the result that these resultant documents are often weak or, even, unenforceable.

21.2   Section 106 of the Town and Country Planning Act 1990

The phrase *"planning obligation"* arose as a result of amendments made to section 106 of the Town and Country Planning Act 1990 by the Planning and Compensation Act 1991.

Planning obligations are of importance because they can be used to overcome the doctrine of *"privity of contract"*. This legal doctrine means, in essence, that the terms of a contract are generally binding only upon the parties to that contract – they are not binding on a party's successors. Thus, a landowner who enters into an ordinary covenant relating to development on his land could sell the land, and the new owner might escape the covenant because he was not a party to the contract. Some types of restrictive covenant may run with the land and bind successors in title, but some do not. Positive covenants (e.g. to carry out works on the land) do not. This situation is manifestly unhelpful to bodies that are seeking to impose restrictive or positive obligations on land (in the public interest), because they need to be sure that such obligations cannot be avoided by a sale of the land.

Hence, the Law Commission's analysis of this doctrine and the emergence of Conservation Covenant Agreements as a means of bypassing privity of contract for the purposes of providing long-term security for the delivery of ecological and historical objectives on land: see Chapter 11 above.

For town and country planning, the current position is that the doctrine of privity of contract can be overcome by way of planning obligations under section 106.

A planning obligation may be created either by a planning agreement or a unilateral undertaking. As its name implies, a planning agreement is a deed entered into between the persons interested in the land and the local planning authority. By contrast, a unilateral undertaking is a deed executed by the persons interested in the land only. It is not executed by the local planning authority, but is delivered to the authority as a deed and thereby becomes a binding statutory planning obligation.

It is imperative that the terms of section 106 are borne in mind at all times when negotiating and settling planning obligations, because section 106 imposes a number of immutable limitations on what can and cannot be done under its aegis.

Section 106(1) states:

> *(1) Any person interested in land in the area of a local planning authority may, by agreement or otherwise, enter into an obligation (referred to in this section and sections 106A to 106C, Schedule 7A[1] as "a planning obligation"), enforceable to the extent mentioned in subsection (3) -*
>
> > *(a) restricting the development or use of the land in any specified way;*
> >
> > *(b) requiring specified operations or activities to be carried out in, on, under or over the land;*
> >
> > *(c) requiring the land to be used in any specified way; or*
> >
> > *(d) requiring a sum or sums to be paid to the authority (or, in a case where section 2E applies, to the Greater London Authority)] on a specified date or dates or periodically.*

21.3   Section 106(1)(a)

Section 106(1)(a) allows the imposition of the restrictive covenants which bind the subject land – for example, "*no buildings shall be constructed on the open space*". However, subsection (1)(a) can also allow for positive outcomes if phrased in the negative or "*Grampian*" form; viz:

> "*No part of the Development shall be begun unless a Biodiversity Management Plan has been submitted to and approved by the local planning authority.*"

Indeed, it might be the case that the planning obligation sets out a specification for the said Biodiversity Management Plan – for example, that the outputs in connection with the identified habitat meet standards which may be measured by the application of the Biodiversity Metric. It should also go on to provide that the approved Biodiversity Management Plan shall then be carried out by reference to a timetable and might provide that long-term financial security is provided by way of a bond or fund of some description.

21.4   Section 106(1)(b)

Requirements under section 106(1)(b) can underpin comprehensive development schemes; for example, requiring the establishment of, or enhancement of, habitats of value etc.

---

[1]   Inserted by Part 2 of Schedule 14 to the Environment Act.

This habitat establishment or enhancement could be on the application site or on another site via *"enabling development"* (see below). If an enabling development approach is taken, both the application site and the site that is the subject of the specified operations or activities should be subject to planning obligations. The works on the recipient site would then be specified *"operations or activities"* for the purposes of section 106(1)(b).

Section 106(1)(b) can also be used to underpin long-term care requirements, and requirements might be secured by bonding arrangements, guarantees etc. It is particularly valuable in connection with securing biodiversity gain on offsite land.

21.5   Section 106(1)(c)

This is a relatively straightforward provision and, effectively, is the obverse of section 106(1)(a). It allows for requirements that land shall be used in a particular positive way, e.g. public open space etc.

21.6   Section 106(1)(d)

This allows a variety of payment arrangements. It could encompass payments towards the achievement of identified ecological objectives and will allow for the creation of bonding arrangements to secure them.

Section 106(1)(d) does not use the word *"specified"*, and so section 106(13)[2] does not appear to apply. Section 106(2)(c) allows any payments under this provision to be calculated by reference to a formula.

It is important to note that section 106(1)(d) states *"sum or sums to be paid to the authority"*. This precludes payments to a third party. Clearly, this limitation raises a problem if the idea behind an *"enabling development"* approach involves a payment to a third party.

One way of overcoming this problem might be for the developer to make the payment to the local authority in the first instance, on the basis that the local authority will then transfer the money to the ultimate recipient. Unfortunately, this device might create more problems than it solves, because the funds might be treated as a capital receipt for the purposes of local authority finance controls, with the result that part of it is clawed back against grant aid from Central Government.

Another approach might be to provide a negative requirement in the obligation that places a constraint upon the use of the property or progress of the development unless the payment is made to the third party. For example, the planning obligation might prevent first occupation of dwellings in a residential development unless the payment is made to the third party. The monies are secured by the use of section 106(1)(a) instead of section 106(1)(d).

---

[2]   See below.

Arguably, section 106(1)(d) allows for *"roof tax"* payments: see below. Section 106(1)(d) would also appear to allow payments calculated by reference to enhanced land values resulting from the development.

Some local planning authorities seek financial contributions by reference to the size of the development or by way of a *"roof tax"*. This type of contribution is often sought as part of a fund that is being built up for future infrastructure works which will be only funded in part by the particular project. For example, the local planning authority may anticipate that the full fund will be generated by a series of separate developments in the locality over a particular period. Each separate developer will then be expected to make payments into the pot as his development progresses. Clearly, there are problems with this approach. The pot could be used in order to fund offsite habitat creation or enhancement, but there is the ever present concern that the total sum needed to do so might not be achieved for many reasons, including a premature ending to the development when many dwellings remain to be completed. This problem of *"marginal viability"*[3] is discussed below. It might be the case that the local planning authority should consider some form of default situation whereby such monies as have been collected can, *in extremis*, be applied to different purposes.

The prudent developer will ensure that, if his contribution is not used, it will be repaid. A properly worded repayment clause will provide for repayment if the specified work is not commenced within a defined period or is subsequently abandoned, and the developer should also ensure that interest upon the sum is also paid to them. Given these difficulties, it might be the case that the *"roof tax"* approach might prove too uncertain if it is deployed in order to discharge the statutory biodiversity net gain condition.

Be that as it may, this approach was examined by the Court of Appeal in *R v South Northamptonshire DC and Another ex parte Crest Homes Plc* [1995] J.P.L. 200 (CA); but Circular 1/97 commented on the *Crest Homes* case as follows:

> *"On the facts of the case, the planning obligations were held to be lawful, but this should not be interpreted as providing a justification for similar arrangements in other circumstances. As Lord Justice Henry explained, the facts of the case were crucial 'because they legitimise a formula which, if used in other factual contexts, could be struck down as an unauthorised local development land tax' (page 12, footnote 3)."*

The *Crest Homes* case indicates that advance payments need to be based on an accurate pre-estimate of the proposed expenditure, and the better course of action, for local planning authorities, would be to try and ensure that any payment arrangements are by reference to accurate pre-estimates.

---

[3]   The author's phrase.

21.7   Section 106(13)

Before moving on to consider section 106 in detail, it is necessary to pause and consider the impact of section 106(13) on section 106(1)(a), (b) and (c), all of which use the word "*specified*". The word has a particular effect within section 106 and it is defined by section 106(13):

> "*In this section 'Specified' means specified in the instrument by which the planning obligation is entered into ...*"

The apparent effect of section 106(13) is that a requirement in a planning obligation may be defective if it leaves essential items to be settled by a later document. This begs the question of whether a requirement to carry out a scheme in a document which is approved after the date of the obligation is valid.

If the scheme approach is adopted via section 106(1)(a), it is difficult to see a problem. This restricts the development or use of the land "*in any specified way*", and the "*specified*" restriction is articulated in the planning obligation itself – namely, that the commencement of development is subject to a clear embargo unless and until the relevant scheme (e.g. a Biodiversity Management Plan) is approved.

21.8   The Community Infrastructure Levy Regulations 2010

Regulation 122 of the 2010 Regulations applies where a "*relevant determination*"[4] is made which results in planning permission being granted for development. A planning obligation (or proposed planning obligation)[5] may only constitute a reason for granting planning permission for the development if the obligation is:

(a)   necessary to make the development acceptable in planning terms;

(b)   directly related to the development; and

(c)   fairly and reasonably related in scale and kind to the development.

Given that the statutory Biodiversity Net Gain condition will require a Biodiversity Gain Plan to be settled in respect of most development sites, it would be safe to presume that any planning obligation which seeks to implement a properly evidenced Biodiversity Gain Plan will meet the tests in this regulation without difficulty. It will, however, be necessary to consider the tests in the regulation where the planning obligation seeks to impose requirements which are not covered by the statutory Biodiversity Gain Plan – for example, provisions relating to fauna, as opposed to habitat only, or a commitment to provide a global financial contribution for unspecified ecological benefits in a wide area.

---

[4]   By regulation 122(3), a "*relevant determination*" means a determination made, on or after 6 April 2010, ((a) under section 70, 73, 76A or 77 of TCPA 1990 of an application for planning permission ; or (b) under section 79 of TCPA 19904 of an appeal.

[5]   See regulation 122(3).

21.9 Regulation 122 and offset sites

The difficulty might arise where offsite biodiversity gain is promised by the developer as a benefit of the proposed development; yet the offset site is remote from the development and is in excess of the statutory 10% requirement. Then, arguably, there might be concerns as to whether the delivery of this promise would breach Regulation 122. It is, in this connection, worth noting that the Environment Act and supporting publications and mechanisms encourage local planning authorities to support Local Nature Recovery Strategies, local biodiversity plans and National Character Area objectives. It should follow that, if such an extraneous benefit is offered in connection with these objectives in mind, then this might be a proper material planning consideration in the determination of the planning application.

Paragraph 5.15 of the *"User Guide"* for the Biodiversity Metric explains that the strategic significance of a habitat is treated as a component of the quality of a habitat parcel in the same way as distinctiveness and condition. The User Guide continues:

> *[5.16]* " *Strategic significance relates to the spatial location of a habitat parcel and works at a landscape scale.* **It gives additional biodiversity unit value**[6] *to habitats that have been identified as habitats of strategic importance to that local area."* (Emphasis added).

> *[5.17]* *"Strategic significance utilises published local strategies and objectives to identify local priorities for targeting biodiversity and nature improvement, such as Local Nature Recovery Strategies, local biodiversity plans, National Character Area objectives."*

21.10 Conservation Covenant Agreements or planning obligations?

This topic is discussed in Chapter 11; however, it is important to say that the use of a Conservation Covenant Agreement is not a magic remedy. Those seeking to ensure that such an agreement is enforceable in reality will have to face many of the problems which have bedevilled the drafting of contracts and planning obligations for many years. If one has entered into an agreement with the proverbial *"man of straw"*,[7] no amount of deft draftsmanship is going to overcome his impecuniosity. It makes no odds whether one is drafting a Conservation Covenant Agreement, a planning obligation or a contract. Thus, one has to draw on ways of ensuring that his impending insolvency will not frustrate the desired outcome. This means deploying time-honoured devices, such as bonding arrangements. Hence, much of that discussed below in connection with planning obligations should be relevant to those drafting Conservation Covenant Agreements.

---

[6] Which may be an addition of up to 15% depending on the quality of the habitat. See further paragraphs 5.19 to 5.23 and Table 5.4 of the User Guide.

[7] In the absence of firm evidence to the contrary, it is worth presuming that the party on the other side of the transaction is always a *"man of straw"*. The author's reply to *"Our client is worth £*******"* is usually *"So was Barings Bank!"*.

21.11   Land transfers under section 106

Planning obligations often provide for the transfer of land to councils or their nominees; however, the validity of this practice was thrown into doubt by the High Court in *Wimpey Homes Holdings Ltd v Secretary of State etc* [1993] J.P.L. 54 and *Jelson v Derby CC* [2000] J.P.L. 521.[8]

If the parties decide that a land transfer is appropriate, the alternative to a positive covenant providing for a land transfer is a negative covenant which has the same practical effect:

> *"No part of the Development shall be occupied unless and until the Ecological Enhancement Land has been transferred to the Council."*

21.12   Planning obligations and *"enabling development"*

In some situations, a local planning authority may be minded to grant a planning permission that it would not normally grant, because that planning permission *"enables"* a desirable consequence to be carried out. This approach is sometimes called the *"principle of overall advantage"*.

The leading case on the point is *R v Westminster CC, ex parte Monahan* [1989] 2 All E.R. 74, concerned a proposed office development which would fund the renovation of the Royal Opera House in Covent Garden. The Court of Appeal held that financial considerations which fairly and reasonably related to a permitted development were a material consideration which a planning authority was entitled to take into account when considering an application for development. Therefore, when considering an application for development which was contrary to planning policy, it was permissible for the planning authority to have regard to the fact that the financial gains from that development would enable a related and desirable development to proceed.

During the course of his judgment, in the *Royal Opera House* case, Nicholls LJ stated:

> *"That a planning authority may properly take into account as a material consideration within section 29 of the Town and Country Planning Act 1971 the practical consequences likely to follow if permission for a particular development is refused seems to me to be self-evident. For example, take a run-down site, littered with derelict buildings. The soil is contaminated from previous industrial use. Preparation of the site for development will be expensive. The planning authority is anxious that such an eyesore shall be removed, and housing the preferred use. An application is submitted for development with high-density housing. In my view it is clear that in considering this application the planning authority is entitled to take into account, first, that a lower density of housing will not be commercially viable, having regard to the heavy cost of site clearance, so that, second, the probable consequence of refusing to permit the*

---

[8]   See T. Graham - *"Planning Obligations and the Transfer of Land"* - The Journal of Planning and Environmental Law, November 1999.

> *development sought will be the absence of any development for the foreseeable future, in which event the eyesore will remain."*

If one transposes references to *"sites for ecological enhancement"* for the references to *"contaminated land"* and *"eyesores"*, the relevance of this approach to ecology is immediately apparent.

21.13   Drafting planning obligations
"Trigger" clauses

It is important that the parties are clear as to the date when the requirements in a planning obligation actually come into force. In the majority of cases, the date of grant of the relevant planning permission might not be the appropriate date, because the planning permission might not be implemented for a considerable period of time – indeed, it might not be implemented at all. In many cases, there is little point in bringing a covenant into force when the planning permission which is the basis of the obligation is lying dormant and may well expire or be superseded by a later permission.

One way of dealing with the point is by way of a *"trigger"* clause, e.g:

> *"This planning obligation shall not come into force until and unless there is commenced*[9] *on the Land a material operation (as defined by section 56(4) of the Town and County Planning Act 1990) pursuant to the Planning Permission."*

The legal meaning of *"material operation"* is well settled by caselaw and can include such minor operations as the pegging out of a highway or the digging of a trench: *Malvern Hills DC v Secretary of State* [1982] J.P.L. 439. Section 56(4)(aa) includes demolition works as a material operation – something which could easily catch the unwary.

It could be that the developer would prefer to have the obligation triggered by more substantial works, or needs to carry out infrastructure works before starting the development itself (e.g. where an access will serve two or more separate sites). In that case, the trigger clause could provide:

> *"This planning obligation shall not come into force until and unless the construction of the foundations of the proposed [   ] has been commenced."*

Another way of dealing with this is to narrow the meaning of *"material operation"*:

> *"For the purposes of this clause [   ], the phrase 'material operation' shall not include any works or operations (including the creation of necessary access arrangements) for or in connection with:*

---

[9]   Some draftsmen say something like: *"This planning obligation shall not come into force until and unless a material operation is implemented [or carried out] on the land"*. But how do you judge when the material operation is *"implemented"* or *"carried out"*? Ergo, keep it simple and refer to *"commencement"*, which should be easy to spot.

a) site clearance or demolition;

b) site security;

c) any site investigation or survey whether involving bore-holes or trenching or otherwise;

d) the diversion and laying of services;

e) the display of advertisements."

21.14   Release clauses

It is important that the position of the parties on any future transfer of the land is addressed (so far as is possible) in the planning obligation itself.

The original landowner might have no intention of carrying out the construction of the project. He may (as is often the case) simply obtain outline planning permission and then sell the site or parts of the site to developers who will finalise the planning position and construct the development. As such, this vendor does not wish to be saddled with ongoing liability once the transfer is complete. Yet, having been one of the signatory parties to the planning obligation, he will remain liable in contract notwithstanding that a transfer has taken place. The purchaser will become liable as a successor in title under section 106(3) of the 1990 Act, and so the local planning authority will be able to sue the vendor and/or the purchaser in the event of breach of the obligation. Effectively, they are jointly and severally liable. So how should the original landowner deal with the point?

Whilst section 106(3) makes a planning obligation enforceable against successors in title, section 106(4) states that the obligation may provide that a person shall not be bound by the obligation in respect of any period during which he no longer has an interest in the land.

Therefore, the usual approach is to require that the planning obligation contains a release clause along the following lines:

> *"No person or body shall be bound by any obligation in this Deed in respect of any period during which he or it no longer has an interest in the Land but without prejudice to liability for any subsisting breach of covenant prior to parting with such interest."*

Finally, it is important to think about the ultimate purchaser. In many cases, the intended final purchaser should not be saddled with any liabilities. The classic example is the purchaser of an individual dwelling in a residential development. An appropriate clause in this case might be:

> *"No person or body shall be bound by any obligation in this Deed:*

a) in respect of any period during which he or it no longer has an interest in the Property but without prejudice to liability for any subsisting breach of covenant prior to parting with such interest; or

b) if that person or body is the owner of a single dwelling within the Development."

Alternatively, if the scheme involves retail provision:

"if that person or body is the owner of a single Retail Unit within the Development".

Herein lies a dormant problem which becomes obvious when it is pointed out.[10] This occurs where the planning obligation not only requires certain requirements to be carried out after the new properties are occupied but also those requirements to be discharged on the land which has just been sold to the said occupiers. In many cases, it may be undesirable to enforce against otherwise innocent occupiers, yet the original developer has put himself out of the firing line by his sale of the freehold. Thus, for example, requiring that certain habitat creation, enhancement or management take place after occupation might prove fruitless. This point can be of considerable importance in the present context where residential gardens and *"green"* roofs are counted towards the score in an application of the Biodiversity Metric; there might, in a particular case, be concerns about the practical enforcement of the relevant mechanisms. There could be both legal and political ramifications for the local authority which seeks to do so, perhaps even a complaint to the Ombudsman[11] on the basis that the authority should have found a way of saddling the developer with the obligation. Hence, the solution, in many cases, might be to ensure that the relevant measures are carried out before occupation or that the relevant land is excluded from plot sales.

21.15   Measurable targets and outputs

It is essential that any clause or condition which provides for the performance of any specified objective should be clear as to the objective which is being sought and should provide a measure of performance to show when the objective has been achieved. It must provide for defined targets and measurable outputs. If it fails to do so, it is difficult to see how it will operate in practice. Take, as a simple example, the following:

"The Owner shall construct changing rooms on land to the north of the sports pitches with 6 months of the date that the sports pitches are substantially completed."

One should see the problem immediately; namely, that no specification is provided for the changing rooms. It is, therefore, impossible to glean from the agreement whether the changing rooms are going to be the size of a small garden shed or something more palatial. This clause is, by itself, largely unworkable and it is difficult to see what a Court would

---

[10]   *You have been in Afghanistan, I perceive*: Mr Sherlock Holmes in A Study in Scarlet (1887).

[11]   The Local Commissioner for Administration. Also, any well-advised aggrieved person would probably submit a freedom of information request to try to unravel what went on before the permission was granted.

make of it, in the event that there is a dispute as to the character of the changing rooms to be erected. It might be argued that it is referring to changing rooms which will be reasonable having regard to the use to be made of them; however, even if this argument were to work, it does not absolve those who are drafting the agreement from the responsibility of doing so properly in the first instance.

Now take an example closer to home:

> *"The Owner shall identify two mixed scrub strips of land to the west of the Site which shall be used for biodiversity objectives for the approval of the Council and the said land shall then be maintained for the purposes of biodiversity for the period of 25 years."*

It might well be the case that, leading up to the negotiation of the agreement, the parties had in mind two particular strips of land. However, simply drafting on the basis that, at some future date, the then parties to the obligation (who might be completely different) will have the same images in their mind is somewhat optimistic. This type of drafting, which is not unusual, is badly flawed.

In this example, nothing is said about the respective sizes of the areas of land in question. It could be the case that the owner offers up two postage stamp-sized areas of land and then asserts that it is required to do no more. It might be argued that one would then look to the background documents (such as an illustrative masterplan). This, of course, presupposes that such documents will have survived to this later date. It is also posited on the perilous assumption that a Court will have regard to extrinsic evidence in the interpretation of what should have been a self-contained legal document. The better alternative, it is suggested, is that, instead of storing up problems for the future, those drafting the agreement should attend to this point at the outset and provide some spatial parameters. Certainly, something will need to be said about the anticipated size of the areas in question. It might also be possible to annex drawings showing the indicative locations of these areas. Furthermore, the *"biodiversity objectives"* should be particularised in some way, perhaps by reference to a biodiversity metric. There would, then, be some measurable targets.

The next question, of course, is whether those drafting the agreement have attended to the matter of performance indicators. Here, again, there is a significant lack of particularity. The agreement gives no indication as to what *"maintenance"* means in this context. It is essential that some form of specification is indicated in the agreement, even if this is in a relatively simplified form at the outset.

Consider, also, the following definition:

> *"'Farmland Bird Strategy' means a written strategy for the management of the effects of the wider masterplan development across the Land to provide long-term compensation for the effects of the Development and the wider masterplan on farmland birds and which may include the identification of an area of land within the wider Site which*

could be suitable to deliver as compensation habitat for the displacement of breeding farmland birds as a result of Development."

In analysing this clause, it is again necessary to break it down into whether there are defined targets and, if so, whether those targets are accompanied by measurable indicators of performance against them.

Whilst the clause provides for a written strategy for the management of the effects of the development, it does not give a clear indication of the contents of the strategy. An alternative (and, it is suggested, better) approach would be to provide some heads of terms for the proposed strategy. These will not need to be voluminous; however, they would provide useful guidance for those who become charged with the task of providing the strategy. The second point concerns the phrase *"long-term compensation"*; namely, that this is too vague in terms of a proposed timescale. At the very least, there should be a reference to a period of years, albeit that it might be the case that this is an indicative period only which can be varied, from time to time, by agreement between the parties. Again, as above, reference to an area of land which might or might not be suitable to deliver a compensation habitat could, perhaps, be accompanied by some spatial parameters – if nothing else, by way of marking on approved master plans.

21.16   Practical enforcement of planning obligations

Section 106(5) and (6) provide the statutory enforcement mechanisms:

"(5) A restriction or requirement imposed under a planning obligation is enforceable by injunction.

(6) Without prejudice to subsection (5), if there is a breach of a requirement in a planning obligation to carry out any operations in, on, under or over the land to which the obligation relates, the authority by whom the obligation is enforceable may–

(a) enter the land and carry out the operations; and

(b) recover from the person or persons against whom the obligation is enforceable any expenses reasonably incurred by them in so doing."

It is important to consider the way in which these mechanisms might apply in real-life situations.

An elegantly drafted planning obligation is of little use to a local planning authority if it is either unenforceable or involves the expenditure of a disproportionate amount of powder and shot in the enforcement process. Yet many authorities fail to recognise that the provision of straightforward and efficient enforcement mechanisms is at the heart of the process. Take, for example, the following clause:

> *"If required by the Council by giving to the applicant at any time within three months from the date of the Commencement of Development at least 28 days' written notice requiring the Applicant to enter into a contract with the Council or person of the Council's nomination for the transfer of an area of land within the Site of not less than 0.3 hectares ('the Enhancement Land') to enter into a contract for the transfer of the Enhancement Land."*

This example is adapted from the real-life planning obligation, yet it is fundamentally flawed because:

(a)   it involves the transfer of land, yet it is not clear whether or not such an obligation can fall within section 106 (see above);

(b)   if it is outwith section 106, it is doubtful whether the clause is effective as an ordinary agreement to transfer under conventional property law principles, because it does not appear to comply with the Law of Property (Miscellaneous Provisions) Act 1986;[12]

(c)   even if (a) and (b) can be overcome, the enforcement of such a clause would be time-consuming and difficult, because it would involve forcing an unwilling applicant to execute a contract and transfer; and

(d)   nothing in the clause prevents the carrying out of the development whilst the applicant is in breach.

All of these criticisms could be avoided by the simple mechanism of imposing an embargo upon the progress of the development by way of a negative obligation:

> *"The Development shall not Commence until the Enhancement Land[13] has been transferred to the Council or a person nominated by the Council PROVIDED that this clause shall be discharged and cease to be of effect in the event that the Council or its nominee fails to accept a transfer of the Enhancement Land when tendered by the Applicant in accordance with the following terms of this clause ..."*

If the Applicant fails to offer the transfer of the Enhancement Land in accordance with the terms of the planning obligation, the solution is straightforward: the Council can apply for an injunction requiring cessation of all work on the development. There is no need to become entangled in difficult legal solutions, such as specific performance.

If the planning obligation is designed to secure the payment of money to the Council, then, again, a positive obligation is not necessarily the most effective approach. For example:

---

[12]   See *Wimpey Homes Holdings Ltd v Secretary of State etc* [1993] J.P.L. 54 and *Jelson v Derby CC* [2000] J.P.L. 521.

[13]   In accordance with the principle of defining measurable targets (see above), the *"Enhancement Land"* should be defined with sufficient particularity as to its identifiable spatial characteristics. The word *"commence"* will be defined in the definitions section of the Agreement, but see comments above on *"trigger clauses"*.

> *"The Applicant shall pay to the Council the Biodiversity Contribution not later than 28 days following [Commencement of the Development] [the issue of a certificate of compliance under the Building Regulations]."*

The theoretical enforcement mechanism for a default is by way of a money judgment, but this is of no use if the money has been spent or the owner has gone into liquidation with no visible assets. Every litigation lawyer will know that obtaining a money judgment is only half the battle, because actually enforcing the judgment will often be a major task in itself.[14] It is possible to cover the matter by way of a negative clause:

> *"The Development shall not be commenced unless and until the Biodiversity Contribution has been paid to the Council."*

But this approach, in turn, has limitations if the embargo is against residential occupation until the sum has been paid. Consider:

> *"No dwelling forming part of the development shall be occupied unless and until the Biodiversity Contribution has been paid."*

It is difficult to believe that a judge would dispossess a family from their home in order to enforce breach of this obligation by a commercial housebuilder. A better approach in this case might be for the Council to require the payment of the money to be secured by a bond or guarantee or, with a phased development, a clause to freeze the commencement of later phases pending the receipt of the money.

21.17   Securing enabling development in theory

It is now clear that many types of enabling development may be prayed in aid in order to obtain planning permission in certain narrowly defined circumstances: see above.

The fact that an approach is lawful does not, however, mean that it is straightforward in practical terms. In reality, there are a number of problems which need to be solved in each case.

Clearly, the appropriate legal mechanisms for ensuring that the funding from the enabling development is paid into the destined project will involve a planning obligation, but it is always extremely difficult to guarantee that the fund will actually reach its proposed destination. For example, if the enabling development is carried out before the fund is paid over (as is usually the case), how can the local planning authority ensure that the money is forthcoming or is not misdirected? What of the dishonest developer who creates a network of *"shell companies"* to siphon off the profits? What if the landowner goes into liquidation and HM Revenue & Customs or trade creditors claim the proceeds of the enabling development as part of the landowner's assets? There is no single solution.

---

[14]   One might need to put the bailiffs in, for instance.

One solution, or partial solution, might be for the local authority to ensure that the obligation is secured by a third party bond or guarantee. The shortcoming of this approach is that a bond or guarantee is designed to operate where the planning authority carries out works in default pursuant to section 106(6), yet it is unlikely that the works which are the subject of the enabling monies will be specified with any great particularity. In the majority of situations, the landowner will have a list of works of which only some will be selected for funding out of the enabling development. The position is even more problematic if the works are to be specified annually on a rolling programme.

Given that one of the reasons put forward for the enabling development will usually be that the landowner is impecunious, the local planning authority might well be concerned that the landowner could go bankrupt, with the result that the proceeds of the enabling development are seized by trade creditors or HM Revenue & Customs. Indeed, a trade creditor holding off due to the fact that the landowner has no money might be prompted to pursue recovery of his debt when he finds out that a large sum of money is about to be placed in the landowner's bank account out of the enabling development. It might, therefore, be necessary to ring fence the proceeds by placing them in a trust fund.

Another approach is the deposit of the net proceeds arising from the enabling development into a special purpose deposit account, and the assignment of all funds in that account to the local planning authority on terms that monies can be drawn down only against proven expenditure on authorised works. Whilst the landowner will protest that the creation of a secured fund is a draconian interference in his commercial activities, this approach is, in all probability, the only one which guarantees that the enabling proposals will be carried into effect.

If the circumstances of the arrangement permit it, it might be possible to arrange for the profits from the enabling development to be paid to a third party trustee as they arise, and then the trustee will be responsible for ensuring that the profits are applied in the agreed way; this could be to the developer against proof that the end project is being carried out (e.g. completion certificates), or to the local authority where the authority carries out the works under a default power in the section 106 obligation.

Another approach may be to structure the development itself in a way which ensures that the money from the enabling development is directed to the desired end project or use. For example, the development could be brought forward in phases and, as each phase is completed, a tranche of the profit is forwarded to the end use. If the proposed development will be a phased development, it might be possible to provide a clause to freeze the commencement of later phases pending the payment of staged payments into the pot for the enabled works or measures.

Ultimately, many of these arrangements may turn on the "*covenant strength*" of the developer. A planning obligation with a major multinational will always be more reliable than one with a "*man of straw*". Indeed, it may be the case that the local authority will only enter into such arrangements with companies of proven financial worth.

If the end project involves defined physical works (e.g. the remediation of derelict land), the planning obligation should, of course, give the local authority power to enter the relevant land to carry out the agreed works. Thus the owner of the site of the end project will have to be party to the obligation. Section 106(6) of the 1990 Act contains a statutory right of entry, but this would be nugatory if the obligation does not involve the relevant landowner as a party. Furthermore, the right to recover *"reasonable expenses"* in section 106(6)(b) is not precise enough for most complex transactions and, as such, the obligation should contain a well-drafted formula providing for the costs of the end project, together with an appropriate expert determination or arbitration clause in order to resolve disputes.

21.18   *"Marginal viability"*

Local planning authorities should be alert to the cash flow strategy for particular developments which are to be subject to planning obligations because the cash flows in the later stages of the development might not be helpful in realising the objectives which the authority is seeking to secure by way of the obligation.

To give an example involving a hypothetical residential scheme[15], the developer may reasonably stall the project because the marginal costs of producing each additional house at that point are more than the net income which can be realised by the sale of the said house. This situation might arise where the final phase of development triggers a substantial requirement in a planning obligation which would cost more to deliver than the net income from the remainder of the scheme would provide.

The local planning authority needs to be aware of the possibility of this phenomenon and guard against any ensuing delivery problems by ensuring that the phasing of the development sits comfortably with the delivery of the requisites which are being sought by the planning obligation. This is particularly the case where there is the temptation to leave the provision of green space, net gain land ct cetera to the end of the project. From the authority's standpoint, it is better to front-load these requirements; however, as noted elsewhere in this book, the front-loading of expensive infrastructure can have its own adverse impacts on the economic viability of the project. Accordingly, the prudent local planning authority and developer will formulate a masterplan which allows for the safe and viable delivery of both the development and the requisites for planning gain in a timely and phased manner throughout the scheme.

21.19   Air quality and planning obligations

To some extent, the existing planning system already has regard to vehicular pollution. Almost all applications for developments which impact on the highway have to be accompanied by some explanation of the likely impacts of those proposals, both in terms of highway impacts and *"sustainable"* transportation.

---

[15]   Albeit a *"hypothetical example"*, which is, in turn, based upon a planning obligation drafted by the author not so long ago!

If those impacts might be significant, a *"travel plan"* might be required. Paragraph 113 of the National Planning Policy Framework states:

> *"All developments that will generate significant amounts of movement should be required to provide a travel plan, and the application should be supported by a transport statement or transport assessment so that the likely impacts of the proposal can be assessed."*

The glossary to the National Planning Policy Framework describes a *"transport assessment"* as:

> *"A comprehensive and systematic process that sets out transport issues relating to a proposed development. It identifies measures required to improve accessibility and safety for all modes of travel, particularly for alternatives to the car such as walking, cycling and public transport, and measures that will be needed deal with the anticipated transport impacts of the development."*

A *"transport statement"* is described as:

> *"A simplified version of a transport assessment where it is agreed the transport issues arising from development proposals are limited and a full transport assessment is not required."*

A *"travel plan"* is:

> *"A long-term management strategy for an organisation or site that seeks to deliver sustainable transport objectives and is regularly reviewed."*

The traditional repository for a travel plan is normally a planning obligation, and there are many examples of how such plans are incorporated into planning obligations.

21.20 Local authority resources

Concerns have been expressed about the ability of local planning authorities to implement the additional burdens imposed by the requirements of the Environment Act, in particular the processing of information relating to Biodiversity Net Gain. The Government has indicated that it will provide support; however, this support should have been provided well in advance of the coming into force of these statutory provisions because, of course, these authorities will need to set up systems, recruit staff, et cetera in anticipation of the trigger date. The Planning Advisory Service has indicated that it is producing a short guide on resourcing Biodiversity Net Gain for local authorities; but, again, there is this problem of meeting the necessary time constraints.

In the absence of this type of timely intervention, it would not be surprising if local planning authorities turn to developers to obtain the funding for the assessment process and the subsequent monitoring of any arrangements which are crystallised in a planning obligation. Indeed, many developers will be minded to provide such funding in order to expedite the delivery of their anticipated planning permissions. Accordingly, consideration needs to be given to the incorporation of these matters into planning obligations and, as noted in connection with the discussion of economic viability at Chapter 19 above, this should form part of an iterative process.[16]

21.21   Modification of obligations

Section 106A(3) of the Town and Country Planning Act 1990 allows a person against whom a planning obligation is enforceable to apply to the local planning authority to modify or discharge a planning obligation within the period of five years beginning with the date on which the obligation is entered into.[17]

Importantly, Part 2 of Schedule 14 to the Environment Act inserts a new subsection (6A) which provides that:

> *"(6A) Except in such cases as may be prescribed, the authority may not under subsection (6) discharge or modify the planning obligation if the authority considers that doing so would -*
>
> *(a) prevent the biodiversity gain objective referred to in paragraph 2 of Schedule 7A from being met in relation to any development, or*
>
> *(b) give rise to a significant risk of that objective not being met in relation to any development."*

The administrative process for the management and determination of the application is set out in the Town and Country Planning (Modification and Discharge of Planning Obligations) Regulations 1992 (S.I. 1992/2832).

An authority is entitled to agree to a modification or discharge within the five-year period on a voluntary basis.

Section 106A(1) provides *(inter alia)* that a planning obligation may not be modified or discharged except by agreement between the appropriate authority and the person or persons against whom the obligation is enforceable.

If one takes these provisions together, they are quite cumbersome and time consuming. Yet it is often the case that changes in the scheme, or the economic viability assessment which underpins the scheme, necessitate a reconfiguration of the provisions of a planning obligation. Take, for example:

---

[16]   See now the Community Infrastructure Levy (Amendment) (England) (No. 2) Regulations 2019 (S.I. 2019/1103). Councils may charge monitoring fees provided they are fairly and reasonably related in scale and kind to the development and do not exceed the authority's estimate of its cost of monitoring the development over the lifetime of the planning obligation.

[17]   Or such period as may be prescribed.

> *"The Owner shall submit a Biodiversity Net Gain Plan not later than [****] for the approval of the Council and the requirements of the approved Biodiversity Net Gain Plan shall be carried out in accordance with the timescales stipulated in that plan."*

This seems innocuous, but consider that the developer had budgeted £30,000 for archaeological investigations but a Saxon hoard, or rare Roman artefacts, are then discovered which push that bill to £300,000 instead.[18] This will have financial ramifications for the economic viability assessment for the scheme and may have significant implications for its build programme. One effect might be that the financial aspects of the approved Biodiversity Net Gain Plan might have to be trimmed as part of an overall financial adjustment, and this might require a modification to the planning obligation, which is a process that will involve delay and cost.

One answer is to add some additional words to the above clause:

> *"The Owner shall submit a Biodiversity Net Gain Plan not later than [****] for the approval of the Council and the requirements of the approved Biodiversity Net Gain Plan shall be carried out in accordance with the timescales stipulated in that plan.* **The approved Biodiversity Net Gain Plan may be varied from time to time by agreement in writing by the Owner and the Council."**
> (Emphasis added).

This may seem to cover the point from the standpoint of those drafting the agreement, but it needs to be borne in mind that the approval of such proposed variations might not, necessarily, be for officers only. If the Biodiversity Net Gain Plan was a significant matter for members, it might be necessary to return the matter to the committee so that they can approve variations to it, or (as the case may) not. This may, in particular, be the case where biodiversity net gain is in a trade-off against another benefit which was secured by the planning obligation, perhaps affordable housing.

---

[18] Drawn from a case which the author was involved with some months ago! The local planning authority had to remove its affordable housing requirement on viability grounds.

Chapter 22

Section 73 Of The Town And Country Planning Act 1990

22.1   Introduction

One of the points of particular concern for both developers and local planning authorities, appears to be the question of how the biodiversity net gain condition will operate in relation to applications for and the grants of planning permissions pursuant to section 73 of the Town and Country Planning Act 1990. This chapter is intended to provide some commentary on this particular point.

The Consultation Document produced by the Department for the Environment, Food and Rural Affairs[1] has indicated that the position will probably be settled by way of regulations; however, this chapter seeks to evaluate the position by reference to the bare terms of the Environment Act for the moment.

It would appear that the main concern, for those who are concerned about section 73 permissions and the biodiversity net gain condition, is whether the application of the condition to the section 73 permission will have the effect of creating a *"double counting"* situation – this is to say, that a biodiversity net gain requirement for 10% net gain on the original scheme will stand upon another condition for another 10% net gain on the grant of a section 73 permission, with the result that the unfortunate developer is saddled with a total burden of 20% net gain. In most cases, this concern does not, however, stand up to analysis. In order to test the point, it is necessary to go back to basics and consider the way in which section 73 operates in the context of the 1990 Act.

22.2   Section 73 of the Town and Country Planning Act 1990

Section 73 relates to the determination of applications to develop land without compliance with conditions which were attached to a planning permission which has already been granted.

For example, it might be the case that, with a residential scheme, the conditions to the planning permission stipulate that the dwellings must be provided in accordance with prescribed house types, but the housebuilder finds that those house types (for whatever reason) are now inappropriate and so wishes to change them. Rather than making an application for a fresh planning permission, with all that this entails in terms of costs, delay and administrative actions, he is able to make an application to substitute a new condition with house types which are more acceptable to him. On such an application, the local planning authority will consider only the question of the condition subject to which the Section 73 planning permission should be granted.

---

[1]   Entitled *"Consultation on Biodiversity Net Gain Regulations and Implementation"* (January 2022).

Whilst many within the planning profession have the habit of describing an application under section 73 of the Town and Country Planning Act 1990 as an application to *"vary"* a planning permission, this is, strictly speaking, a misuse of language. An application pursuant to section 73 will, if granted, not vary an existing planning permission, but will provide for the grant of an entirely new permission. That is to say, the applicant will be left with the original planning permission and the planning permission granted pursuant to section 73 on the table. Sullivan J explained this in *Pye v Secretary of State for Environment* (1998) 3 P.L.R. 72:

> *"An application made under section 73 is an application for planning permission: see section 73(1). ... While section 73 applications are commonly referred to as applications to 'amend' the conditions attached to a planning permission, a decision under section 73(2) leaves the original planning permission intact and unamended. That is so whether the decision is to grant planning permission unconditionally or subject to different conditions under para (a), or to refuse the application under para (b), because planning permission should be granted subject to the same conditions. In the former case, the applicant may choose whether to implement the original planning permission or the new planning permission; in the latter case, he is still free to implement the original planning permission. Thus, it is not possible to 'go back on the original planning permission' under section 73. It remains as a baseline, whether the application under section 73 is approved or refused, in contrast to the position that previously obtained."*

Whilst section 73 allows the local planning authority to revisit certain of the conditions of the original planning permission, the authority is not entitled to impose fresh conditions which fundamentally alter the original position. To put it another way, it is not open to the local planning authority unilaterally to impose fresh conditions relating to ecology so as to incorporate ideas which are fundamental to the scheme and which were missed at the time that the original permission was granted: see *R (Arrowcroft Group) v Coventry CC* [2001] P.L.C.R. 7 and *Finney v Welsh Ministers* [2018] EWHC 3073 (Admin).

Section 73 planning permissions are something of a vexed subject for local planning authorities and developers because, if the original planning permission is subject to a section 106 agreement, a new section 106 agreement will have to be provided for the section 73 planning permission or, alternatively, the original section 106 agreement will have to be varied by way of a deed of variation. A local planning authority which fails to catch this requirement might find that the developer implements the section 73 planning permission free of the original section 106 agreement.

Clearly, one needs to consider the application of these principles when looking to the statutory biodiversity net gain condition, and also any section 106 agreement which might be associated with the development scheme.

22.3   The statutory net gain condition

It is, also, useful to recall the way in which biodiversity net gain is secured by way of the Environment Act. The Act imports a deemed condition into most planning permissions granted after the trigger date for the Act.[2] For this part of the Act, the deemed condition will provide that the relevant development may not be begun unless a Biodiversity Gain Plan has been submitted to and approved by the local planning authority. The objective of the Biodiversity Gain Plan is to set out how biodiversity net gain will be delivered during, and as a result of, the proposed development. The object is to ensure that a net gain of at least 10% is achieved in the "*post-development*" situation. This "*net gain*" will, of course, be measured by way of the Biodiversity Metric.

Section 98 of the Environment Act provides that Schedule 14 makes provision for biodiversity gain to be a condition of planning permission in England. The Schedule will (when it comes into force) amend the Town and Country Planning Act 1990 so that a new section 90A is inserted after section 90. New section 90A of the 1990 Act will provide, in turn, a new Schedule 7A which "*makes provision for grants of planning permission in England to be subject to a condition to secure that the biodiversity gain objective is met*": paragraph 1(1).

There seems to be little doubt that a permission granted pursuant to section 73 of the Town and Country Planning Act 1990 will be caught by the statutory net gain condition. A section 73 permission will be subject to the statutory biodiversity net gain condition because it is a "*planning permission*" within the meaning of the 1990 Act. If the original planning permission was granted subject to the statutory condition, then, the original permission will be subject to its own 10% requirement, and the later section 73 permission will be subject to its own, separate, 10% requirement.

22.4   The concerns
There would appear to be three separate cases:

- First, where the original planning permission is granted after these provisions of the Act come into force, and is, accordingly, subject to the statutory condition.

- Secondly, where the original planning permission pre-dates the implementation of the statutory requirement, made provision for biodiversity net gain and the section 73 application is made after the relevant provisions come into force.

- Thirdly, where the original planning permission predates the implementation of the statutory requirement, made no provision for biodiversity net gain and the section 73 application made after the relevant provisions come into force.

22.5   The current position
By way of a baseline to this chapter, provides for consequential amendments to the Town and Country Planning Act 1990 and, in connection with section 73 of the 1990 Act, paragraph 3(5) of Part 2 to Schedule 14 to the Environment Act provides that:

---

[2]   Currently two years from November 2021 – see "*Consultation on Biodiversity Net Gain Regulations and Implementation*" (Defra, January 2022).

"In section 73 (determination of applications to develop land after non-compliance) [sic], after subsection (2A) insert–

'(2B) Nothing in this section authorises the disapplication of the condition under paragraph 13 of Schedule 7A (biodiversity gain condition).

(2C) Subsection (2D) applies where–

> *(a) for the purposes of paragraph 13 of Schedule 7A a biodiversity gain plan was approved in relation to the previous planning permission ("the earlier biodiversity gain plan"),*

> *(b) planning permission is granted under this section, and*

> *(c) the conditions subject to which the planning permission is granted under this section do not affect the post-development biodiversity value of the onsite habitat as specified in the earlier biodiversity gain plan.*

(2D) Where this subsection applies, the earlier biodiversity gain plan is regarded as approved for the purposes of paragraph 13 of Schedule 7A in relation to the planning permission granted under this section."

This saving should cover the position where the original planning permission is granted after these provisions of the Act come into force, is, accordingly, subject to the statutory condition and a biodiversity net gain plan is approved for the purposes of Schedule 7A by the local planning authority. The biodiversity net gain plan which was approved in connection with that permission should be an *"earlier biodiversity gain plan"* for the purposes of the above statutory provision and, thereby, regarded as approved. There is no suggestion in this statutory provision that it is necessary to repeat the previous exercise of evaluating the earlier biodiversity gain plan by reference to the then latest version of the Biodiversity Metric. The words of the statute are manifestly clear on this point and there is no good reason to add gloss to them; however, one is left to wonder how this will operate in practice.

Importantly, the saving provides that the conditions subject to which the section 73 permission is granted must not affect the post-development biodiversity value of the onsite habitat as specified in the earlier biodiversity gain plan: section 73(2C)(c). Unfortunately, it might be the case that the only way in which the local planning authority can satisfy itself that the saving may be applied is by inviting the developer to apply the Biodiversity Metric in any event. In practice, the reality is that the majority of applications under section 73 are for relatively minor variations to pre-existing schemes, such as house types, fenestration etc. As such, they will probably rely upon the masterplan which was originally agreed for the site at the outset in any event. It might, of course, be the case that a proposed section

73 amendment will bite into the original arrangements for biodiversity net gain.[3] If this is the case, it would be surprising if the local planning authority presses ahead with the determination of the application without requiring a new biodiversity net gain plan which ensures that the reconfigured scheme provides not less than 10% net gain.

As to the case where the original planning permission pre-dates the implementation of the statutory requirement, made provision for at least 10% biodiversity net gain and the section 73 application is made after the relevant provisions come into force, it is arguable that much depends upon how the developer and the local planning authority have approached biodiversity in the development scheme.

If the answer is that a minimum of 10% biodiversity net gain was incorporated into the original scheme on a non-statutory basis, it is difficult to see how the imposition of the statutory condition will cause problems when one comes to a section 73 application. As noted above, the developer will be put in the position of having to supply a Biodiversity Gain Plan. There is nothing to suggest that the plan should not amount to the adoption of a previously submitted plan which provides the necessary 10% net gain. The only practical difficulty would appear to be that, of course, it would be necessary to input the data from the original scheme into the current version of the Biodiversity Metric to ensure that the output figures coincide. Beyond this, it would be bizarre if a local planning authority argued that an additional 10% should be supplied when the development is already doing so – that is to say, that the developer should end up supplying 20% biodiversity net gain. It is doubtful whether any reasonable construction of the statute would allow for such double counting.

However, the difficulty arises when the original planning permission did not provide an enforceable mechanism for the provision of 10% net gain. As noted above, the section 73 planning permission will be subject to the statutory condition. The local planning authority will not have power to vary the statutory percentage, which would suggest that, in many cases, the developer and the local planning authority might have to revisit the overall scheme itself in order to generate the requisite net gain. One answer might be that the developer purchases biodiversity credits rather than amend his scheme. However, in either case, revisiting the scheme means revisiting the financial parameters which underpinned the original economic viability assessment. The worst-case scenario might be that it is not economically viable to go ahead with the section 73 adjustments in any event.

The answer would thus appear to be something of a curate's egg. The Secretary of State does, of course, have power to adjust the statutory regime by way of regulations, and it is understood that a consultation will take place in an effort to try and resolve this particularly tricky issue. Unfortunately, it does not appear, at the moment, that the Secretary of State will be willing to provide for adjustments in connection with viability problems. This might be something of an own goal because, if the developer has to accommodate the costs of providing biodiversity net gain, one might find that this is at the expense of affordable

---

[3]   Then the question might arise whether or not this amounts to a fundamental alteration to the scheme see *R (Arrowcroft Group) v Coventry CC* [2001] P.L.C.R. 7 and *Finney v Welsh Ministers* [2018] EWHC 3073 (Admin).

housing or some other benefits of the scheme. Arguably, this is something that is best left to the discretion of local planning authorities on a case-by-case basis. But, at the moment, it does not appear to be the plan.

The Consultation Document sets out the Department's proposals for settling the detail of the framework provided by the 2021 Act and includes a section dealing with the application of the biodiversity gain objective to different types of development. The subtitle to the section is *"phased development and development subject to subsequent applications"*: see page 33.

The Consultation Document contains certain proposals in relation to permissions granted under section 73, although they do not seem to be much of an advance on the provisions in the bare statute:

> *In the case of an application for permission under section 73, if:*
>
> > *a) a biodiversity net gain plan has been approved in relation to the earlier permission, and*
> >
> > *b) the conditions subject to which the new permission is granted under section 73 do not affect the post-development biodiversity value of the onsite habitat as specified in the earlier plan*
>
> *Then the earlier plan is regarded as approved for the purposes of the new permission and another biodiversity gain plan or approval is not required.*
>
> *For section 73 proposals that affect the post-development biodiversity value, the local planning authority will need to approve a new biodiversity gain plan for the proposal. This biodiversity gain plan should apply the same baseline as the previous development. This means that the achievement of at least a 10% net gain can be secured without requiring the applicant to deliver further gains on top of their original 10% net gain.*
>
> *In the case of an application for permission under section 73, if a biodiversity net gain plan has been approved in relation to the early permission, and the conditions subject to which the new permission is granted under section 73 do not affect the proposed post-development biodiversity value of the onsite habitat, as specified in the earlier Biodiversity Gain Plan, the earlier Biodiversity Gain Plan is regarded as approved for the purposes of the new permission and another Biodiversity Gain Plan or approval is not required.*

This begs the question of how one tests the post-development scenario without re-running the Metric and then re-assessing the results. It might be the case that, with a proposal for relatively small amendments, the answer is self-evident. Nor is it clear how this approach will work where the site is partly built out. It might be, and probably will be, the case that the local planning authority and the developer can work out solutions between themselves, but this does beg the question of why central Government feels the need to provide this advice in the first place.

Be that as it may, this proposal does provide one advantage; namely, that it reduces the administrative burden on both the developer and the local planning authority. If a biodiversity net gain condition is imposed upon a new section 73 planning permission which is identical to the original planning permission, save for relatively minor alterations (for example, the substitution of house types) and the arrangements for biodiversity net gain are predicted to be the same in both cases, the process of submitting and approving a Biodiversity Gain Plan which is identical in all respects to the earlier Biodiversity Gain Plan (save for a different front sheet) would be a pointless, costly and time-consuming exercise.

22.6   Section 106 agreements and section 73 permissions

It is worth, at this point, considering the relationship between section 73 permissions and planning obligations.

If the original planning permission is granted following the execution of a planning obligation, that planning obligation will, without more, normally be tied to that original planning permission only. It follows that the subsequent section 73 permission will, unless preventative measures are taken, not be bound by the same planning obligation. It is, therefore, necessary for the local planning authority to take prophylactic action so as to apply the extant planning obligation to the new section 73 planning permission and to ensure that a failure to do so does not put them into difficulty.

One way of seeking to do so is to require that a deed of variation is entered into with the landowner prior to the grant of the section 73 permission. This is a fairly routine matter for local planning authorities; however, it is not without its difficulties. First, settling and executing a deed of variation is not necessarily a speedy process, and this could cause an undesirable delay to the issue of the section 73 planning permission, particularly where the variation agreement requires execution by multiple parties. Secondly, it might be the case that the local planning authority and/or the developer miss this point of apparent detail, in the melee of organising and processing the section 73 planning permission, with the result that the section 73 permission is not caught by the original planning obligation at all.

One way of avoiding these difficulties is to include within the original planning obligation what is now known as a "*section 73 clause*". This has the effect of providing that any section 73 planning permissions which are granted by reference to the original planning permission are caught, automatically, by the original planning obligation. It might be the case that, in practice, the parties would prefer a bespoke deed of variation, and most properly drafted section 73 clauses will provide for just such an eventuality. If nothing else, a section 73 clause will act as a default position and a long-stop in the event that the parties failed to provide for a deed of variation.

It follows that these problems, which might arise in connection with a planning obligation which is intended to secure biodiversity net gain, are neither unusual nor insuperable. Again, they arise in practice on a regular basis, in any event, albeit with different subject materials.

Chapter 23

Phased Schemes/Outline Planning Permissions

Paragraph 19 to Schedule 14 of the Environment Act allows for modifications for particular kinds of planning permission, including phased schemes and outline planning permissions:

> *"(1) The Secretary of State may by regulations make provision modifying the application of this Part of this Schedule in relation to–*
>
> *(a) the grant of outline planning permission, where the reservation of matters for subsequent approval has the effect of requiring or permitting development to proceed in phases, or*
>
> *(b) the grant of any kind of planning permission, where the grant is subject to conditions (whether requiring the subsequent approval of any matters or otherwise) having that effect.*
>
> *(2) Regulations under this paragraph may include provision for a grant of planning permission referred to in sub-paragraph (1)(a) or (b) to be subject to conditions relating to meeting the biodiversity gain objective referred to in paragraph 2."*

It is, again, useful to refer to the Consultation Document. This contains a number of proposals in relation to the delivery of biodiversity net gain when the proposed scheme involves a phased delivery or an outline planning permission (pages 33-34):

> *"As with all applications, those for outline planning permission and phased development will require the submission of biodiversity gain information.*
>
> *We propose that for outline and phased permissions we will ask the applicant to explain the strategy to achieve the biodiversity gain objective across the whole site and to demonstrate how this could be delivered on a phase-by-phase basis. This would include:*
>
> - *the key principles that will be followed to ensure biodiversity gain commitments are achieved through subsequent detailed design*
>
> - *how biodiversity net gain delivery will be tracked on a phase-to-phase basis, including the target percentage gains to be delivered at each stage. For most phased developments, we intend to state in guidance that biodiversity gains should be 'front-loaded' into earlier stages. This will help to avoid the risk of net losses being caused by later stages being delayed or cancelled*
>
> - *the approach to be taken in the event that subsequent phases do not proceed or fail to achieve their biodiversity net gain targets*

- *that the pre-development biodiversity value for the whole site will be agreed as part of the framework plan and used as the basis for agreeing the detailed proposals through subsequent applications pursuant to the approved development*

- *a mechanism to link the framework plan to subsequent applications pursuant to the approved development"*

Whilst these proposals provide a useful framework, it is necessary to make some comments about them.

The second bullet point suggests that, for most phased developments, biodiversity gains should be *"front-loaded"* into the early stages of the scheme. This approach could be problematic because the business model for almost all property development schemes is a negative cash flow one, in the sense that large financial investments must be made before any income starts to flow into the site.[1]

With a residential scheme, a housebuilder does not start realising a revenue stream until the first dwelling is sold. This could be a considerable period into the implementation of the development, during which time the developer will have burned working capital by carrying construction costs, the cost of financing, sales costs, etc.

This proposal to front-load appears to be predicated on the basis that it will help avoid the risk of net losses being caused by a later stage, or of being delayed or cancelled. This is nothing new in the context of planning obligations and it is difficult to see why biodiversity net gain is, in some way, separated out. There is always the risk of a development slowing for legitimate reasons (e.g. to allow the market to catch up), because the marginal profitability of producing later stages in the development is outweighed by the costs of proceeding further at that time. Local planning authorities are, or should be, already aware of this problem in connection with many types of scheme, and the prudent ones can come up with realistic strategies for minimising or obviating the risk.[2]

One way of dealing with this problem is to ensure that, so far as is possible, biodiversity net gain is provided on a phase-by-phase basis and that the scheme is so conditioned that phases cannot leapfrog one another. Thus, the developer can be required to complete all earlier phases before moving on to later ones. This phase-by-phase approach does not do away with all concerns in relation to the marginal viability of later phases; however, it will mitigate the risk to, perhaps, an acceptable level.

The Consultation Document proposes regulations which would require Biodiversity Gain Plans to be submitted for approval prior to the commencement of individual phases of development. Presumably, this will still allow local planning authorities to require an

---

[1]   See discussion of financial viability in Chapter 19.

[2]   For example, bonding arrangements.

overarching Biodiversity Gain Plan which covers the whole of the development and is particularised in masterplan, timetable and schedule of structural works. The phase-by-phase submission of Biodiversity Gain Plans would then be conditioned by, and have to fall within, the framework set by the masterplan.

Again, it is worth considering the tools which are currently available to those involved in the development process and which may achieve the objectives which are being sought by the Consultation Document in any event.

As noted above, there is nothing new in securing the delivery of an overall target across a phased development. Local planning authorities and developers have been entering into planning obligations to do this for many years. The formula is well known (for example, in connection with affordable housing). There, a planning obligation may require the development not to be commenced unless and until an affordable housing scheme has been approved in writing by the local planning authority. A well-drafted clause will set out the number of affordable dwellings to be provided, along with their types, tenures, locations and similar details,[3] and the programme for the delivery of them on a phase-by-phase basis. It is difficult to see why such a mechanism cannot be applied in the case of biodiversity net gain or why it is, in some way, a special case.

The relevant clauses can provide that the features which provide biodiversity net gain are delivered on a phase-by-phase basis against an overall net gain requirement for the site as a whole. In turn, each phase should be required to provide a defined proportion of that overall target and, in all cases, the measuring of progress towards that target can, if necessary, be provided by using the Biodiversity Metric. One is then in a proper position where the planning obligation supplies defined targets and measurable outputs.

One can allude to British Standard BS42020:2013, Annex D (informative), "*Standard or model planning conditions and planning informatives*" at this point for useful guidance in connection with both planning obligations and planning conditions.

Model D.4.5 refers to Landscape and Ecological Management Plans (LEMPs):[4]

> "*A landscape and ecological management plan (LEMP) shall be submitted to, and be approved in writing by, the local planning authority prior [... to the commencement or occupation ...] of the development [or specified phase of development]. The content of the LEMP shall include the following.*
>
> *a) Description and evaluation of features to be managed.*
>
> *b) Ecological trends and constraints on site that might influence management.*

---

[3]   Often by way of an affordable housing plan which is superimposed onto a site masterplan.

[4]   Also referred to as "*Habitat or Biodiversity Management Plans*".

c) Aims and objectives of management.

d) Appropriate management options for achieving aims and objectives.

e) Prescriptions for management actions.

f) Preparation of a work schedule (including an annual work plan capable of being rolled forward over a five-year period).

g) Details of the body or organization responsible for implementation of the plan.

h) Ongoing monitoring and remedial measures.

The LEMP shall also include details of the legal and funding mechanism(s) by which the long-term implementation of the plan will be secured by the developer with the management body(ies) responsible for its delivery. The plan shall also set out (where the results from monitoring show that conservation aims and objectives of the LEMP are not being met) how contingencies and/or remedial action will be identified, agreed and implemented so that the development still delivers the fully functioning biodiversity objectives of the originally approved scheme. The approved plan will be implemented in accordance with the approved details."

The model condition is a useful starting point, but it is not perfect; it would be helpful if the mantra *"defined targets, measurable outputs"* could be applied to this central condition in order to assist in the application and enforcement of it.

First, the phrase *"A landscape and ecological management plan (LEMP) shall be submitted to, and be approved in writing by, the local planning authority prior [... to the commencement or occupation ...] of the development"* is unclear in terms of enforcement. The notion is, presumably, to replicate the *"Grampian"* formula and so it is, perhaps, best to do so with clarity; for example: *"No part of the development shall be [commenced] [occupied] unless and until the LEMP has been submitted to and approved in writing by the local planning authority"*.

Secondly, the LEMP now provides an opportunity to import objectivity by making reference to hard targets which are based on the Biodiversity Metric.[5] For example, sub-paragraph (c) refers to aims and objectives of management, and it would be possible to add a reference to the metric, viz:

*"(c) aims and objectives of **management which will (without limitation) include the provision of not less than 15% biodiversity net gain within the Site as calculated by the Biodiversity Metric 3.0.** "*(Emphasis added).

---

[5] BS42020 was, of course, drafted whilst the Biodiversity Metric was in draft form only.

The Consultation Document goes on to say (page 34):

> *"With respect to securing delivery of the biodiversity gain requirement, we propose to require through secondary legislation that a biodiversity gain plan would be submitted for approval prior to the commencement of individual phases of development."*

It is questionable whether this is over-kill because, again, this proposal alludes to techniques which are used by developers and local planning authorities in any event. Ergo, this should be something that they can work out for themselves.

Chapter 24

Section 73A Of The Town And Country Planning Act 1990

As with section 73, there seems to be little doubt that a permission granted pursuant to section 73A of the Town and Country Planning Act 1990 will be caught by the statutory net gain condition.

Section 73A(1) provides that, on an application made to a local planning authority, the planning permission which may be granted includes planning permission for development carried out before the date of the application. Thus, retrospective planning permission may be granted for development already carried out.

This procedure applies to development carried out without planning permission in accordance with planning permission granted for a limited period or without complying with some condition subject to which planning permission was granted: section 73A(2).

The operation of the provision is not, however, limited to processes initiated by application and may come into play in the context of planning enforcement.

Section 173(11) of the 1990 Act provides as follows:

> *"Where–*
>
> *(a) an enforcement notice in respect of any breach of planning control could have required any buildings or works to be removed or any activity to cease, but does not do so; and*
>
> *(b) all the requirements of the notice have been complied with,*
>
> *then, so far as the notice did not so require, planning permission shall be treated as having been granted by virtue of section 73A in respect of development consisting of the construction of the buildings or works or, as the case may be, the carrying out of the activities."*

Retrospective planning permission may be granted so as to have effect from the date on which the development was carried out or, if it was carried out in accordance with planning permission granted for a limited period, the end of that period: section 73A(3).

As a simple matter of interpretation, it follows that a section 73A permission which is granted after the trigger date for the biodiversity net gain provisions in the Environment Act, but is dated so as to take effect before that date, should not be caught by the statutory condition. The apparent difficulty lies where the permission is granted so as to take effect after the trigger date.

Paragraph 20 of Schedule 14 to the Environment Act provides that the Secretary of State may by regulations make provision modifying or excluding the application of this Part of the Schedule in relation to development for which planning permission is granted under section 73A. The Consultation Document does not include any commentary or proposals on the anticipated use of this power and this would suggest that the matter will be left open.

The position would appear to be that, where the section 73A permission is granted so as to take effect after the trigger date, it will be subject to the mandatory condition. Arguably, this is fair when development has been carried out without permission and without the benefit of any assessments relating to the material considerations which would apply to the development. In practice, one would not expect a local planning authority to grant retrospective planning permission so as to allow the applicant to leapfrog all the assessments which would normally be required in relation to the site.

Chapter 25

Minerals Sites

The Biodiversity Net Gain condition provisions of the Environment Act will apply to minerals permissions; however, the proposed content of regulations which will affect minerals permissions is unclear.

The Consultation Document states:

> *"We recognise that minerals sites can, within one planning permission, contain several phases of extraction and restoration and we are considering the additional discretion or considerations that mineral planning authorities might need to apply in considering mineral sites' biodiversity gain plans.*
>
> *This would be supported with guidance and might include looking at iterations of the biodiversity metric as it is applied at various extraction phases or applying the biodiversity metric in a way that better acknowledges the effects of habitats created in advance or at later stages in the scheme.*
>
> *We also know that Reviews of Old Minerals Permissions (ROMPs) typically result in the amendment of planning conditions and attaching modern conditions to old planning permissions. As a new permission is not being granted, we do not generally consider it reasonable to attach the mandatory biodiversity gain requirement to old permissions during these reviews."*

This suggests that there will be adjustments to the basic position so far as minerals permissions are concerned.

Chapter 26

Marine Net Gain

The Consultation Document does not deal with marine net gain substantively but states:

> *"The requirements for biodiversity net gain will apply to development projects, or components of projects, as far as the low-water mark, including the intertidal zone. Projects, or components of projects, in the marine environment beyond the intertidal zone are not included within the scope of the mandatory requirements for biodiversity net gain.*
>
> *The Environment Act does, however, provide options for introducing such a requirement for Nationally Significant Infrastructure Projects when a suitable approach has been developed and consulted upon. We are currently working with a wide range of stakeholders towards a consultation on the principles for marine net gain early this year."*

Appendix: Annotated Extracts From
The Environment Act 2021

CHAPTER 1

IMPROVING THE NATURAL ENVIRONMENT

Environmental targets

1 Environmental targets

(1) The Secretary of State may by regulations set long-term targets in respect of any matter which relates to—

(a) the natural environment, or

(b) people's enjoyment of the natural environment.

> The use of the word "*may*" means that the Secretary of State is not obliged to set these long-term targets. The "*natural environment*" is a defined term: section 44.[1]

(2) The Secretary of State must exercise the power in subsection (1) so as to set a long-term target in respect of at least one matter within each priority area.

> Here the operative word is "*must*". This is, therefore, a mandatory requirement on the Secretary of State. The priority areas are listed below. A "*long-term target*" is a target for a period of not less than 15 years: see subsection (6) below.

(3) The priority areas are—

(a) air quality;

(b) water;

(c) biodiversity;

---

[1]   In this Part the "*natural environment*" means – "*(a) plants, wild animals and other living organisms,(b) their habitats,(c) land (except buildings or other structures), air and water, and the natural systems, cycles and processes through which they interact.*": section 44.

(d) resource efficiency and waste reduction.

(4) A target set under this section must specify—

(a) a standard to be achieved, which must be capable of being objectively measured, and

(b) a date by which it is to be achieved.

> The first question is whether the targets can be specified in a way which is objectively measurable, as opposed to being a matter of expert opinion. Setting targets is one thing but achieving them is another, and there is nothing in the Act or supporting documentation to show how the Secretary of State is expected to achieve these objectives in real life.

(5) Regulations under this section may make provision about how the matter in respect of which a target is set is to be measured.

(6) A target is a "long-term" target if the specified date is no less than 15 years after the date on which the target is initially set.

(7) A target under this section is initially set when the regulations setting it come into force.

(8) In this Part the "specified standard" and "specified date", in relation to a target under this section, mean the standard and date (respectively) specified under subsection (4).

(9) ...

2 Environmental targets: particulate matter

(1) The Secretary of State must by regulations set a target ("the $PM_{2.5}$ air quality target") in respect of the annual mean level of $PM_{2.5}$ in ambient air.

(2) The $PM_{2.5}$ air quality target may, but need not, be a long-term target.[2]

(3) In this section "$PM_{2.5}$" means particulate matter with an aerodynamic diameter not exceeding 2.5 micrometres.

(4) Regulations setting the $PM_{2.5}$ air quality target may make provision defining "ambient air".

---

[2]   See Section 1(6) for "*long-term target*".

(5) The duty in subsection (1) is in addition to (and does not discharge) the duty in section 1(2) to set a long-term target in relation to air quality.

(6) Section 1(4) to (9) applies to the $PM_{2.5}$ air quality target and to regulations under this section as it applies to targets set under section 1 and to regulations under that section.

(7) In this Part "the $PM_{2.5}$ air quality target" means the target set under subsection (1).

> This provision is of the utmost importance but, unfortunately, the antecedents to it have shown up a number of uncertainties and the Secretary of State will have to grapple with them – for example, the meaning of "*ambient air*"; is this to be, in some way, throughout the UK, or by way of proxy air monitoring stations situated within particular sensitive locations? Be that as it may, it is realistic to say that the achievement of air quality targets is something which is capable of being a material planning consideration, because most proposals for built development or mining will carry with them some form of impact on air quality, even if it is simply by way of construction traffic. Likewise, there will be many cases where a proposed material change of use will include changed traffic patterns (for example, "*drive through*" fast food outlets).

3 Environmental targets: species abundance

(1) The Secretary of State must by regulations set a target (the "species abundance target") in respect of a matter relating to the abundance of species.

(2) The specified date for the species abundance target must be 31 December 2030.

(3) Accordingly, the species abundance target is not a long-term target and the duty in subsection (1) is in addition to (and does not discharge) the duty in section 1(2) to set a long-term target in relation to biodiversity.

(4) Before making regulations under subsection (1) which set or amend a target the Secretary of State must be satisfied that meeting the target, or the amended target, would halt a decline in the abundance of species.

(5) Section 1(4) to (9) applies to the species abundance target and to regulations under this section as it applies to targets set under section 1 and to regulations under that section.

(6) In this Part "the species abundance target" means the target set under subsection (1).

> The definition of "*species abundance*" is left to regulations and this leaves a major uncertainty. For example, it is well known that increasing the abundance of one species within a habitat can have the effect of causing harm to others within the same habitat. The

introduction of a rare predator might be seen as beneficial but, by definition, it will have an adverse impact on those native, transitive and local species which are then predated. Furthermore, a given habitat has an ecological capacity for specific species which depends on the natural resources available within the habitat from time to time and competition or predation from other species.

Accordingly, it is difficult to see how measurable targets can be set, for the simple reason that (as every farmer knows) the establishment of flora and fauna is in the hands of nature. If something is expected of the development industry, it is difficult to see how property developers can go beyond the creation of beneficial habitats for particular species, which is covered elsewhere in the Act in any event.

4 Environmental targets: process

(1) Before making regulations under sections 1 to 3 the Secretary of State must seek advice from persons the Secretary of State considers to be independent and to have relevant expertise.

(2) Before making regulations under sections 1 to 3 which set or amend a target the Secretary of State must be satisfied that the target, or amended target, can be met.

This might be the fly in the ointment. The Secretary of State is faced with not only attempting to define what is meant by these concepts by reference to objectively measurable criteria, but also then coming up with mechanisms whereby this can be achieved. It can reasonably be speculated that some form of burden will fall on the property development sector.

(3) The Secretary of State may make regulations under sections 1 to 3 which revoke or lower a target (the "existing target") only if satisfied that—

(a) meeting the existing target would have no significant benefit compared with not meeting it or with meeting a lower target, or

(b) because of changes in circumstances since the existing target was set or last amended the environmental, social, economic or other costs of meeting it would be disproportionate to the benefits.

The reference to *"social, economic or other costs"* appears to allow for the reduction of targets for ethnocentric reasons.

(4) Before making regulations under sections 1 to 3 which revoke or lower a target the Secretary of State must lay before Parliament, and publish, a statement explaining why the Secretary of State is satisfied as mentioned in subsection (3).

(5) Regulations lower a target if, to any extent, they—

(a) replace the specified standard with a lower standard, or

(b) replace the specified date with a later date.

(6) Regulations under section 2 may not revoke the $PM_{2.5}$ air quality target (but may amend it in accordance with this section).

(7) For the purposes of this Part a target is met if the specified standard is achieved by the specified date.

(8) Regulations under sections 1 to 3 are subject to the affirmative procedure.

(9) A draft of a statutory instrument (or drafts of statutory instruments) containing regulations setting—

(a) each of the targets required by section 1(2),

(b) the $PM_{2.5}$ air quality target, and

(c) the species abundance target,

must be laid before Parliament on or before 31 October 2022.

5 Environmental targets: effect

It is the duty of the Secretary of State to ensure that—

(a) targets set under section 1 are met,

(b) the $PM_{2.5}$ air quality target set under section 2 is met, and

(c) the species abundance target set under section 3 is met.

Again, it is difficult to see how the Secretary of State can procure the achievement of these targets without involving landowners and developers.

---

6 Environmental targets: reporting duties

(1) Regulations under section 1, 2 or 3 must specify a reporting date for any target set under that section.

(2) On or before the reporting date the Secretary of State must lay before Parliament, and publish, a statement containing the required information about the target.

(3) The required information about a target is (as appropriate)—

(a) that the target has been met,

(b) that the target has not been met, or

(c) that the Secretary of State is not yet able to determine whether the target has been met, the reasons for that and the steps the Secretary of State intends to take in order to determine whether the target has been met.

(4) Where the Secretary of State makes a statement that the target has not been met the Secretary of State must, before the end of the 12 month period beginning with the date on which the statement is laid, lay before Parliament, and publish, a report.

(5) The report must—

(a) explain why the target has not been met, and

(b) set out the steps the Secretary of State has taken, or intends to take, to ensure the specified standard is achieved as soon as reasonably practicable.

(6) Where the Secretary of State makes a statement that the Secretary of State is not yet able to determine whether the target has been met the Secretary of State must, before the end of the 6 month period beginning with the date on which the statement is laid, lay before Parliament, and publish, a further statement containing the required information.

(7) Subsections (3) to (6) apply to further statements under subsection (6) as they apply to a statement under subsection (2).

7 Environmental targets: review

(1) The Secretary of State must review targets set under sections 1 to 3 in accordance with this section.

(2) The purpose of the review is to consider whether the significant improvement test is met.

(3) The significant improvement test is met if meeting—

(a) the targets set under sections 1 to 3, and

(b) any other environmental targets which meet the conditions in subsection (8) and which the Secretary of State considers it appropriate to take into account,

would significantly improve the natural environment in England.

(4) Having carried out the review the Secretary of State must lay before Parliament, and publish, a report stating—

(a) whether the Secretary of State considers that the significant improvement test is met, and

(b) if the Secretary of State considers that the test is not met, the steps the Secretary of State intends to take in relation to the powers in sections 1 to 3 to ensure that it is met.

(5) The first review must be completed by 31 January 2023.

(6) Subsequent reviews must be completed before the end of the 5 year period beginning with the day on which the previous review was completed.

(7) A review is completed when the Secretary of State has laid and published the report.

(8) The conditions mentioned in subsection (3)(b) are that—

(a) the target relates to an aspect of the natural environment in England or an area which includes England,

(b) it specifies a standard to be achieved which is capable of being objectively measured,

(c) it specifies a date by which the standard is to be achieved, and

(d) it is contained in legislation which forms part of the law of England and Wales.

(9) In this section "England" includes—

(a) the English inshore region, and

(b) the English offshore region,

within the meaning of the Marine and Coastal Access Act 2009 (see section 322 of that Act).

8 Environmental improvement plans

(1) The Secretary of State must prepare an environmental improvement plan.

(2) An "environmental improvement plan" is a plan for significantly improving the natural environment in the period to which the plan relates.

Definitions:

For "*natural environment*", see section 44.

---

(3) That period must not be shorter than 15 years.

(4) An environmental improvement plan must set out the steps Her Majesty's Government intends to take to improve the natural environment in the period to which the plan relates.

(5) It may also set out steps Her Majesty's Government intends to take to improve people's enjoyment of the natural environment in that period (and if it does so references in this Part to improving the natural environment, in relation to that plan, include improving people's enjoyment of it).

(6) …

(7) The document entitled "A green future: our 25 year plan to improve the environment" published by Her Majesty's Government on 11 January 2018 is to be treated as an environmental improvement plan prepared by the Secretary of State under this section.

(8) References in this Part—

(a) to the first environmental improvement plan, are to that document;

(b) to the current environmental improvement plan, are to the environmental improvement plan for the time being in effect.

Notwithstanding that this environmental improvement plan will, no doubt, be prayed in aid at numerous planning inquiries, the reality is that the current version sets out very broad policy objectives which do not lend themselves to application on a site-specific basis.

---

9 Annual reports on environmental improvement plans

(1) The Secretary of State must prepare annual reports on the implementation of the current environmental improvement plan.

(2) An annual report must—

(a) describe what has been done, in the period to which the report relates, to implement the environmental improvement plan, and

(b) consider, having regard to any data obtained under section 16, whether the natural environment has, or particular aspects of it have, improved during that period.

(3) In considering the matters in subsection (2)(b) an annual report must consider the progress that has been made towards achieving—

(a) any targets, or any relevant targets, set under sections 1 to 3, and

(b) any interim targets, or any relevant interim targets, set under sections 11 and 14.

(4) The first annual report on the first environmental improvement plan may relate to any 12 month period that includes the day on which this section comes into force.

(5) The first annual report on a subsequent environmental improvement plan must relate to the first 12 months of the period to which the plan relates.

(6) Subsequent annual reports on an environmental improvement plan must relate to the 12 month period immediately following the 12 month period to which the previous annual report relates.

(7) An annual report must be laid before Parliament before the end of the 4 month period beginning immediately after the last day of the period to which the report relates.

(8) The Secretary of State must publish annual reports laid before Parliament under this section.

10 Reviewing and revising environmental improvement plans

(1) The Secretary of State must—

(a) review the current environmental improvement plan in accordance with this section, section 11 and section 12, and

(b) if the Secretary of State of State is required to revise the plan under section 11, or considers it appropriate to revise the plan as a result of the review, revise the plan.

(2) The period to which a revised plan relates must end at the same time as the period to which the current plan relates.

(3) The first review of the first environmental improvement plan must be completed by 31 January 2023.

(4) The first review of a subsequent environmental improvement plan must be completed before the end of the 5 year period beginning with the day on which it replaces the previous plan (see section 13(4)).

(5) Subsequent reviews of an environmental improvement plan must be completed before the end of the 5 year period beginning with the day on which the previous review was completed.

(6) If as a result of a review the Secretary of State revises the environmental improvement plan, the Secretary of State must lay before Parliament—

(a) the revised environmental improvement plan, and

(b) a statement explaining the revisions and the reasons for them.

(7) If as a result of a review the Secretary of State does not revise the environmental improvement plan, the Secretary of State must lay before Parliament a statement explaining that and the reasons for it.

(8) The Secretary of State must publish the documents laid under subsection (6) or (7).

(9) A review is completed when the Secretary of State has laid and published the documents mentioned in subsection (6) or (7).

(10) References in this Act to an environmental improvement plan include a revised environmental improvement plan.

11 Reviewing and revising plans: interim targets

(1) On the first review of the first environmental improvement plan, the Secretary of State must revise the plan so as to—

(a) set at least one interim target in respect of each relevant matter, and

(b) secure that there is at all times, until the end of the 5 year period beginning with the relevant date, an interim target set by the plan in respect of each relevant matter.

(2) On any other review of an environmental improvement plan, the Secretary of State must make any revisions to the plan which are necessary in order to—

(a) set at least one interim target in respect of any matter that has become a relevant matter since the previous review, and

(b) secure that there is at all times, until the end of the 5 year period beginning with the relevant date, an interim target set by the plan in respect of each relevant matter.

(3) A "relevant matter" means any matter in respect of which there is a target under sections 1 to 3.

(4) Subsection (2)(b) does not apply in respect of a matter if the specified date for the target under sections 1 to 3 in respect of that matter is before the end of the 5 year period beginning with the relevant date.

(5) On a review of an environmental improvement plan, the Secretary of State may revise or replace any interim targets set by the plan in respect of a relevant matter (subject to subsection (2)(b), where it applies in respect of the matter).

(6) An interim target in respect of a matter must specify—

(a) a standard to be achieved, which must be capable of being objectively measured, and

(b) a date by which it is to be achieved.

(7) The date must be no later than the end of the 5 year period beginning with—

(a) for the first interim target in respect of a matter, the relevant date;

(b) for subsequent interim targets in respect of a matter, the later of the relevant date and the date specified for the previous interim target.

(8) Before setting or revising an interim target in respect of a matter the Secretary of State must be satisfied that meeting the target, or the revised target, would make an appropriate contribution towards meeting the target under sections 1 to 3 in respect of that matter.

(9) The "relevant date" is the date on which the review is completed.

12 Reviewing and revising plans: other requirements

(1) In reviewing an environmental improvement plan under section 10, the Secretary of State must consider—

(a) what has been done to implement the plan in the period since it was published or (if it has been reviewed before) last reviewed,

(b) whether, having regard to data obtained under section 16 and reports made by the OEP[3] under section 28, the natural environment has, or particular aspects of it have, improved during that period, and

---

[3]   The Office for Environmental Protection.

(c) whether Her Majesty's Government should take further or different steps to improve the natural environment (compared to those set out in the plan) in the remainder of the period to which the plan relates.

(2) In considering the matters in subsection (1)(b) the Secretary of State must consider the progress that has been made towards meeting—

(a) any targets, or any relevant targets, set under sections 1 to 3, and

(b) any interim targets, or any relevant interim targets, set under sections 11 and 14.

(3) In considering the matters in subsection (1)(c) the Secretary of State must consider whether Her Majesty's Government should take further or different steps towards meeting those targets (compared to those set out in the plan).

13 Renewing environmental improvement plans

(1) Before the end of the period to which an environmental improvement plan (the "old plan") relates, the Secretary of State must prepare a new environmental improvement plan (the "new plan") for a new period in accordance with this section, section 14 and section 15.

(2) The new period must begin no later than immediately after the end of the period to which the old plan relates.

(3) At or before the end of the period to which the old plan relates the Secretary of State must lay before Parliament, and publish, the new plan.

(4) The new plan replaces the old plan when—

(a) it has been laid and published, and

(b) the period to which it relates has begun.

14 Renewing plans: interim targets

(1) A new plan prepared by the Secretary of State under section 13 must—

(a) set at least one interim target in respect of each relevant matter, and

(b) secure that there is at all times, until the end of the 5 year period beginning with the relevant date, an interim target set by the plan in respect of each relevant matter.

(2) A "relevant matter" means any matter in respect of which there is a target under sections 1 to 3.

(3) Subsection (1) does not apply in respect of a matter if the specified date for the target under sections 1 to 3 in respect of that matter is before the end of the 5 year period beginning with the relevant date.

(4) An interim target in respect of a matter must specify—

(a) a standard to be achieved, which must be capable of being objectively measured, and

(b) a date by which it is to be achieved.

(5) The date must be no later than the end of the 5 year period beginning with—

(a) for the first interim target set by the new plan in respect of a matter, the relevant date;

(b) for subsequent interim targets set by the new plan in respect of a matter, the date specified for the previous interim target.

(6) Before setting an interim target in respect of a matter, the Secretary of State must be satisfied that meeting it would make an appropriate contribution towards meeting the target under sections 1 to 3 in respect of that matter.

(7) The "relevant date" is the first day of the period to which the new plan relates.

(8) In this section references to the "new plan" are to be read in accordance with section 13.

15 Renewing plans: other requirements

(1) In preparing a new plan under section 13 the Secretary of State must consider—

(a) what has been done to implement the old plan,

(b) whether, having regard to data obtained under section 16 and reports made by the OEP under section 28, the natural environment has improved since the beginning of the period to which the old plan relates, and

(c) whether Her Majesty's Government should take further or different steps(compared to those set out in the old plan) to improve the natural environment in the period to which the new environmental improvement plan relates.

(2) In considering the matters in subsection (1)(b) the Secretary of State must consider the progress that has been made towards meeting—

(a) any targets set under sections 1 to 3, and

(b) any interim targets set under sections 11 and 14.

(3) In considering the matters in subsection (1)(c) the Secretary of State must consider whether Her Majesty's Government should take further or different steps (compared to those set out in the old plan) towards meeting any targets set under sections 1 to 3.

(4) In this section references to the "new plan" and the "old plan" are to be read in accordance with section 13.

16 Environmental monitoring

(1) The Secretary of State must make arrangements for obtaining such data about the natural environment as the Secretary of State considers appropriate for the purpose of monitoring—

(a) whether the natural environment is, or particular aspects of it are, improving in accordance with the current environmental improvement plan,

(b) the progress being made towards meeting any targets set under sections 1 to 3, and

(c) the progress being made towards meeting any interim targets set under sections 11 and 14.

(2) The Secretary of State must lay before Parliament, and publish, a statement setting out the kinds of data to be obtained under subsection (1).

(3) The first statement must be laid before the end of the 4 month period beginning with the day on which this section comes into force.

(4) The Secretary of State may revise the statement at any time (and subsection (2) applies to any revised statement).

(5) The Secretary of State must publish any data obtained under subsection (1).

17 Policy statement on environmental principles

(1) The Secretary of State must prepare a policy statement on environmental principles in accordance with this section and section 18.

(2) A "policy statement on environmental principles" is a statement explaining how the environmental principles should be interpreted and proportionately applied by Ministers of the Crown when making policy.

The reference to *"proportionality"* means balancing the costs and environmental benefits of the implementation of such a policy. Paragraph 186 of the Explanatory Memorandum states:

> *"The policy statement will explain how Ministers of the Crown should interpret and proportionately apply the environmental principles when developing policies. Proportionate application means ensuring that action taken on the basis of the principles balances the potential for environmental benefit against other benefits and costs associated with the action. This means that a policy where there is the potential for high environmental damage would require more stringent action than a policy where the potential environmental damage is low. This consideration of the principles policy statement throughout the policy-making process may be carried out by policy-makers on behalf of Ministers of the Crown, though Ministers will retain the responsibility to have due regard to the policy statement."*

(3) It may also explain how Ministers of the Crown, when interpreting and applying the environmental principles, should take into account other considerations relevant to their policy.

(4) The Secretary of State must be satisfied that the statement will, when it comes into effect, contribute to—

(a) the improvement of environmental protection, and

(b) sustainable development.

(5) In this Part "environmental principles" means the following principles—

(a) the principle that environmental protection should be integrated into the making of policies,

(b) the principle of preventative action to avert environmental damage,

(c) the precautionary principle, so far as relating to the environment,

(d) the principle that environmental damage should as a priority be rectified at source, and

(e) the polluter pays principle.

The point to bear in mind here is that the policies to which these provisions will apply will include planning policy (in particular, the National Planning Policy Framework). The policies in the National Planning Policy Framework will, in turn, trickle down to local development control by way of incorporation into local plans and in site-specific development control decisions. One problem is that the meaning of the concepts relating to preventative action and the precautionary principle are very complex and not readily digested by the average planning committee. Presumably, the answer is that these principles will have, already, been taken into account at policy level and, as such, they need not be *"double counted"*.

18 Policy statement on environmental principles: process

(1) The Secretary of State must prepare a draft of the policy statement on environmental principles.

(2) The Secretary of State must consult such persons as the Secretary of State considers appropriate in relation to the draft statement.

(3) The Secretary of State must lay the draft statement before Parliament.

(4) If before the end of the 21 day period—

(a) either House of Parliament passes a resolution in respect of the draft statement, or

(b) a committee of either House of Parliament, or a joint committee of both Houses, makes recommendations in respect of the draft statement,

the Secretary of State must produce a response and lay it before Parliament.

(5) The Secretary of State must prepare and lay before Parliament the final statement, but not before—

(a) if subsection (4) applies, the day on which the Secretary of State lays the response required by that subsection, or

(b) otherwise, the end of the 21 day period.

(6) The final statement has effect when it is laid before Parliament.

(7) The Secretary of State must publish the statement when it comes into effect.

(8) The "21 day period" is the period of 21 sitting days beginning with the first sitting day after the day on which the draft statement is laid under subsection (3).

(9) "Sitting day" means a day on which both Houses of Parliament sit.

(10) The requirements in subsections (1) and (2) may be met by the preparation of a draft statement, and consultation, before this section comes into force.

(11) The Secretary of State may prepare a revised policy statement on environmental principles at any time (and subsections (1) to (9) apply in relation to any revised statement).

19 Policy statement on environmental principles: effect

(1) A Minister of the Crown must, when making policy, have due regard to the policy statement on environmental principles currently in effect.

> As noted above, this provision seems to encompass the content of future iterations of the National Planning Policy Framework. The words *"have due regard"* do not necessarily import a particularly high hurdle. Arguably, it should be enough for a Minister who is minded to depart from the policy statement to show that he has heeded the policy statement, given it proper consideration and noted why he departs from it.

(2) Nothing in subsection (1) requires a Minister to do anything (or refrain from doing anything) if doing it (or refraining from doing it)—

(a) would have no significant environmental benefit, or

(b) would be in any other way disproportionate to the environmental benefit.

(3) Subsection (1) does not apply to policy so far as relating to—

(a) the armed forces, defence or national security,

(b) taxation, spending or the allocation of resources within Government, or

(c) Wales.

(4) ...

(5) ...

(6) ...

CHAPTER 3

INTERPRETATION OF PART 1

44 Meaning of "natural environment"

In this Part the "natural environment" means—

(a) plants, wild animals and other living organisms,

(b) their habitats,

(c) land (except buildings or other structures), air and water,

and the natural systems, cycles and processes through which they interact.

The use of the phrase "*other living organisms*" might come back to bite[4] those who procured the drafting of the legislation. This is because the question whether or not a particular organism is "*living*" is a vexed one. For example, does the concept of being "*alive*" incorporate the notion of sentience? If so, there is a disjunction within this apparently generic provision unless it is somehow presumed that plants are, in some way, sentient. Paragraph 390 of the Explanatory Memorandum states:

> "*In setting out the matters that are each considered to be environmental protection, section 44 uses the term 'natural environment'. The definition provided in the section includes living elements of the environment, namely plants, wild animals, other living organisms, and their habitats – both terrestrial and marine. However, it is not intended to include domesticated animals such as livestock and pets. The definition also includes non-living elements, namely air, water and land. This includes both the marine and terrestrial environments. 'Water' will include seawater, freshwater and other forms of water, while 'air' will include the atmosphere (including, for example, the ozone layer) and 'land' will include soil, geological strata and other features. In addition, 'land', as defined in the Interpretation Act 1978, includes 'land covered with water' and therefore will include the sea bed. Buildings and other structures are excluded from the meaning of 'land', however water and air are included regardless of whether they are outside or inside a building or other structure.*"

Paragraph 391 states:

> "*The section also sets out that systems, cycles and processes through which the elements listed above interact are also included within this definition of the natural environment. This therefore includes ecosystems, and hydrological and geomorphological processes.*"

---

[4] No pun intended!

45 Meaning of "environmental protection"

In this Part "environmental protection" means—

(a) protection of the natural environment from the effects of human activity;

(b) protection of people from the effects of human activity on the natural environment;

(c) maintenance, restoration or enhancement of the natural environment;

(d) monitoring, assessing, considering, advising or reporting on anything in paragraphs (a) to (c).

> The stark reality is that it is not possible to "*protect*" the natural environment from the effects of human activity. Even if one were to exclude farming, mining etc as permissible activities, one is still left with the collateral damage caused by air pollution etc. It follows that the references to "*protection*" must, more readily, be construed as meaning "*mitigation*".

46 Meaning of "environmental law"

(1) In this Part "environmental law" means any legislative provision to the extent that it—

(a) is mainly concerned with environmental protection, and

(b) is not concerned with an excluded matter.

(2) Excluded matters are—

(a) disclosure of or access to information;

(b) the armed forces or national security;

(c) taxation, spending or the allocation of resources within Government.

(3) The reference in subsection (1) to "legislative provision" does not include devolved legislative provision, except for the purposes of section 20.

(4) "Devolved legislative provision" means—

(a) legislative provision contained in, or in an instrument made under, an Act of the Scottish Parliament, an Act or Measure of Senedd Cymru, or Northern Ireland legislation, and

(b) legislative provision not within paragraph (a) which—

(i) if contained in an Act of the Scottish Parliament, would be within the legislative competence of the Parliament;

(ii) if contained in an Act of Senedd Cymru, would be within the legislative competence of the Senedd, or

(iii) if contained in an Act of the Northern Ireland Assembly, would be within the legislative competence of the Assembly and would not require the Secretary of State's consent.

(5) The Secretary of State may by regulations provide that a legislative provision specified in the regulations is, or is not, within the definition of "environmental law" in subsection (1) (and this Part applies accordingly).

(6) Before making regulations under subsection (5) the Secretary of State must consult—

(a) the OEP, and

(b) any other persons the Secretary of State considers appropriate.

(7) Regulations under subsection (5) are subject to the affirmative procedure.

47 Interpretation of Part 1: general

In this Part—

"application for judicial review" is to be read in accordance with section 39(8);

"current environmental improvement plan" has the meaning given by section 8(8);

"decision notice" means a notice given under section 36;

[...]

"environmental improvement plan" has the meaning given by section 8 (and see also section 10(10));

"environmental principles" has the meaning given by section 17;

"environmental review" has the meaning given by section 38;

"first environmental improvement plan" has the meaning given by section 8(8);

"improving the natural environment", in relation to an environmental improvement plan, is to be read in accordance with section 8(5);

"information notice" means a notice given under section 35;

"judicial review" means—

(a) in England and Wales or Northern Ireland, an application to the High Court for judicial review, or

(b) in Scotland, an application to the supervisory jurisdiction of the Court of Session;

"making" policy includes developing, adopting or revising policy;

"met", in relation to a target set under sections 1 to 3, has the meaning given by section 4(7);

"Minister of the Crown" has the same meaning as in the Ministers of the Crown Act 1975;

[...]

"OEP" has the meaning given by section 22;

"parliamentary function" means a function in connection with proceedings in Parliament or a devolved legislature;

"policy" includes proposals for legislation, but does not include an administrative decision taken in relation to a particular person or case (for example, a decision on an application for planning permission, funding or a licence, or a decision about regulatory enforcement);

"policy statement on environmental principles" has the meaning given by section 17;

"public authority" has the meaning given by section 31(3);

"relevant Minister" has the meaning given by section 33;

"relevant ombudsman" has the meaning given by section 23;

[...]

"specified date" and "specified standard", in relation to a target set under sections 1 to 3, have the meaning given by section 1(8);

"statutory review" has the meaning given by section 39(8).

[...]

PART 4

AIR QUALITY AND ENVIRONMENTAL RECALL

Air quality

72 Local air quality management framework

Schedule 11 contains amendments of Part 4 of the Environment Act 1995 (air quality).

PART 6

NATURE AND BIODIVERSITY

Biodiversity gain in planning

98 Biodiversity gain as condition of planning permission.

Schedule 14 makes provision for biodiversity gain to be a condition of planning permission in England.

> These provisions are discussed in the notes to Schedule 14 below.

99 Biodiversity gain in nationally significant infrastructure projects

Schedule 15 makes provision about biodiversity gain in relation to development consent for nationally significant infrastructure projects.

100 Biodiversity gain site register

(1) The Secretary of State may by regulations make provision for and in relation to a register of biodiversity gain sites ("the biodiversity gain site register").

(2) A biodiversity gain site is land where—

(a) a person is required under a conservation covenant or planning obligation to carry out works for the purpose of habitat enhancement,

> The term "*habitat enhancement*" has the same meaning as in Schedule 7A to the Town and Country Planning Act 1990.

(b) that or another person is required to maintain the enhancement for at least 30 years after the completion of those works, and

Defra has indicated that it might review this 30-year period, once the Act and associated administration have bedded down: see the Consultation Document.

(c) for the purposes of Schedule 7A to the Town and Country Planning Act 1990 the enhancement is made available to be allocated (conditionally or unconditionally, and whether for consideration or otherwise) in accordance with the terms of the covenant or obligation to one or more developments for which planning permission is granted.

The term *"development"* has the same meaning as in Schedule 7A to the Town and Country Planning Act 1990.

A *"planning obligation"* is a planning agreement or unilateral undertaking pursuant to section 106 of the 1990 Act.

In many (if not most) cases, a biodiversity gain site will be land separate from a development site and the measurable net gain required of the developer will be achieved by way of *"offset"* on this separate land. However, it should be borne in mind that biodiversity net gain can be achieved by way of the enhancement of an existing habitat, which may also be part of a development site. For example, it might be the case that the developer of a site affected by contamination may choose to allocate part of the site to remediation by a method which also allows for a new or enhanced habitat. The creation of a retention pond for SUDS might also present opportunities for onsite biodiversity net gain, where the pond may attract species which are capable of withstanding infrequent inundations. These benefits will be recorded in the register and taken into account when the relevant application for planning permission is considered.

(3) Regulations under this section must provide for the information in the register to be accessible to members of the public.

(4) Regulations under this section may in particular make provision about—

(a) the person who is to establish and maintain the biodiversity gain site register(who may be the Secretary of State, Natural England or another person);

(b) circumstances in which land is or is not eligible to be registered;

(c) applications to register land in the register;

(d) the information to be recorded in relation to any land that is registered;

(e) amendments to the register;

(f) removal of land from the register;

(g) fees payable in respect of any application under the regulations.

(5) Provision under subsection (4)(c) may in particular include provision about—

(a) who is entitled to apply to register land in the biodiversity gain site register;

(b) the procedure to be followed in making an application;

(c) the information to be provided in respect of an application;

(d) how an application is to be determined;

(e) appeals against the rejection of an application;

(f) financial penalties for the supply of false or misleading information in connection with an application.

(6) Provision under subsection (4)(d) may in particular require the recording of the following in relation to any land registered in the biodiversity gain site register—

(a) the location and area of the land;

(b) the works to be carried out on the land and the habitat enhancement to be achieved by them;

> Presumably, there would be some reference to a measurement of net biodiversity gain by way of the Biodiversity Metric: see Consultation Document.

(c) information about the habitat of the land before the commencement of those works;

(d) the person who applied to register the land and (if different) the person by whom the requirement to carry out the works or maintain the habitat enhancement is enforceable;

(e) any development to which any of the habitat enhancement has been allocated;

(f) the biodiversity value (for the purposes of Schedule 7A to the Town and Country Planning Act 1990 or Schedule 2A to the Planning Act 2008) of any such habitat enhancement in relation to any such development.

> Again, presumably, there would be some reference to a measurement of net biodiversity gain by way of the Biodiversity Metric: see Consultation Document.

(7) Regulations under this section may amend subsection (2)(b) so as to substitute for the period for the time being specified there a different period of at least 30 years.

(8) Regulations under this section making provision under subsection (4)(g) or (5)(f) are subject to the affirmative procedure.

(9) Other regulations under this section are subject to the negative procedure.

(10) The Secretary of State must keep under review—

(a) the supply of land for registration in the biodiversity gain site register;

(b) whether the period specified in subsection (2)(b) or in paragraph 9(3) of Schedule 7A to the Town and Country Planning Act 1990 can be increased under subsection (7) or paragraph 9(4) of that Schedule without adversely affecting that supply.

(11) In this section "development", "habitat enhancement", "planning obligation" and "planning permission" have the same meanings as in Schedule 7A to the Town and Country Planning Act 1990.

> The creation of the register is one of the key instruments which will underpin the application of these biodiversity provisions. Importantly, a landowner who wishes to create a bank of biodiversity gain land for sale to developers will be able to register this land bank, thereby assisting nearby developers who are in need of offset land in order to meet the biodiversity net gain condition.
>
> Paragraph 913 of the Explanatory Memorandum states (inter alia):
>
> *"... Subsection (6) sets out further information requirements which will be fundamental to the register, such as the location and area of land and who will be responsible for carrying out the works to enhance biodiversity. Subsection (6) also explicitly references the allocation of biodiversity enhancement to a particular development, which will be important in preventing the 'double-counting' of a given enhancement (or the units that it creates)."*

101 Biodiversity credits

(1) The Secretary of State may make arrangements under which a person who is entitled to carry out the development of any land may purchase a credit from the Secretary of State for the purpose of meeting the biodiversity gain objective referred to in Schedule 7A to the Town and Country Planning Act 1990 or Schedule 2A to the Planning Act 2008.

> Biodiversity Credits are discussed in Chapter 13 above. The *"biodiversity gain objective"* is set out in Chapter 14.
>
> Whilst giving a developer the ability to purchase Biodiversity Credits in lieu of onsite measures, this facility is an option of last resort in terms of the mitigation hierarchy. Accordingly, a developer must show that the mitigation hierarchy has been applied to their particular proposals and show why they are proposing to resort to the purchase of Biodiversity Credits.
>
> Paragraph 917 of the Explanatory Memorandum states:
>
> *"917 Subsections (1) to (5) make provision for the Secretary of State to set up a system to sell a supply of statutory biodiversity credits to the habitat compensation market. The provision of statutory credits will be made in England only. The sold credits will be equivalent to a specified gain in biodiversity value, which will be eligible for inclusion in a biodiversity gain plan. ... Subsection (4) requires the Secretary of State, in considering the price of a biodiversity credit, to set this at a level that does not discourage the development of local market schemes and non-credit habitat creation projects. The Government intends to conduct a further review of the price of units, following engagement with stakeholders, before setting a price. The intention is that the price of biodiversity credits will be higher than prices for equivalent biodiversity gain on the market. Subsection (5) will require the Secretary of State to make information on the price of the units and their operation publicly available."*
>
> Paragraph 918 of the Explanatory Memorandum states (inter alia):
>
> *"918 Subsection (6) sets the framework that the Secretary of State must consider when handling the proceeds of the credits. Proceeds from the sale of credits will contribute to strategic ecological networks and provide long-term environmental benefits, and would be additional to existing requirements. This framework includes a provision that funds collected via this mechanism must be used for the purpose of securing biodiversity gain. Subsection (7) makes provision to exclude works to enhance habitat from the system where there is an existing requirement for the Secretary of State to act – for example, where land is subject to alternative legislative requirements such as where a public body manages a Site of Special Scientific Interest ..."*

(2) A credit is to be regarded for the purposes of that Schedule as having such biodiversity value as is determined under the arrangements.

> An important point to bear in mind here is that Biodiversity Credits and Biodiversity Units are different things. It follows that, whilst a Biodiversity Credit might be valued in Biodiversity Units, one credit does not necessarily equate to one unit.

(3) The arrangements may in particular include arrangements relating to—

(a) applications to purchase credits;

(b) the amount payable in respect of a credit of a given value;

(c) proof of purchase;

(d) reimbursement for credits purchased for development which is not carried out.

(4) In determining the amount payable under the arrangements for a credit of a given value the Secretary of State must have regard to the need to determine an amount which does not discourage the registration of land in the biodiversity gain sites register.

(5) The Secretary of State must publish information about the arrangements, including in particular the amount payable for credits.

(6) The Secretary of State may use payments received under arrangements under this section for the following purposes (only)—

(a) carrying out works, or securing the carrying out of works, for the purpose of habitat enhancement (within the meaning of Part 7A of the Town and Country Planning Act 1990) on land in England;

(b) purchasing interests in land in England with a view to carrying out works, or securing the carrying out of works, for that purpose;

(c) operating or administering the arrangements.

> There is nothing to suggest that all of a developer's purchase of biodiversity credits must be used for a single offset site or that credits cannot be pooled.

(7) The references to works in subsection (6) do not include works which the Secretary of State is required to carry out apart from this section by virtue of any enactment.

(8) The Secretary of State must publish reports relating to the discharge of the Secretary of State's functions under subsections (1) and (6).

(9) A report must relate to a period not exceeding a year which—

(a) in the case of the first report, begins on the date on which Schedule 7A to the Town and Country Planning Act 1990 comes into force in relation to any development (within the meaning of Part 3 of that Act), and

(b) in the case of any subsequent report, begins on the day after the last day of the period to which the previous report related.

(10) A report must set out—

(a) the total payments received under arrangements under this section in the period to which the report relates,

(b) how those payments have been used, and

(c) where those payments have been used for the purpose of carrying out or securing the carrying out of works for the purpose of habitat enhancement, the projected biodiversity value of the habitat enhancement at such time or times after completion of the works as the Secretary of State considers it appropriate to specify.

102 General duty to conserve and enhance biodiversity

(1) Section 40 of the Natural Environment and Rural Communities Act 2006 (duty to conserve biodiversity) is amended in accordance with subsections (2) to (7).

(2) In the heading, after "conserve" insert "and enhance".

(3) For subsections (A1) and (1) substitute –

"(A1) For the purposes of this section "the general biodiversity objective" is the conservation and enhancement of biodiversity in England through the exercise of functions in relation to England.

> The functions mentioned above should include town and country planning.
>
> Paragraph 920 of the Explanatory Memorandum states:
>
> *"920 Section 40 of the Natural Environment and Rural Communities Act 2006 ('the NERC Act') places a duty on public authorities to have regard for the conservation of biodiversity when delivering their functions. This section makes textual amendments to section 40 of that Act, to avoid repeating definitions. The revisions make more explicit the requirement for public authorities to assess how they can take action to conserve and enhance biodiversity,*

> *and then take these actions. This section also sets out how public authorities should abide by the revised duty."*

Paragraphs 921 and 922 of the Explanatory Memorandum state:

> *"921 Subsection (2) adds to the heading of the biodiversity duty in the NERC Act, setting out that this duty is changing from 'conserving' to 'conserving and enhancing' biodiversity.*
>
> *922 Subsection (3) replaces existing subsections (A1) and (1) of the NERC Act with new subsections."*

NB: The duty in section 40 of the NERC Act has always encompassed enhancement.

(1) A public authority which has any functions exercisable in relation to England must from time to time consider what action the authority can properly take, consistently with the proper exercise of its functions, to further the general biodiversity objective.

> It is not clear whether this provision is intended to lead to a directly enforceable legal duty, which must be applied in day-to-day development control functions, or whether it simply acts as a feed to the reporting function mentioned below. Arguably, it might be prayed in aid as a material planning consideration, but the position is not clear.

(1A) After that consideration the authority must (unless it concludes there is no new action it can properly take)—

(a) determine such policies and specific objectives as it considers appropriate for taking action to further the general biodiversity objective, and

(b) take such action as it considers appropriate, in the light of those policies and objectives, to further that objective.

> Paragraph 923 of the Explanatory Memorandum states:
>
> *"923 New subsection (A1) defines the term 'general biodiversity objective', which is used in section 40 to direct the activity taken by public authorities under this duty. This extends the duty of public authorities beyond the original NERC Act, which referred only to conservation, so that it includes the enhancement of biodiversity in England. The aim is to provide for the enhancement or improvement of biodiversity, not just its maintenance in its current state. These provisions would appear to give rise to material planning considerations for the determination of applications for planning permission."*

> Again, this is wrong.
>
> Be that as it may, the salient question is whether this gives rise to a material consideration which must be taken into account by those determining planning applications.

(1B) The requirements of subsection (1A)(a) may be satisfied (to any extent) by revising any existing policies and specific objectives for taking action to further the general biodiversity objective.

(1C) The first consideration required by subsection (1) must be completed by the authority within the period of one year beginning with the day on which section 102 of the Environment Act 2021 comes into force.

> This time period of one year is a relatively short one.

(1D) Any subsequent consideration required by subsection (1) must be completed no more than five years after the completion of the authority's previous consideration.

(1E) A determination required by subsection (1A)(a) must be made as soon as practicable after the completion of the consideration to which it relates.

(1F) Nothing in this section prevents the authority from—

(a) determining or revising policies and specific objectives at any time, or

(b) taking action to further the general biodiversity objective at any time."

(4) In subsection (2) for "subsection (1)" substitute "subsections (1) and (1A)".

(5) After subsection (2) insert—

"(2A) In complying with subsections (1) and (1A) the authority must in particular have regard to—

(a) any relevant local nature recovery strategy, and

(b) any relevant species conservation strategy or protected site strategy prepared by Natural England.

(2B) The Secretary of State must issue guidance to local planning authorities as to how they are to comply with their duty under subsection (2A)(a) when complying with subsections (1) and (1A) in their capacity as such authorities.

(2C) Guidance under subsection (2B) must be—

(a) published by the Secretary of State in such manner as the Secretary of State thinks fit,

(b) kept under review, and

(c) revised where the Secretary of State considers it appropriate.

(2D) The first guidance under subsection (2B) must be published by the Secretary of State within the period of two years beginning with the day on which section 102 of the Environment Act 2021 comes into force."

Paragraph 930 of the Explanatory Memorandum states:

"*930 Subsection (5) of section 102 requires that public authorities must have regard to any relevant Local Nature Recovery Strategies (LNRSs), Species Conservation Strategies and Protected Site Strategies as part of their strategic assessment of their functions, establishing the relationship between the measures. LNRSs map existing important areas for nature and show the opportunities that exist in an area to recover and enhance nature. LNRSs will support public authorities in deciding the most appropriate and effective action to take to further the biodiversity objective under new section 40(1A) of the NERC Act, and in turn subsection (5) will support the implementation of LNRSs. Species Conservation Strategies and Protected Site Strategies (introduced in sections 109 and 110 respectively) are more targeted measures intended to address a range of impacts on species and protected sites. They will also support public authorities in determining the most appropriate and effective action to take in those areas where such a strategy is in operation.*"

Paragraph 931 of the Explanatory Memorandum states:

"*931 Subsection (5) also adds a requirement for the Secretary of State to give guidance to local planning authorities. The guidance will specify how they are to take a local nature recovery strategy into account when discharging their duties under new section 40(1) and (A1) of the NERC Act 2006 concerning the conservation and enhancement of biodiversity. The Secretary of State is required to publish this guidance within two years from when this section comes into force, in such manner as the Secretary of State thinks fit. The Secretary of State is then required to keep the guidance under review and revise it when they consider it appropriate.*"

(6) For subsection (3) substitute—

"(3) The action which may be taken by the authority to further the general biodiversity objective includes, in particular, action taken for the purpose of—

(a) conserving, restoring or otherwise enhancing a population of a particular species, and

(b) conserving, restoring or otherwise enhancing a particular type of habitat."

Paragraph 932 of the Explanatory Memorandum states:

"*932 Subsection (6) updates the existing explanation of 'conserving biodiversity' by directing public authorities to give particular focus to the conservation, restoration and enhancement of species and habitats when deciding the actions to take under the biodiversity objective. This particular emphasis on species and habitats reflects their significance within biodiversity overall, and the wider benefits for nature and society that can be accrued through actions for species and habitats.*"

As noted above, this is misleading.

---

(7) After subsection (5) insert—

"(6) This section has effect in relation to Her Majesty's Revenue and Customs with the following modifications—

(a) the omission from subsection (A1) of the words "in England" and "in relation to England";

(b) the omission from subsection (1) of the words from "which" to "England".

(7) In this section references to England include the territorial sea adjacent to England."

(8) In section 41 of that Act (biodiversity lists and action (England))—

(a) in subsection (1), after "conserving" insert "or enhancing";

(b) in subsection (3) for "and (2)" substitute "and (1A)".

These provisions do not refer to measurable biodiversity outcomes, but, if the relevant authority is using a biodiversity metric for development control, this means of measurement could, presumably, be incorporated.

Paragraph 934 of the Explanatory Memorandum states:

"*934 Subsection (8) amends section 41 of the NERC Act so that its references to section 40 correctly reflect the amendments made by this Act. It also adds a reference to enhancing biodiversity to section 41(1) of that Act. This reflects the increased level of ambition set out*"

> *in the Act, for not only conserving the existing biodiversity of England but also enhancing biodiversity, where appropriate."*

103 Biodiversity reports

(1) After section 40 of the Natural Environment and Rural Communities Act 2006 insert—

"40A Biodiversity reports

(1) This section applies to—

(a) a local authority in England other than a parish council,

(b) a local planning authority in England, and

(c) a designated authority (see subsection (8)(a)).

(2) A public authority to which this section applies ('the authority') must publish biodiversity reports in accordance with this section.

(3) A biodiversity report so published must contain—

(a) a summary of the action which the authority has taken over the period covered by the report for the purpose of complying with its duties under section 40(1) and (1A),

(b) a summary of the authority's plans for complying with those duties over the period of five years following the period covered by the report,

(c) any quantitative data required to be included in the report by regulations under subsection (8)(b), and

(d) any other information that the authority considers it appropriate to include in the report.

(4) If the authority is a local planning authority, its biodiversity report must also contain—

(a) a summary of the action taken by the authority in carrying out its functions under Schedule 7A to the Town and Country Planning Act 1990 (biodiversity gain as condition of planning permission) over the period covered by the report,

(b) information about any biodiversity gains resulting or expected to result from biodiversity gain plans approved by the authority during that period, and

(c) a summary of the authority's plans for carrying out those functions over the five year period following the period covered by the report.

Paragraph 935 of the Explanatory Memorandum states:

"935 This section adds new section 40A to the NERC Act, which creates a power for the Secretary of State to designate public authorities who are required to report on the action they have taken under the biodiversity objective set out in section 102. It also defines, at a high level, the content of the biodiversity reports and their frequency. These reports will capture how public authorities with significant landholdings have sought to conserve and enhance biodiversity, and will contribute to the improvement of information on protected sites, priority habitats and priority species."

The requirements relating to the local planning authority in subsection (4) would seem to point to the notion that biodiversity reports will be material planning considerations in the determination of site-specific planning applications. As always in this type of interaction, it is important to ensure that nebulous aspirations are, somehow, separated from deliverable targets.

---

(5) A biodiversity report—

    (a) must specify the period covered by the report, and

    (b) must be published within the period of 12 weeks following the last day of that period.

(6) The authority's first biodiversity report must cover a period chosen by the authority which—

    (a) is no longer than three years, and

    (b) begins with the day on which the authority first becomes subject to the duty under subsection (2).

(7) A subsequent biodiversity report made by the authority must cover a period chosen by the authority which—

    (a) is no longer than five years, and

    (b) begins with the day after the last day of the period covered by its most recent biodiversity report.

(8) The Secretary of State may by regulations—

(a) provide for specified public authorities, or public authorities of a specified description, to be designated authorities for the purposes of this section;

(b) require biodiversity reports to include specified quantitative data relating to biodiversity in any area of land in England in relation to which the authority exercises any functions.

In this subsection 'specified' means specified in the regulations.

(9) Public authorities with no functions exercisable in relation to England may not be designated under subsection (8)(a).

(10) The power to make regulations under subsection (8) is exercisable by statutory instrument.

(11) A statutory instrument containing regulations under subsection (8) is subject to annulment in pursuance of a resolution of either House of Parliament.

(12) Terms used in this section and section 40 have the same meaning as in that section."

Local nature recovery strategies

104 Local nature recovery strategies for England

(1) There are to be local nature recovery strategies for areas in England.

(2) Together the local nature recovery strategies are to cover the whole of England.

(3) The Secretary of State is to determine the areas within England to which individual local nature recovery strategies are to relate.

See Chapter 6.

Paragraph 944 of the Explanatory Memorandum states:

"944 This section provides for the creation of Local Nature Recovery Strategies (LNRSs) in England, for how the geographical coverage of each LNRS will be determined, and for the relationship between LNRSs and the biodiversity duty under the NERC Act."

---

(4) The area of a local authority, other than a county council, may not be split between local nature recovery strategies.

(5) Section 40(2A) of the Natural Environment and Rural Communities Act 2006 (duty to conserve biodiversity) makes provision about the duties of public authorities in relation to local nature recovery strategies.

105 Preparation of local nature recovery strategies

(1) A local nature recovery strategy for an area ("the strategy area") is to be prepared and published by the responsible authority.

> Paragraphs 951 and 952 of the Explanatory Memorandum state:
>
> *"951 This section sets out the process by which LNRSs are to be prepared, published, reviewed and republished. It also provides a power for the Secretary of State to make regulations regarding this process.*
>
> *952 Subsection (1) sets out that each LNRS will be prepared and published by a 'responsible authority'. The requirement to publish the LNRS is to ensure that the LNRS is a publicly available document."*

(2) The responsible authority for a local nature recovery strategy is such one of the following authorities as is appointed by the Secretary of State—

(a) a local authority whose area is, or is within, the strategy area;

(b) the Mayor of London;

(c) the mayor for the area of a combined authority established under section 103 of the Local Democracy, Economic Development and Construction Act 2009;

(d) a National Park authority in England;

(e) the Broads Authority;

(f) Natural England.

(3) A local nature recovery strategy is to be reviewed and republished from time to time by the responsible authority.

(4) The Secretary of State may by regulations make provision about the procedure to be followed in the preparation and publication, and review and republication, of local nature recovery strategies.

(5) Regulations under this section may, for example, include provision—

(a) requiring the provision of information by a local authority whose area is, or is within, the strategy area but which is not the responsible authority;

(b) for a local nature recovery strategy to be agreed by all of the local authorities whose areas are within the strategy area;

(c) for the procedure for reaching such agreement and for the resolution of disagreements (including resolution by the Secretary of State or by a public inquiry);

(d) for consultation, including consultation of members of the public;

(e) for the times at or after which a local nature recovery strategy is to be reviewed and republished.

(6) Regulations under this section are subject to the negative procedure.

106 Content of local nature recovery strategies

> Paragraph 959 of the Explanatory Memorandum states:
>
> *"959 This section defines the required content of an LNRS, setting out the general nature of the documents that each LNRS must comprise and the information that these documents must contain. It also provides for the Secretary of State to issue statutory guidance to provide further detail."*

(1) A local nature recovery strategy relating to an area ("the strategy area") is to include—

(a) a statement of biodiversity priorities for the strategy area, and

(b) a local habitat map for the whole strategy area or two or more local habitat maps which together cover the whole strategy area.

(2) The statement of biodiversity priorities referred to in subsection (1)(a) is to include—

(a) a description of the strategy area and its biodiversity,

(b) a description of the opportunities for recovering or enhancing biodiversity, in terms of habitats and species, in the strategy area,

(c) the priorities, in terms of habitats and species, for recovering or enhancing biodiversity (taking into account the contribution that recovering or enhancing biodiversity can also make to other environmental benefits), and

(d) proposals as to potential measures relating to those priorities.

(3) A local habitat map referred to in subsection (1)(b) is a map identifying—

(a) national conservation sites in the strategy area,

(b) any nature reserves in the strategy area provided under section 21 of the National Parks and Access to the Countryside Act 1949, and

(c) other areas in the strategy area which in the opinion of the responsible authority—

(i) are, or could become, of particular importance for biodiversity, or

(ii) are areas where the recovery or enhancement of biodiversity could make a particular contribution to other environmental benefits.

Paragraph 965 of the Explanatory Memorandum states:

"965 Subsection (3)(c)(i) is what is sometimes referred to as 'biodiversity opportunity mapping'. The Government is aware of more than a dozen different examples of biodiversity opportunity maps that have been produced by local authorities or on their behalf – such as Surrey Nature Partnership's Biodiversity Opportunity Areas: the basis for realising Surrey's ecological network. It is intended that LNRSs will build on and seek to accommodate existing best practice."

---

(4) A local habitat map which does not relate to the whole of the strategy area must relate to the area of one or more local authorities within the strategy area.

(5) The Secretary of State may issue guidance as to—

(a) information to be included in a local nature recovery strategy pursuant to the requirements in subsections (1) to (3), and

(b) any other matters to be included in a local nature recovery strategy.

(6) A responsible authority must have regard to the guidance when preparing a local nature recovery strategy.

(7) The Secretary of State must lay before Parliament, and publish, the guidance.

> These strategies will, no doubt, be referred to in future planning applications and public inquiries, and there is no reason why they should not carry weight in the context of individual applications.

107 Information to be provided by the Secretary of State

(1) For the purpose of assisting responsible authorities in their preparation of local nature recovery strategies, the Secretary of State must prepare and publish a national habitat map for England.

(2) The national habitat map must in particular identify—

(a) national conservation sites, and

(b) other areas that in the opinion of the Secretary of State are of particular importance for biodiversity.

(3) The Secretary of State may from time to time review and republish the national habitat map.

(4) The Secretary of State must inform a responsible authority of any area in the authority's strategy area which falls within subsection (5).

(5) An area falls within this subsection if in the Secretary of State's opinion—

(a) the area could be of greater importance for biodiversity, or is an area where the recovery or enhancement of biodiversity could make a contribution to other environmental benefits, and

(b) the area could contribute to the establishment of a network of areas across England for the recovery and enhancement of biodiversity in England as a whole.

(6) The Secretary of State must provide a responsible authority with any other information—

(a) that is held by the Secretary of State, and

(b) that the Secretary of State considers might assist the authority in preparing a local nature recovery strategy.

108 Interpretation

(1) This section has effect for the purposes of sections 104 to 107.

(2) "Local authority" means—

(a) a county or district council in England;

(b) a London borough council;

(c) the Common Council of the City of London;

(d) the Council of the Isles of Scilly.

(3) "National conservation site" means—

(a) a site of special scientific interest, within the meaning of Part 2 of the Wildlife and Countryside Act 1981;

(b) a national nature reserve declared in accordance with section 35 of that Act;

(c) a Ramsar site, within the meaning of section 37A of that Act;

(d) a marine conservation zone designated under section 116 of the Marine and Coastal Access Act 2009;

(e) a European site, within the meaning of regulation 8 of the Conservation of Habitats and Species Regulations 2017 (SI 2017/1012).

Conservation

109 Species conservation strategies

(1) Natural England may prepare and publish a strategy for improving the conservation status of any species of fauna or flora.

Paragraph 985 of the Explanatory Memorandum states:

"985 This section establishes species conservation strategies, which may be prepared by Natural England with the purpose of improving the conservation status of a specified species. It further requires local planning authorities, and any other public authority specified in regulations by the Secretary of State, to cooperate with Natural England in preparing and implementing a strategy. It then establishes that these authorities must consider any relevant strategy as they carry out their functions."

(2) A strategy under subsection (1) is called a "species conservation strategy".

(3) A species conservation strategy must relate to an area (the "strategy area") consisting of—

(a) England, or

(b) any part of England.

(4) A species conservation strategy for a species may in particular—

(a) identify areas or features in the strategy area which are of importance to the conservation of the species,

(b) identify priorities in relation to the creation or enhancement of habitat for the purpose of improving the conservation status of the species in the strategy area,

(c) set out how Natural England proposes to exercise its functions in relation to the species across the whole of the strategy area or in any part of it for the purpose of improving the conservation status of the species in the strategy area,

(d) include Natural England's opinion on the giving by any other public authority of consents or approvals which might affect the conservation status of the species in the strategy area, and

(e) include Natural England's opinion on measures that it would be appropriate to take to avoid, mitigate or compensate for any adverse impact on the conservation status of the species in the strategy area that may arise from a plan, project or other activity.

(5) Natural England may, from time to time, amend a species conservation strategy.

(6) A local planning authority in England and any prescribed authority must co-operate with Natural England in the preparation and implementation of a species conservation strategy so far as relevant to the authority's functions.

This duty of a local planning authority to co-operate in the implementation of the strategy is important in relation to site-specific planning applications.

Paragraph 994 of the Explanatory Memorandum states:

"994. Subsection (6) places a duty on local planning authorities and other prescribed authorities (as established by the Secretary of State through regulations as set out in subsection (9)) to cooperate with Natural England in preparing and implementing a strategy. The duty only applies if the cooperation required is relevant to the functions of the authority. This duty is a proportionate way to ensure Natural England has the data and support required to efficiently and effectively establish and lead a strategy."

---

(7) The Secretary of State may give guidance to local planning authorities in England and to prescribed authorities as to how to discharge the duty in subsection (6).

> Paragraph 995 of the Explanatory Memorandum states:
>
> *"995 Subsection (7) provides a power for the Secretary of State to produce guidance for authorities setting out what is required by the duty to cooperate in subsection (6). The power allows bespoke guidance to be prepared for each strategy, as the cooperation required will vary for different species and strategy areas."*

(8) The Secretary of State must lay before Parliament, and publish, the guidance.

(9) A local planning authority in England and any prescribed authority must in the exercise of its functions have regard to a species conservation strategy so far as relevant to its functions.

> This would seem to make a species conservation strategy a material consideration in the determination of relevant planning applications. It is, therefore, important that templates for committee reports include this as a heading.

(10) In this section—

"England" includes the territorial sea adjacent to England, which for this purpose does not include—

(a) any part of the territorial sea adjacent to Wales for the general or residual purposes of the Government of Wales Act 2006 (see section 158 of that Act), or

(b) any part of the territorial sea adjacent to Scotland for the general or residual purposes of the Scotland Act 1998 (see section 126 of that Act);

"local planning authority" means a person who is a local planning authority for the purposes of any provision of Part 3 of the Town and Country Planning Act 1990;

"prescribed authority" means an authority exercising functions of a public nature in England which is specified for the purposes of this section by regulations made by the Secretary of State.

(11) Regulations under subsection (10) are subject to the negative procedure.

110 Protected site strategies

(1) Natural England may prepare and publish a strategy for—

(a) improving the conservation and management of a protected site, and

(b) managing the impact of plans, projects or other activities (wherever undertaken) on the conservation and management of the protected site.

Paragraph 1001 of the Explanatory Memorandum states:

"*1001 This section establishes Protected Site Strategies, which may be prepared by Natural England with the purpose of improving the conservation and management of a protected site, and managing the impact of activity, such as offsite development, on those sites. It requires local planning authorities and other appropriate public bodies to cooperate with Natural England in preparing a strategy. It then establishes that public bodies must consider any relevant strategy as they carry out their functions.*"

This suggests that a Protected Site Strategy will be a material consideration in the determination of relevant planning applications.

Paragraph 1002 of the Explanatory Memorandum states:

"*1002 Suitable Alternative Natural Green spaces (SANGs) in the Thames Basin Heaths are an example of a strategic approach established by Natural England in cooperation with local planning authorities and other appropriate public bodies. The section will place Protected Site Strategies prepared by Natural England on a legislative footing.*"

The provision of SANGs in connection with planning proposals has now spread well beyond the Thames Basin, and the usual concerns arise as to how long-term maintenance etc can be secured on a site-specific basis.

---

(2) A strategy under subsection (1) is called a "protected site strategy".

(3) A "protected site" means—

(a) a European site,

(b) a site of special scientific interest, or

(c) a marine conservation zone,

to the extent the site or zone is within England.

(4) A protected site strategy for a protected site may in particular—

(a) include an assessment of the impact that any plan, project or other activity may have on the conservation or management of the protected site (whether assessed individually or cumulatively with other activities),

(b) include Natural England's opinion on measures that it would be appropriate to take to avoid, mitigate or compensate for any adverse impact on the conservation or management of the protected site that may arise from a plan, project or other activity,

(c) identify any plan, project or other activity that Natural England considers is necessary for the purposes of the conservation or management of the protected site, and

(d) cover any other matter which Natural England considers is relevant to the conservation or management of the protected site.

(5) In preparing a protected site strategy for a protected site, Natural England must consult—

(a) any local planning authority in England which exercises functions in respect of an area—

(i) within which any part of the protected site is located, or

(ii) within which a plan, project or other activity that Natural England considers may have an adverse impact on the conservation or management of the protected site is being, or is proposed to be, undertaken,

(b) any public authority in England—

(i) that is undertaking, or proposing to undertake, a plan, project or other activity that Natural England considers may have an adverse impact on the conservation or management of the protected site,

(ii) the consent or approval of which is required in respect of a plan, project or other activity that Natural England considers may have an adverse impact on the conservation or management of the protected site, or

(iii) that Natural England considers may otherwise be affected by the strategy,

(c) any IFC authority in England which exercises functions in respect of an area—

(i) the conservation or management of which Natural England considers may be affected by the strategy, or

(ii) the sea fisheries resources of which Natural England considers may be affected by the strategy,

(d) the Marine Management Organisation, where—

(i) any part of the protected site is within the MMO's area, or

(ii) Natural England considers any part of the MMO's area may otherwise be affected by the strategy,

(e) the Environment Agency,

(f) the Secretary of State, and

(g) any other person that Natural England considers should be consulted in respect of the strategy, including the general public or any section of it.

(6) In subsections (4) and (5), a reference to an adverse impact on the conservation or management of a protected site includes—

(a) in relation to a European site, anything which adversely affects the integrity of the site,

(b) in relation to a site of special scientific interest, anything which is likely to adversely affect the flora, fauna or geological or physiographical features by reason of which the site is of special interest,

(c) in relation to a marine conservation zone, anything which hinders the conservation objectives stated for the zone pursuant to section 117(2) of the Marine and Coastal Access Act 2009, and

(d) any other thing which causes deterioration of natural habitats and the habitats of species as well as disturbance of the species in the protected site, in so far as such disturbance could be significant in relation to the conservation or management of the protected site.

(7) A person whom Natural England consults under subsection (5)(a) to (e) must co-operate with Natural England in the preparation of a protected site strategy so far as relevant to the person's functions.

(8) The Secretary of State may give guidance as to how to discharge the duty in subsection (7).

(9) The Secretary of State must lay before Parliament, and publish, the guidance.

(10) A person must have regard to a protected site strategy so far as relevant to any duty which the person has under—

(a) the Conservation of Habitats and Species Regulations 2017 (SI 2017/1012),

(b) sections 28G to 28I of the Wildlife and Countryside Act 1981, or

(c) sections 125 to 128 of the Marine and Coastal Access Act 2009.

(11) Natural England may, from time to time, amend a protected site strategy.

(12) The duty to consult a person under subsection (5) also applies when Natural England amends a protected site strategy under subsection (11) so far as the amendment is relevant to the person's functions.

(13) In this section—

"England" has the meaning given in section 109;

"European site" has the meaning given in regulation 8 of the Conservation of Habitats and Species Regulations 2017;

"IFC authority" means an inshore fisheries and conservation authority created under section 150 of the Marine and Coastal Access Act 2009;

"local planning authority" has the meaning given in section 109;

"marine conservation zone" means an area designated as a marine conservation zone under section 116(1) of the Marine and Coastal Access Act 2009;

"MMO's area" has the meaning given in section 2(12) of the Marine and Coastal Access Act 2009;

"public authority" has the meaning given in section 40(4) of the Natural Environment and Rural Communities Act 2006;

"sea fisheries resources" has the meaning given in section 153(10) of the Marine and Coastal Access Act 2009;

"site of special scientific interest" means an area notified under section 28(1) of the Wildlife and Countryside Act 1981.

111 Wildlife conservation: licences

(1) In section 10 of the Wildlife and Countryside Act 1981 (exceptions to section 9 of that Act), in subsection (1)—

(a) in paragraph (a), omit the final "or";

(b) at the end insert

"or

(c) anything done in relation to an animal of any species pursuant to a licence granted by Natural England under regulation 55 of the Conservation of Habitats and Species Regulations 2017 (SI 2017/1012) in respect of an animal or animals of that species".

(2) In section 16 of that Act (power to grant licences), in subsection (3)—

(a) in paragraph (h), omit the final "or";

(b) at the end insert "or (j) in England, for reasons of overriding public interest".

(3) In that section, after subsection (3A) insert—

"(3B) In England, the appropriate authority shall not grant a licence under subsection (3) unless it is satisfied—

(a) that there is no other satisfactory solution, and

(b) that the grant of the licence is not detrimental to the survival of any population of the species of animal or plant to which the licence relates."

(4) In that section, in subsections (5A)(c) and (6)(b), after "two years," insert "or in the case of a licence granted by Natural England five years,".

(5) In that section, in subsection (9)(c), after "to (e)" insert "or (j)".

(6) In the Conservation of Habitats and Species Regulations 2017 (SI 2017/1012), in regulation 55(10), for "two years" substitute—

"(a) five years, in the case of a licence granted by Natural England, or

(b) two years, in any other case."

Habitats Regulations

112 Habitats Regulations: power to amend general duties

(1) The Secretary of State may by regulations amend the Conservation of Habitats and Species Regulations 2017 (SI 2017/1012) (the "Habitats Regulations"), as they apply in relation to England, for the purposes in subsection (2).

(2) The purposes are—

(a) to require persons within regulation 9(1) of the Habitats Regulations to exercise functions to which that regulation applies—

(i) to comply with requirements imposed by regulations under this section, or

(ii) to further objectives specified in regulations under this section,

instead of exercising them to secure compliance with the requirements of the Directives;

(b) to require persons within regulation 9(3) of the Habitats Regulations, when exercising functions to which that regulation applies, to have regard to matters specified by regulations under this section instead of the requirements of the Directives.

(3) The regulations may impose requirements, or specify objectives or matters, relating to—

(a) targets in respect of biodiversity set by regulations under section 1 or 3;

(b) improvements to the natural environment which relate to biodiversity and are set out in an environmental improvement plan.

(4) The regulations may impose any other requirements, or specify any other objectives or matters, relating to the conservation or enhancement of biodiversity that the Secretary of State considers appropriate.

(5) Regulations under this section may also, in connection with provision made for the purposes in subsection (2), amend other provisions of the Habitats Regulations, as they apply in relation to England, which refer to requirements, objectives or provisions of the Directives.

(6) In making regulations under this section the Secretary of State must have regard to the particular importance of furthering the conservation and enhancement of biodiversity.

(7) The Secretary of State may make regulations under this section only if satisfied that the regulations do not reduce the level of environmental protection provided by the Habitats Regulations.

(8) Before making regulations under this section the Secretary of State must lay before Parliament, and publish, a statement explaining why the Secretary of State is satisfied as mentioned in subsection (7).

(9) Before making regulations under this section the Secretary of State must consult such persons as the Secretary of State considers appropriate.

(10) Regulations under this section may not come into force before 1 February 2023.

(11) In this section—

"the Directives" has the same meaning as in the Habitats Regulations (see regulation 3(1));

"England" includes the territorial sea adjacent to England, which for this purpose does not include—

(a) any part of the territorial sea adjacent to Wales for the general or residual purposes of the Government of Wales Act 2006 (see section 158 of that Act), or

(b) any part of the territorial sea adjacent to Scotland for the general or residual purposes of the Scotland Act 1998 (see section 126 of that Act);

"environmental improvement plan" has the same meaning as in Part 1.

(12) Regulations under this section are subject to the affirmative procedure.

113 Habitats Regulations: power to amend Part 6

(1) The Secretary of State may by regulations amend Part 6 of the Conservation of Habitats and Species Regulations 2017 (SI 2017/1012) (the "Habitats Regulations") (assessment of plans and projects) as they apply in relation to England.

(2) In making regulations under this section the Secretary of State must have regard to the particular importance of furthering the conservation and enhancement of biodiversity.

(3) The Secretary of State may make regulations under this section only if satisfied that the regulations do not reduce the level of environmental protection provided by the Habitats Regulations.

> There have been concerns that this power to amend the Habitats Regulations might mean that they are watered down; however, the provisions in section 113(2) and (3) seem to suggest that the Secretary of State would have to provide good reasons for loosening the protections provided by these regulations.

(4) Before making regulations under this section the Secretary of State must lay before Parliament, and publish, a statement explaining why the Secretary of State is satisfied as mentioned in subsection (3).

> This provision makes it clear that the Secretary of State is subject to an oversight by Parliament. Again, this goes to the concerns as to whether the Habitats Regulations might be watered down.

(5) Before making regulations under this section the Secretary of State must consult such persons as the Secretary of State considers appropriate.

(6) In this section "England" has the same meaning as in section 112.

(7) Regulations under this section are subject to the affirmative procedure.

PART 7

CONSERVATION COVENANTS

Creation of conservation covenant

117 Conservation covenant agreements

(1) For the purposes of this Part, a "conservation covenant agreement" is an agreement between a landowner and a responsible body where—

(a) the agreement contains provision which—

(i) is of a qualifying kind,

(ii) has a conservation purpose, and

(iii) is intended by the parties to be for the public good,

(b) it appears from the agreement that the parties intend to create a conservation covenant, and

(c) the agreement is executed as a deed by the parties.

> *"Landowner"* is not defined in the Act, but *"responsible body"* is defined in section 119. Provisions of a *"qualifying kind"* are defined in section 117(2), and *"conservation purpose"* is defined in section 117(3).
>
> There are a number of formalities to be observed in drafting and executing a Conservation Covenant Agreement. The late introduction of the requirement for the agreement to be by way of a deed was, in some way, intended to make it more robust when, instead, it simply adds an unnecessary requirement which could trip up the unwary. It will be important for the recitals to the agreement to set out how it seeks to meet these objectives and make it crystal clear that the agreement is a Conservation Covenant Agreement. As with a section 106 agreement, the putative landowner should deduce title in the usual way.

(2) The reference in subsection (1)(a) to provision of a qualifying kind is to provision—

(a) requiring the landowner—

(i) to do, or not to do, something on land in England specified in the provision in relation to which the landowner holds a qualifying estate specified in the agreement for the purposes of the provision, or

(ii) to allow the responsible body to do something on such land, or

(b) requiring the responsible body to do something on such land.

"Qualifying estate" is defined in section 117(4).

The provision in paragraph (a)(i) is similar to the ambit of a planning obligation; however, paragraphs (a)(ii) and (b) go further in that they, respectively, allow or require the responsible body to do something on the subject land.

Those familiar with section 106 agreements will know that the imposition of a requirement on a landowner is one thing, but enforcement is another. The reality is that, if the agreement requires the expenditure of money, this might prove problematic if the landowner is a *"man of straw"*.

---

(3) For the purposes of subsection (1)(a)(ii), provision has a conservation purpose if its purpose is—

(a) to conserve the natural environment of land or the natural resources of land,

(b) to conserve land as a place of archaeological, architectural, artistic, cultural or historic interest, or

(c) to conserve the setting of land with a natural environment or natural resources or which is a place of archaeological, architectural, artistic, cultural or historic interest.

"Conservation" is defined in section 119(9) and, presumably, informs *"conserve"*; and *"natural environment"* is defined in section 119.

Clearly, the statutory purposes go beyond biodiversity and encompass places of archaeological, architectural, artistic, cultural or historic interest.

---

(4) In this Part—

a reference to conserving something includes a reference to protecting, restoring or enhancing it;

> This provision makes it clear that the Conservation Covenant Agreement can include requirements to protect, restore and enhance.

"qualifying estate" means—

(a) an estate in fee simple absolute in possession, or

(b) a term of years absolute granted for a term of more than seven years from the date of the grant and in the case of which some part of the period for which the term of years was granted remains unexpired;

a reference to "the qualifying estate", in relation to an obligation under a conservation covenant, is to the estate in land by virtue of which the condition in subsection (1)(a)(i) was met in relation to—

(a) if the obligation is not an ancillary obligation, the provision giving rise to the obligation, or

(b) if the obligation is an ancillary obligation, the provision giving rise to the obligation to which it was ancillary;

(and for this purpose "ancillary obligation" means an obligation under provision falling within section 118(2)(b));

"natural environment", in relation to land, includes—

(a) its plants, animals and other living organisms;

(b) their habitats;

(c) its geological features.

118 Conservation covenants

(1) A conservation covenant is so much of a conservation covenant agreement as is given statutory effect by this section.

(2) The following provisions of a conservation covenant agreement have statutory effect as a conservation covenant—

(a) provisions in respect of which the conditions in section 117(1)(a) are met, and

(b) provisions ancillary to any provision falling within paragraph (a).

The reference to ancillary provisions meets one of the shortcomings in section 106 of the Town and Country Planning Act 1990; namely, that, for some reason, section 106 sets out the objectives of a planning obligation but does not include necessary ancillary measures, thus leading to clumsy drafting solutions to include them.

(3) If the agreement includes provision for public access to land to which other provision of the agreement (being provision which meets the conditions in section 117(1)(a))relates, the provision for public access is to be treated as ancillary to that other provision.

(4) In this Part—

(a) references to an obligation under a conservation covenant are to an obligation of the landowner or the responsible body given statutory effect by this section as part of the conservation covenant, and

(b) references to the land to which an obligation under a conservation covenant relates are, in the case of an obligation given statutory effect by this section by virtue of being ancillary to another provision, to the land to which the obligation under the other provision relates.

119 Responsible bodies

(1) The following are responsible bodies for the purposes of this Part—

(a) the Secretary of State;

(b) bodies which are designated under this section (referred to in this Part as "designated bodies").

(2) The Secretary of State may, on the application of a local authority or other body, designate it as a responsible body for the purposes of this Part.

(3) The Secretary of State may only designate a local authority if satisfied that it is suitable to be a responsible body.

"*Local authority*" is defined in section 119(9).

A local authority is not, automatically, a responsible body, but must gain this status (if minded to do so) by way of an application to the Secretary of State.

Subsection (3) is, frankly, bizarre. Local authorities have been trusted with a wide range of statutory duties for many years and it is odd that entry into a Conservation Covenant Agreement should have magical properties which put them outwith the scope of local authorities as a matter of course. This restriction may, by itself, tempt local authorities to seek to cover these matters by way of conventional planning obligations, so as to retain some control over them.

(4) The Secretary of State may only designate a body that is not a local authority if satisfied that it—

(a) meets the condition in subsection (5), and

(b) is suitable to be a responsible body.

(5) The condition is that—

(a) in the case of a public body or a charity, at least some of its main purposes or functions relate to conservation, or

(b) in any other case, at least some of the body's main activities relate to conservation.

(6) The Secretary of State may revoke a designation by notice to the body concerned if—

(a) the body has applied to the Secretary of State for its designation to be revoked,

(b) the Secretary of State is satisfied that the body is not suitable to remain as a responsible body, or

(c) in the case of a body other than a local authority, the Secretary of State is satisfied that the body does not meet the condition in subsection (5).

(7) The Secretary of State may determine the criteria to be applied in deciding whether a body is suitable to be or to remain a responsible body (which may include criteria relating to the body's connection with the United Kingdom).

(8) The Secretary of State must publish (and keep up to date)—

(a) a document setting out the criteria applicable for the purposes mentioned in subsection (7), and

(b) a list of the bodies who are designated under this section.

(9) In this section—

"charity" means a charity registered under the Charities Act 2011 or an exempt charity (within the meaning of that Act);

"conservation" means conservation of—

(a) the natural environment or natural resources of land,

(b) places of archaeological, architectural, artistic, cultural or historic interest, or

(c) the setting of land with a natural environment or natural resources or which is a place of archaeological, architectural, artistic, cultural or historic interest;

"local authority" means—

(a) a county or district council in England;

(b) a London borough council;

(c) the Common Council of the City of London;

(d) the Council of the Isles of Scilly.

Effect of conservation covenant

120 Local land charge

(1) A conservation covenant is a local land charge.

(2) For the purposes of the Local Land Charges Act 1975 the originating authority, as respects a conservation covenant, is the person by whom an obligation of the landowner under the covenant is enforceable.

(3) In section 2 of the Local Land Charges Act 1975 (matters which are not local land charges), the references in paragraphs (a) and (b) to a covenant or agreement made between a lessor and a lessee do not include a conservation covenant.

(4) In its application to a conservation covenant, section 10(1) of the Local Land Charges Act 1975 (compensation for non-registration or defective official search certificate) has effect as if—

(a) in the words preceding paragraph (a), the words from the beginning to "but" were omitted,

(b) paragraph (a) (non-registration) were omitted, and

(c) in paragraph (b), for the words from "in existence" to the end there were substituted the words "registered in that register at the time of the search but was not shown by the official search certificate as so registered".

121 Duration of obligation under conservation covenant

(1) An obligation under a conservation covenant has effect for the default period, unless the covenant provides for a shorter period.

(2) The default period for the purposes of subsection (1) is—

(a) if the qualifying estate in relation to the obligation is an estate in fee simple absolute in possession, a period of indefinite duration, and

(b) if the qualifying estate in relation to the obligation is a term of years absolute, a period corresponding in length to the remainder of the period for which the term of years was granted.

122 benefit and burden of obligation of landowner

(1) An obligation of the landowner under a conservation covenant is owed to the responsible body under the covenant.

(2) Subject to the following provisions, an obligation of the landowner under a conservation covenant binds—

(a) the landowner under the covenant, and

(b) any person who becomes a successor of the landowner under the covenant.

(3) In subsection (2)(b) "successor" (in relation to the landowner under the covenant) means a person who holds, in respect of any of the land to which the obligation relates—

(a) the qualifying estate, or

(b) an estate in land derived (whether immediately or otherwise) from the qualifying estate after the creation of the covenant.

(4) An obligation of the landowner under a conservation covenant ceases to bind the landowner under the covenant, or a person who becomes a successor of that landowner, in respect of—

(a) land which ceases to be land to which the obligation relates,

(b) in the case of the landowner under the covenant, land in relation to which the landowner ceases to be the holder of the qualifying estate, or

(c) in the case of a successor, land in relation to which the successor ceases to be the holder of the qualifying estate or of the estate derived from the qualifying estate, as the case may be.

(5) Subsection (2)(b) does not apply if—

(a) the obligation is positive and the person becomes a successor by virtue of holding a term of years absolute granted for a term of seven years or less from the date of the grant,

(b) the conservation covenant was not registered in the local land charges register at the time when the successor acquired the estate in land concerned, or

(c) the successor's immediate predecessor was not bound by the obligation in respect of the land to which the successor's interest relates.

(6) In the case of a conservation covenant relating to land in an area in relation to which section 3 of the Local Land Charges Act 1975 (as substituted by paragraph 3 of Schedule 5 to the Infrastructure Act 2015) does not yet have effect, the reference in subsection (5)(b) to the local land charges register is to the appropriate local land charges register.

(7) The reference in subsection (5)(b) to the time when the successor acquired the estate in land concerned is, if the successor acquired that interest under a disposition which took effect at law only when registered in the register of title kept under the Land Registration Act 2002, to be read as a reference to the time when the disposition was made.

(8) In subsection (5)(c) the successor's "immediate predecessor" is, unless subsection (9) applies, the successor's immediate predecessor in title.

(9) If the successor is the first holder of an estate in land which is derived from another estate in land (whether the other estate is the qualifying estate or an estate derived, immediately or otherwise, from it) the successor's immediate predecessor is the holder of that other estate when the derived estate was created.

123 Benefit of obligation of responsible body

(1) Subject to the following provisions, an obligation of the responsible body under a conservation covenant is owed—

(a) to the landowner under the covenant, and

(b) to any person who becomes a successor of the landowner under the covenant.

(2) In this section "successor" (in relation to the landowner under the covenant) means a person who holds, in respect of any of the land to which the obligation relates—

(a) the qualifying estate, or

(b) an estate in land derived (whether immediately or otherwise) from the qualifying estate after the creation of the covenant.

(3) An obligation of the responsible body under a conservation covenant ceases to be owed to the landowner under the covenant, or to a person who becomes a successor of that landowner, in respect of—

(a) land which ceases to be land to which the obligation relates,

(b) in the case of the landowner under the covenant, land in relation to which the landowner ceases to be the holder of the qualifying estate, or

(c) in the case of a successor, land in relation to which the successor ceases to be the holder of the qualifying estate or of the estate derived from the qualifying estate, as the case may be.

(4) Subsection (1)(b) does not apply if the obligation is ancillary to an obligation of the landowner under the covenant which does not bind the successor.

124 Breach of obligation

(1) A person bound by a negative obligation under a conservation covenant breaches the obligation by—

(a) doing something which it prohibits, or

(b) permitting or suffering another person to do such a thing.

(2) A person bound by a positive obligation under a conservation covenant breaches the obligation if it is not performed.

125 Enforcement of obligation

(1) In proceedings for the enforcement of an obligation under a conservation covenant, the available remedies are—

(a) specific performance,

(b) injunction,

(c) damages, and

(d) order for payment of an amount due under the obligation.

> Whilst the Courts have granted mandatory injunctions for planning enforcement, an order for specific performance may be difficult to enforce where the landowner is, or becomes, impecunious – likewise, orders for payments or for the payment of damages. The prudent responsible authority should, therefore, consider whether the commitments in a Conservation Covenant Agreement should be secured by way of a bond or other form of financial guarantee: see Chapters 18 and 21.
>
> As noted above, this type of enforcement mechanism is of limited value where the landowner is a "*man of straw*". There are no provisions for the imposition of financial securities, such as bonds or guarantees.

(2) On an application for a remedy under subsection (1)(a) or (b), a Court must, in considering what remedy is appropriate, take into account any public interest in the performance of the obligation concerned.

> To put it another way, it would seem to be the case that there is no guarantee that a Court will uphold a covenant once it has assessed the public interest and found this consideration to be of little weight.

(3) Subject to subsection (4), contract principles apply to damages for breach of an obligation under a conservation covenant.

(4) In the case of breach of an obligation of the landowner under a conservation covenant, a Court may award exemplary damages in such circumstances as it thinks fit.

(5) For the purposes of the Limitation Act 1980, an action founded on an obligation under a conservation covenant is to be treated as founded on simple contract.

> Whether by way of an oversight or not, this is inconsistent with the usual rule that the limitation period for deeds is 12 years from the breach, not the six years in connection with simple contracts.

126 Defences to breach of obligation

(1) In proceedings for breach of an obligation under a conservation covenant it is a defence to show—

(a) that the breach occurred as a result of a matter beyond the defendant's control,

(b) that the breach occurred as a result of doing, or not doing, something in an emergency in circumstances where it was necessary for that to be done, or not done, in order to prevent loss of life or injury to any person, or

(c) that at the time of the breach—

(i) the land to which the obligation relates was, or was within an area, designated for a public purpose, and

(ii) compliance with the obligation would have involved a breach of any statutory control applying as a result of the designation.

(2) If the only reason for the application of subsection (1)(c) was failure to obtain authorisation, the defendant must also show that all reasonable steps to obtain authorisation had been taken.

(3) The defence under subsection (1)(c) does not apply if the designation was in force when the conservation covenant was created.

Paragraphs 1100 and 1101 of the Explanatory Memorandum state:

"1100 The latter defence will only be available if the land was designated for a public purpose after the conservation covenant was created (subsection (3)) and, in the event that the defence is relied on only because of a failure to obtain authorisation that would have enabled compliance with the obligation, the defendant can show that he or she took all reasonable steps to obtain such an authorisation (subsection (2)).

1101 For example, land may be subject to a conservation covenant which requires the landowner to carry out specified works, and the land, or part of it, may be subsequently designated as a Site of Special Scientific Interest (SSSI). The works specified in the conservation covenant are likely to damage the special interest features for the site and cannot be done without the consent of Natural England. Natural England refuses consent. If the landowner carries out the works required by the conservation covenant he or she will commit an offence under section 28P of the Wildlife and Countryside Act 1981. In these circumstances the landowner could rely on this latter defence."

---

(4) The defence of statutory authority (which applies in relation to the infringement of rights such as easements by a person acting under statutory authority) applies in relation to breach of an obligation under a conservation covenant.

> Paragraph 1102 of the Explanatory Memorandum states:
>
> *"1102 Subsection (4) provides that the defence of statutory authority applies to conservation covenants. The intention is that when a public body such as a local authority acquires, and uses, land in accordance with its statutory powers it can override a conservation covenant that binds the land, in the same way that it can override an easement affecting the land."*

(5) In this section—

"authorisation" means any approval, confirmation, consent, licence, permission or other authorisation (however described), whether special or general;

"statutory control" means control imposed by provision contained in, or having effect under, an Act.

> A local authority with experience of enforceable planning obligations may be concerned that the landowner is provided with a suite of defences when the existence of the conservation covenant was a material consideration which was taken into account in the grant of planning permission. A cynical developer might argue that a breach occurred as a result of a matter beyond their control and thus precipitate the authority into an extended dispute about whether this was the case. The problem is compounded, for the authority, if it is not the responsible body and the responsible body then takes a less robust view.

127 Discharge of obligation of landowner by agreement

(1) The responsible body under a conservation covenant and a person who holds the qualifying estate in respect of any of the land to which an obligation of the landowner under the covenant relates may, by agreement, discharge from the obligation any of the land in respect of which the person holds that estate.

> This discharge provision is one reason why local planning authorities might be wary of accepting a Conservation Covenant Agreement instead of a planning obligation; namely, that control is ceded to a third-party responsible body which might not share the authority's aspirations for the offset site.

(2) Subsection (3) applies to—

(a) the responsible body under a conservation covenant, and

(b) a person who is a successor of the landowner under the covenant by virtue of holding an estate in land which—

(i) is an estate in respect of any of the land to which an obligation of the landowner under the covenant relates, and

(ii) is derived (whether immediately or otherwise) from the qualifying estate.

(3) Those persons may, by agreement, discharge the estate in land mentioned in subsection (2)(b) from the obligation in respect of any of the land to which the obligation relates.

(4) Any power under this section is exercisable by agreement executed as a deed by the parties which specifies—

(a) the obligation to which the discharge relates,

(b) the land to which the discharge relates, and

(c) the estate in land by virtue of which the power is exercisable.

128 Discharge of obligation of responsible body by agreement

(1) A person to whom an obligation of the responsible body under a conservation covenant is owed by virtue of the person holding an estate in land may, by agreement with the responsible body, discharge the obligation, so far as owed in relation to that estate, in respect of any of the land in respect of which the person is entitled to the benefit of the obligation.

> Likewise, the same objection arises in that the local planning authority does not have any statutory right to intervene.

(2) The power under this section is exercisable by agreement executed as a deed by the parties which specifies—

(a) the obligation to which the discharge relates,

(b) the land to which the discharge relates, and

(c) the estate in land by virtue of which the power is exercisable.

129 Modification of obligation by agreement

(1) A person bound by, or entitled to the benefit of, an obligation under a conservation covenant may, by agreement with the responsible body under the covenant, modify the

obligation in its application to any of the land in respect of which the person is bound by, or entitled to the benefit of, it.

(2) The power under subsection (1) does not include power to make a change which, had it been included in the original agreement, would have prevented the provision of the agreement that gave rise to the obligation being provision in relation to which the conditions in section 117(1) were met.

(3) The power under this section is exercisable by agreement executed as a deed by the parties which specifies—

(a) the obligation to which the modification relates,

(b) the land to which the modification relates, and

(c) the estate in land by virtue of which the power is exercisable.

(4) If an obligation under a conservation covenant is modified by an agreement under this section, the modification binds—

(a) the parties to the agreement, and

(b) any person who, as respects any of the land to which the modification relates, becomes a successor of a person bound by the modification.

Paragraphs 1110 and 1111 of the Explanatory Memorandum state (inter alia):

"*1110 ... Subsection (4) provides that any modification will bind the parties to the agreement and their successors in respect of any of the land to which the modification relates.*

1111 For example, X enters into a conservation covenant and then transfers part of the land to Y, leases another part to Z, and retains part of the land. The original obligation may, following devolution of parts of the original landowner's interest, bind X, Y and Z. X then enters into an agreement with the responsible body to modify the obligation. This particular modification will only bind X. It will not bind Y and Z as they are not parties to the modification agreement. In the case of X (and his or her successors), the obligation under the conservation covenant is then read with the modification. In the case of Y and Z (and their successors), the obligation under the covenant has effect without modification."

---

(5) In subsection (4)(b) "successor of a person bound by the modification", means a person who holds, in respect of any of the land to which the modification relates—

(a) the estate held by the person bound by the modification when the modification was agreed, or

(b) an estate in land derived (whether immediately or otherwise) from that estate after the modification is agreed.

130 Discharge or modification of obligation by Upper Tribunal

(1) Schedule 18 makes provision about the discharge or modification of an obligation under a conservation covenant on application to the Upper Tribunal.

> At the risk of repetition, the Act does not provide any rights of consultation with interested parties and it is to be hoped that the forthcoming regulations will rectify this situation.

(2) Where any proceedings by action or otherwise are taken to enforce an obligation under a conservation covenant, any person against whom the proceedings are taken may in such proceedings apply to the High Court or the County Court for an order giving leave to apply to the Upper Tribunal under Schedule 18 and staying the proceedings in the meantime.

(3) No application under section 84(1) of the Law of Property Act 1925 (which enables the Upper Tribunal on application to discharge or modify a restriction arising under covenant or otherwise) may be made in relation to an obligation under a conservation covenant.

Replacement etc of responsible body

131 Power of responsible body to appoint replacement

(1) The responsible body under a conservation covenant may appoint another responsible body to be the responsible body under the covenant, unless the covenant otherwise provides.

(2) The power under subsection (1) is exercisable by agreement executed as a deed by the appointor and appointee.

(3) In the case of a conservation covenant registered in the local land charges register, an appointment under subsection (1) only has effect if the appointor supplies to the Chief Land Registrar the information necessary to enable the Registrar to amend the registration.

(4) In the case of a conservation covenant relating to land in an area in relation to which section 3 of the Local Land Charges Act 1975 (as substituted by paragraph 3 of Schedule 5 to the Infrastructure Act 2015) does not yet have effect—

(a) the references in subsection (3) to the local land charges register and the Chief Land Registrar are to the appropriate local land charges register and the authority responsible for that register, but

(b) subsection (3) does not apply to an appointment by that authority.

(5) Appointment under subsection (1) has effect to transfer to the appointee—

(a) the benefit of every obligation of the landowner under the conservation covenant, and

(b) the burden of every obligation of the responsible body under the covenant.

(6) Appointment under subsection (1) does not have effect to transfer any right or liability in respect of an existing breach of obligation.

(7) A body appointed under subsection (1) as the responsible body under a conservation covenant must notify its appointment to every person who is bound by an obligation of the landowner under the covenant.

132 Body ceasing to be a responsible body

(1) Subsections (2) and (3) apply if a body which is the responsible body under a conservation covenant ceases to be a designated body.

(2) The body ceases to be the responsible body under the conservation covenant.

(3) The following transfer to the Secretary of State—

(a) the benefit of every obligation of the landowner under the covenant, and

(b) the burden of every obligation of the responsible body under the covenant.

(4) Subsection (3) does not have effect to transfer any right or liability in respect of an existing breach of obligation.

(5) If subsection (3) has effect in relation to a conservation covenant, the Secretary of State becomes custodian of the covenant until—

(a) an appointment under section 131(1) by the Secretary of State has effect in relation to the covenant, or

(b) the Secretary of State makes an election under subsection (6) in relation to the covenant.

(6) If custodian of a conservation covenant, the Secretary of State may elect to be the responsible body under the covenant by giving written notice of election to every person who is bound by an obligation of the landowner under the covenant.

(7) The Secretary of State may, as custodian of a conservation covenant—

(a) enforce any obligation of the landowner under the covenant, and

(b) exercise in relation to the covenant any power conferred by this Part on the responsible body under the covenant.

(8) In relation to any period as custodian of a conservation covenant, the Secretary of State has no liability with respect to performance of any obligation of the responsible body under the covenant.

Miscellaneous

133 Effect of acquisition or disposal of affected land by responsible body

If the responsible body under a conservation covenant acquires an estate in land to which an obligation under the covenant relates (whether an obligation of the landowner or of the responsible body under the covenant)—

(a) the acquisition does not have effect to extinguish the obligation,

(b) section 122(2)(b) applies to the body as it would apply to any other person acquiring the estate in land in the same circumstances, and

(c) any obligation of the responsible body under the covenant continues to bind the body in accordance with this Part.

134 Effect of deemed surrender and re-grant of qualifying estate

(1) Subsection (2) applies if a term of years absolute which is the qualifying estate in relation to an obligation under a conservation covenant is deemed to be surrendered and re-granted by operation of law.

(2) In the application of sections 122, 123 and 127 to the period after the deemed surrender, references to the qualifying estate are to be read as including a reference to the term of years deemed to be granted.

> To put this another way, if a qualifying lease is surrendered and re-granted, the covenant will bind the new lease.

135 Declarations about obligations under conservation covenants

(1) The court or Upper Tribunal may on the application of any person interested declare—

(a) whether anything purporting to be a conservation covenant is a conservation covenant,

(b) whether any land is land to which an obligation under a conservation covenant relates,

(c) whether any person is bound by, or entitled to the benefit of, an obligation under a conservation covenant and, if so, in respect of what land,

(d) what, upon the true construction of any instrument by means of which an obligation under a conservation covenant is created or modified, is the nature of the obligation.

> The reference to *"any person interested"* is not limited to persons interested in the relevant land only. This would suggest that interested persons such as local authorities, local residents etc may have rights of audience.

(2) No application under section 84(2) of the Law of Property Act 1925 (which enables the court on application to make declarations about restrictions under instruments) may be made in relation to an obligation under a conservation covenant.

(3) In this section "the court" means the High Court or the county court.

136 Duty of responsible bodies to make annual return

(1) A designated body must make an annual return to the Secretary of State stating whether, during the period to which the return relates, there were any conservation covenants under which an obligation was owed to it as the responsible body.

(2) If there were any such conservation covenants, the annual return must—

(a) state the number of conservation covenants;

(b) state, for each conservation covenant, the area of the land in relation to which the body was owed any obligation as the responsible body.

(3) The annual return must also give any information that is prescribed under subsection (4).

(4) The Secretary of State may by regulations make provision about annual returns to be made by a designated body.

(5) The provision which may be made under subsection (4) includes, in particular, provision—

(a) prescribing information to be included in an annual return (but see subsection (10)), and

(b) provision as to the period to which an annual return is to relate and the date by which an annual return is to be made.

(6) Subject to any provision made as mentioned in subsection (5)(b)—

(a) the period to which an annual return is to relate, and

(b) the date by which an annual return is to be made,

are such period and date as the Secretary of State may direct.

(7) On giving a direction under subsection (6) the Secretary of State must take all reasonable steps to draw the direction to the attention of each responsible body affected by it.

(8) A direction under subsection (6) may be varied or revoked by a further such direction.

(9) Regulations under subsection (4) and directions under subsection (6) may make—

(a) provision of general application, or

(b) provision applicable only to one or more particular responsible bodies or to responsible bodies of a particular description.

(10) Any information prescribed for inclusion in an annual return made by a designated body must be information about or connected with—

(a) the designated body;

(b) its activities over the period to which the return relates;

(c) any conservation covenant under which an obligation was owed to it as the responsible body during that period;

(d) the land in relation to which it was owed such an obligation.

(11) Regulations under this section are subject to the negative procedure.

Supplementary

137 Crown application

Schedule 19 makes provision about the application of this Part to Crown land.

138 Index of defined terms in Part 7

The following Table sets out expressions defined or explained in this Part for general purposes.

Expression	Provision
conservation covenant	section 118(1)
conservation covenant agreement	section 117(1)
conservation purpose	section 117(3)
conserving (something)	section 117(4)
designated body	section 119(1)(b)
natural environment (in relation to land)	section 117(4)
qualifying estate (generally)	section 117(4)
the qualifying estate (in relation to an obligation under a conservation covenant)	section 117(4)
responsible body	section 119

139 Consequential amendments relating to Part 7

Schedule 20 makes consequential amendments relating to this Part.

General provisions

142 Consequential provision

(1) The Secretary of State may by regulations make provision that is consequential on this Act or regulations under this Act.

(2)–(5) …

(6) Regulations under this section may amend or repeal provision made by or under any legislation (whenever passed or made).

(7) Regulations under this section are subject to the affirmative procedure if they amend or repeal any provision of—

(a) an Act of Parliament,

(b) a Measure or Act of Senedd Cymru,

(c) an Act of the Scottish Parliament,

(d) Northern Ireland legislation, or

(e) retained direct principal EU legislation.

(8) Regulations under this section to which subsection (7) does not apply are subject to the negative procedure.

(9)–(10) …

143 Regulations

(1) A power to make regulations under any provision of this Act includes power to make—

(a) supplementary, incidental, transitional or saving provision;

(b) different provision for different purposes or areas.

(2) Subsection (1) does not apply to regulations under section 147 or 148.

(3) Regulations under this Act made by—

(a) the Secretary of State, or

(b) …

are to be made by statutory instrument.

(4) …

(5) Where regulations under this Act made or to be made by the Secretary of State—

(a) are subject to the negative procedure, the statutory instrument containing them is subject to annulment in pursuance of a resolution of either House of Parliament;

(b) are subject to the affirmative procedure, they may not be made unless a draft of the statutory instrument containing them has been laid before, and approved by a resolution of, each House of Parliament.

It is worth adding a note on, respectively, the negative procedure and the affirmative procedure. In essence, draft regulations which are subject to the negative procedure are laid before Parliament; however, they are not discussed unless the matter is raised by a member for that purpose. If, as a result of those discussions, Parliament takes the view that the regulations should not go forward in their current form, a negative resolution will be passed. The affirmative procedure is different, in that draft regulations are laid before Parliament but cannot be adopted until Parliament has resolved accordingly.

(6)–(9) …

144 Crown application

(1) This Act binds the Crown, subject to subsection (2).

(2) An amendment or repeal made by this Act binds the Crown to the same extent as the provision amended or repealed.

146 Extent

(1) In Part 1 of this Act (environmental governance)—

(a) the following provisions extend to England and Wales—

(i) Chapter 1 (improving the natural environment), except for sections 17 to 20;

(ii) section 28 (monitoring and reporting on environmental improvement plans and targets);

(b) sections 17 to 19 (policy statement on environmental principles) extend to England and Wales and Scotland;

(c) the remaining provisions extend to England and Wales, Scotland and Northern Ireland.

(2) Part 2 of this Act (environmental governance: Northern Ireland) extends to Northern Ireland, except that—

(a) in Part 1 of Schedule 3, paragraphs 16 and 17(7) extend to England and Wales, Scotland and Northern Ireland;

(b) an amendment or repeal made by Part 2 of Schedule 3 has the same extent as the provision amended or repealed.

(3) In Part 3 of this Act (waste and resource efficiency)—

(a) the following provisions extend to England and Wales, Scotland and Northern Ireland—

(i) section 50 and Schedule 4 (producer responsibility obligations);

(ii) section 51 and Schedule 5 (producer responsibility for disposal costs);

(iii) section 52 and Schedule 6 (resource efficiency information);

(iv) section 53 and Schedule 7 (resource efficiency requirements);

(v) section 63 (procedure for regulations under the Environmental Protection Act 1990);

(b) the following provisions extend to England and Wales and Northern Ireland—

(i) section 54 and Schedule 8 (deposit schemes);

(ii) sections 55 and Schedule 9 (charges for single use items);

…

(6) Part 6 of this Act (nature and biodiversity) extends to England and Wales, except that—

(a) the amendments made by Schedule 15 (biodiversity gain in nationally significant infrastructure projects) have the same extent as the provisions amended, and

(b) section 116 and Schedule 17 (use of forest risk commodities in commercial activity) extend to England and Wales, Scotland and Northern Ireland.

(7) Part 7 of this Act (conservation covenants) extends to England and Wales.

(8) This Part (miscellaneous and general provisions) extends to England and Wales, Scotland and Northern Ireland.

147 Commencement

(1) The following provisions of this Act come into force on the day on which this Act is passed—

(a) section 63 (procedure for regulations under the Environmental Protection Act 1990);

(b) …

(2) The following provisions of this Act come into force at the end of the period of 2 months beginning with the day on which this Act is passed—

(a) section 51 and Schedule 5 (producer responsibility for disposal costs) so far as relating to England and Wales and Scotland;

(b) section 52 and Schedule 6 (resource efficiency information) so far as relating to England and Wales and Scotland;

(c) section 53 and Schedule 7 (resource efficiency requirements) so far as relating to England and Wales and Scotland;

...

(3) The following provisions of this Act come into force on such day as the Secretary of State may by regulations appoint —

(a) Part 1 (environmental governance);

...

(c) section 57 (separate collection of waste);

...

(f) section 64 (charging powers), so far as relating to the Environment Agency;

...

(i) section 72 and Schedule 11 (local air quality management framework);

...

(s) Part 6 (nature and biodiversity);

(t) Part 7 (conservation covenants).

(4)–(10) ...

148 Transitional or saving provision

(1) The Secretary of State may by regulations make transitional or saving provision in connection with the coming into force of any provision of this Act.

(2)–(7) ...

(8) A power to make regulations or an order under this section includes power to make different provision for different purposes or areas.

SCHEDULE 11

LOCAL AIR QUALITY MANAGEMENT FRAMEWORK

Section 72

1 The Environment Act 1995 is amended as follows.

2(1) Section 80 (national air quality strategy) is amended as follows.

(2) Omit subsection (3).

(3) After subsection (4) insert—

"(4A) The strategy must be reviewed, and if appropriate modified—

(a) within the period of 12 months beginning with the day on which this subsection comes into force, and

(b) within each period of 5 years beginning with the day on which the person carrying out the review completed their most recent review under this subsection."

3 After that section insert—

"80A Duty to report on air quality in England

As soon as reasonably practicable after the end of each financial year, beginning with the financial year in which this section comes into force, the Secretary of State must lay a statement before Parliament that sets out—

(a) the Secretary of State's assessment of the progress made in meeting air quality objectives, and air quality standards, in relation to England, and

(b) the steps the Secretary of State has taken in that year in support of the meeting of those objectives and standards."

Paragraph 1551 of the Explanatory Memorandum states:

"1551 New section 80A requires the Secretary of State to lay a statement annually before Parliament which sets out an assessment of progress made towards meeting air quality objectives and standards in England, as well as the steps the Secretary of State has taken in support of meeting those standards and objectives. These are the standards and objectives for local air quality that the Secretary of State must include in the National Air Quality

> *Strategy and enact in secondary legislation, which are then the levels that local authorities must assess against under the Local Air Quality Management Framework."*

4 After section 81 insert—

"81A Functions of relevant public authorities etc

(1) The following persons must have regard to the strategy when exercising any function of a public nature that could affect the quality of air—

(a) relevant public authorities;

(b) local authorities in England;

(c) county councils for areas in England for which there are district councils.

(2) In this Part, "relevant public authority" means a person designated in accordance with subsection (3) as a relevant public authority in relation to an area in England.

> It would seem logical that a local planning authority would become a *"relevant public authority"* when the Secretary of State carries out this designation exercise.

(3) The Secretary of State may by regulations designate a person as a relevant public authority in relation to an area in England if the person's functions include functions of a public nature in relation to that area.

(4) Before making regulations under subsection (3) the Secretary of State must consult—

(a) the person that is proposed to be designated, and

(b) such other persons as the Secretary of State considers appropriate.

(5) The requirement in subsection (4) may be met by consultation carried out before this section comes into force.

(6) For the purposes of subsections (2) and (3), reference to England includes the territorial sea adjacent to England, which for this purpose does not include—

(a) any part of the territorial sea which is adjacent to Wales for the purposes of the Government of Wales Act 2006 (see section 158 of that Act), or

(b) any part of the territorial sea which is adjacent to Scotland for the purposes of the Scotland Act 1998 (see section 126 of that Act)."

5(1) Section 82 (local authority reviews) is amended as follows.

(2) In subsection (3)—

(a) for "If" substitute "This subsection applies to a local authority where";

(b) omit the words from ", the local authority shall" to the end.

(3) After subsection (3) insert—

"(4) Where subsection (3) applies to a local authority, it must identify any parts of its area in which it appears that air quality standards or objectives are not likely to be achieved within the relevant period.

(5) Where subsection (3) applies to a local authority in England, it must also—

(a) identify relevant sources of emissions that it considers are, or will be, responsible (in whole or in part) for any failure to achieve air quality standards or objectives in its area,

(b) in the case of a relevant source within the area of a neighbouring authority, identify that authority, and

(c) in the case of a relevant source within an area in relation to which a relevant public authority or the Agency has functions of a public nature, identify that person in relation to that source.

(6) For the purposes of subsection (5), a source is 'relevant' if—

(a) it is within the area of the local authority,

(b) it is within the area of a neighbouring authority in England, or

(c) it is within an area in relation to which a relevant public authority or the Agency has functions of a public nature and the local authority considers that the exercise of those functions is relevant to the source of the emissions."

6 After section 83 insert—

"83A Duties of English local authorities in relation to designated areas

(1) This section applies in relation to a local authority in England.

(2) A local authority must, for the purpose of securing that air quality standards and objectives are achieved in an air quality management area designated by that authority, prepare an action plan in relation to that area.

Paragraph 1566 of the Explanatory Memorandum states:

"1566 Subsection (2) applies a duty on local authorities to prepare an action plan to ensure air quality standards and objectives are achieved in the Air Quality Management Area it has designated in accordance with section 83. This tightens the requirement to ensure that action plans should secure the required standards and objectives."

---

(3) An action plan is a written plan that sets out how the local authority will exercise its functions in order to secure that air quality standards and objectives are achieved in the area to which the plan relates.

(4) An action plan must also set out how the local authority will exercise its functions to secure that air quality standards and objectives are maintained after they have been achieved in the area to which the plan relates.

(5) An action plan must set out particular measures the local authority will take to secure the achievement, and maintenance, of air quality standards and objectives in the area to which the plan relates, and must in relation to each measure specify a date by which it will be carried out.

The question for this book is whether, if at all, an air quality action plan will impact upon the development control functions of a local planning authority. Arguably, the existence of such a plan must be a material planning consideration, and the achievements of the objectives of that plan, or failure to do so, should be a factor which will be taken into account in determining site-specific planning applications. Furthermore, it must be the case that the existence of an air quality action plan for a particular locality will be reflected in the provisions of the relevant local plan.

---

(6) A local authority may revise an action plan at any time, and must revise an action plan if it considers that there is a need for further or different measures to be taken to secure that air quality standards and objectives are achieved or maintained in the area to which the plan relates.

(7) Subsections (8) to (10) apply where a district council in an area for which there is a county council is preparing an action plan, or a revision of an action plan.

(8) Where the county council disagrees with the contents of the proposed plan, or the proposed revision of a plan, a referral of the matter may be made to the Secretary of State by—

(a) the county council;

(b) the district council preparing the plan or revision.

(9) The Secretary of State may, on a reference made under subsection (8),confirm (with or without modifications) or reject the proposed action plan, or revision of an action plan.

(10) Where a reference has been made under subsection (8), the district council may not finally determine the proposed action plan or revision of an action plan, except in accordance with the decision of the Secretary of State on the reference or in pursuance of a direction made by the Secretary of State under section 85."

7(1) Section 84 (duties of local authorities in relation to designated areas) is amended as follows.

(2) In the heading, after "of" insert "Scottish and Welsh".

(3) Before subsection (2) insert—

"(1A) This section applies in relation to a local authority in Scotland or Wales."

(4) Omit subsection (5).

8 After section 85 insert—

"85A Duty of air quality partners to co-operate

(1) For the purposes of this Part, an 'air quality partner' of a local authority means a person identified by that authority in accordance with section 82(5)(b) or (c).

(2) An air quality partner of a local authority must provide the authority with such assistance in connection with the carrying out of any of the authority's functions under this Part as the authority requests.

(3) An air quality partner may refuse a request under subsection (2) to the extent it considers the request unreasonable.

85B Role of air quality partners in relation to action plans

(1) Where a local authority in England intends to prepare an action plan it must notify each of its air quality partners that it intends to do so.

(2) Where an air quality partner of a local authority has been given a notification under subsection (1) it must, before the end of the relevant period, provide the authority with proposals for particular measures the partner will take to contribute to the achievement, and maintenance, of air quality standards and objectives in the area to which the plan relates.

(3) An air quality partner that provides proposals under subsection (2) must—

(a) in those proposals, specify a date for each particular measure by which it will be carried out, and

(b) as far as is reasonably practicable, carry out those measures by those dates.

(4) An action plan prepared by a local authority in England must set out any proposals provided to it by its air quality partners under subsection (2)(including the dates specified by those partners by virtue of subsection (3)(a)).

(5) The Secretary of State may direct an air quality partner to make further proposals under subsection (2) by a date specified in the direction where the Secretary of State considers the proposals made by the partner under that subsection are insufficient or otherwise inappropriate.

(6) A direction under subsection (5) may make provision about the extent to which the further proposals are to supplement or replace any other proposals made under subsection (2) by the air quality partner.

(7) An air quality partner must comply with any direction given to it under this section."

9(1) Section 86 (functions of county councils for areas for which there are district councils) is amended as follows.

(2) Omit subsection (1).

(3) In subsection (2), for the words before paragraph (a) substitute "A county council for an area in England for which there are district councils may make recommendations to any of those district councils with respect to the carrying out of—".

(4) After subsection (2) insert—

"(2A) Where a district council of a district in England for which there is a county council intends to prepare an action plan it must notify the county council that it intends to do so."

(5) For subsections (3) to (5) substitute—

"(3) Where a county council has been given a notification by a district council under subsection (2A) it must, before the end of the relevant period, provide the district council with proposals for particular measures the county council will take to contribute to the achievement, and maintenance, of air quality standards and objectives in the area to which the plan relates.

(4) A county council that provides proposals under subsection (3) must—

(a) in those proposals, specify a date for each particular measure by which it will be carried out, and

(b) as far as is reasonably practicable, carry out those measures by those dates.

(5) An action plan prepared by a district council of a district in England for which there is a county council must set out any proposals provided to it by the county council under subsection (3) (including the dates specified by the county council by virtue of subsection (4)(a))."

(6) In subsection (6), in paragraph (a), after "district council" insert "of a district in England for which there is a county council".

(7) In subsection (7)—

(a) in paragraph (a), omit the words from "above or" to the end;

(b) in paragraph (b)—

(i) omit "or statement";

(ii) omit "or (4) above";

(c) in paragraph (c)—

(i) omit "or statement";

(ii) omit "or (4) above".

10 For section 86A substitute—

"86A Role of the Mayor of London in relation to action plans

(1) Where a local authority in London intends to prepare an action plan it must notify the Mayor of London (referred to in this section as 'the Mayor').

(2) Where the Mayor has been given a notification under subsection (1) by a local authority in London the Mayor must, before the end of the relevant period, provide the authority with proposals for particular measures the Mayor will take to contribute to the achievement, and maintenance, of air quality standards and objectives in the area to which the plan relates.

(3) Where the Mayor provides proposals under subsection (2), the Mayor must—

(a) in those proposals, specify a date for each particular measure by which it will be carried out, and

(b) as far as is reasonably practicable, carry out those measures by those dates.

(4) An action plan prepared by a local authority in London must set out any proposals provided to it by the Mayor under subsection (2) (including the dates specified by the Mayor by virtue of subsection (3)(a)).

86B Role of combined authorities in relation to action plans

(1) Where a local authority in the area of a combined authority intends to prepare an action plan it must notify the combined authority.

(2) Where a combined authority has been given a notification under subsection (1) by a local authority, the combined authority must, before the end of the relevant period, provide the local authority with proposals for particular measures the combined authority will take to contribute to the achievement, and maintenance, of air quality standards and objectives in the area to which the plan relates.

(3) Where a combined authority provides proposals under subsection (2), the combined authority must—

(a) in those proposals, specify a date for each particular measure by which it will be carried out, and

(b) as far as is reasonably practicable, carry out those measures by those dates.

(4) An action plan prepared by a local authority in the area of a combined authority must set out any proposals provided to it under subsection (2)(including the dates specified by virtue of subsection (3)(a)).

(5) In this section 'combined authority' has the meaning it has in Part 6 of the Local Democracy, Economic Development and Construction Act 2009 (see section 120 of that Act)."

11(1) Section 87 (regulations) is amended as follows.

(2) In subsection (2)—

    (a) in paragraph (c), after "authorities" insert ", relevant county councils, relevant public authorities or the Agency";

    (b) in paragraph (j), after "otherwise)" insert ", relevant county councils, relevant public authorities, the Agency";

    (c) in paragraph (l), after "authorities" insert ", relevant county councils, relevant public authorities or the Agency";

    (d) in paragraph (m)—

        (i) after "local authority" insert ", a relevant county council, a relevant public authority or the Agency";

        (ii) after "the authority", in both places it occurs, insert ", council or Agency".

(3) After that subsection insert—

    "(2A) In subsection (2) "relevant county council" means a county council for an area in England for which there are district councils."

12 In section 88, in subsection (3), after "district councils" insert ", relevant public authorities and the Agency".

13 In section 91 (interpretation), in subsection (1)—

    (a) for the definition of "action plan" substitute—

    "'action plan' is to be construed—

        (a) in relation to England, in accordance with section 83A;

        (b) otherwise, in accordance with section 84(2);";

    (b) at the appropriate places insert—

    "'air quality partner' has the meaning given by section 85A(1);";

    "'neighbouring authority', in relation to a local authority ('the principal authority'), means another local authority whose area is contiguous with the area of the principal authority;";

    "'relevant public authority' has the meaning given by section 81A(2);"

SCHEDULE 14

SECTION 98

BIODIVERSITY GAIN AS CONDITION OF PLANNING PERMISSION

PART 1

BIODIVERSITY GAIN CONDITION

1 In the Town and Country Planning Act 1990, after section 90 insert—

"Biodiversity gain

90A Biodiversity gain in England

Schedule 7A (biodiversity gain in England) has effect."

> The 2021 Act does not contain the provisions for biodiversity net gain in itself. Instead, it makes amendments to the somewhat overburdened Town and Country Planning Act 1990. Accordingly, practitioners will need to track these amendments into the 1990 Act with a view to understanding how they operate in the context of the provisions of that Act.

2 In that Act, after Schedule 7 insert—

"SCHEDULE 7A   Section 90A

BIODIVERSITY GAIN IN ENGLAND

PART 1

OVERVIEW AND INTERPRETATION

Overview

1(1) This Schedule makes provision for grants of planning permission in England to be subject to a condition to secure that the biodiversity gain objective is met.

"*Biodiversity gain objective*" is defined in paragraphs 1(1) to 1(3) of new Schedule 7A to the 1990 Act below.

See Chapter 14 for discussion.

(2) Paragraphs 2 to 12 have effect for the purposes of this Schedule.

It is important to emphasise that the "*grant of planning permission*" within the 1990 Act covers a number of actions which might, at first blush, appear not to fall within this specific rubric. For example, so-called "*variations*" under section 73 of the 1990 Act do, in fact, take effect by way of the grant of a new planning permission and, on the face of it, they will be caught by this provision.

Biodiversity gain objective

2(1) The biodiversity gain objective is met in relation to development for which planning permission is granted if the biodiversity value attributable to the development exceeds the pre-development biodiversity value of the onsite habitat by at least the relevant percentage.

The "*relevant percentage*" is defined at paragraph 1(3) below.

The provisions of this paragraph can be satisfied only by the application of a biodiversity metric which provides data to evaluate the pre-development and post-development biodiversity value of the site and any offset land.

(2) The biodiversity value attributable to the development is the total of—

(a) the post-development biodiversity value of the onsite habitat,

(b) the biodiversity value, in relation to the development, of any registered offsite biodiversity gain allocated to the development, and

(c) the biodiversity value of any biodiversity credits purchased for the development.

(3) The relevant percentage is 10%.

(4) The Secretary of State may by regulations amend this paragraph so as to change the relevant percentage.

This is the central provision of this Part of the Act. It is an attempt to incorporate some measure of objectivity into the process of assessing whether or not biodiversity net gain is being provided on a site-by-site basis. The methodology is set out in the Biodiversity Metric which is, now, incorporated into the legislation (see below).

Biodiversity value and the biodiversity metric

3 References to the biodiversity value of any habitat or habitat enhancement are its value as calculated in accordance with the biodiversity metric.

The "*biodiversity metric*" is, currently, the Biodiversity Metric 3.0, although it may be revised after a consultation exercise in 2022.

4(1) The biodiversity metric is a document for measuring, for the purposes of this Schedule, the biodiversity value or relative biodiversity value of habitat or habitat enhancement.

(2) The biodiversity metric is to be produced and published by the Secretary of State.

(3) The Secretary of State may from time to time revise and republish the biodiversity metric.

(4) Before publishing or republishing the biodiversity metric the Secretary of State must consult such persons as the Secretary of State considers appropriate.

(5) The Secretary of State may by regulations make transitional provision in relation to the revision and republication of the biodiversity metric.

(6) The Secretary of State must lay the biodiversity metric, and any revised biodiversity metric, before Parliament.

Paragraph 1734 of the Explanatory Memorandum states:

"*1734 Paragraph 4 makes provision for the Secretary of State to publish the biodiversity metric, the tool which is used to measure the relative biodiversity value of habitats as relevant to this schedule. Sub-paragraphs (3) and (5) give the Secretary of State the power to update the biodiversity metric, and set out any arrangements for transition when the metric is updated so that developers and planning authorities are clear what is required where, for example, a planning application is under consideration on the date the updated version of the metric comes into effect. Updates to the metric will allow technical improvements, reflecting improved ecological understanding and further evaluation of the metric's application in practice, to the metric to be incorporated into the approach. Updates will be infrequent to avoid creating unnecessary uncertainty for the planning system. The intention is to publish a timeline of planned updates. The provision also enables the Secretary of State to make transitional provision where the metric is revised and republished. Sub-paragraph (6) requires the biodiversity metric published for mandatory biodiversity net gain, which will be used for measuring the biodiversity value of land and enhancements, to be laid before Parliament. This will ensure that the document is clearly published and is available for scrutiny."*

The definition of *"biodiversity metric"* as a *"document"* appears to miss the point, which is that, in fact, the metric is, actually, a methodology which utilises a number of resources, including an electronic spreadsheet and an electronic mapping system. Be that as it may, Defra is proposing to amend the Biodiversity Metric 3.0 in 2022 following a consultation exercise.

Pre-development biodiversity value

5(1) In relation to any development for which planning permission is granted, the pre-development biodiversity value of the onsite habitat is the biodiversity value of the onsite habitat on the relevant date.

(2) The relevant date is—

(a) in a case in which planning permission is granted on application, the date of the application, and

(b) in any other case, the date on which the planning permission is granted.

These provisions do not appear to mesh well with applications which are granted in outline and then followed by reserved matters approvals, because it will often be the case that the layout of the scheme will not be clear until the reserved matters are considered. This would suggest that a prudent local planning authority will set out the spatial parameters of the scheme at the outline stage by way of *"Rochdale"* type conditions. Defra has promised, via the consultation document, to examine ways of dealing with this problem by way of regulations (see the Consultation Document).

(3) But the person submitting the biodiversity gain plan for approval and the planning authority may agree that the relevant date is to be a date earlier than that specified in sub-paragraph (2)(a) or (b) (but not a date which is before the day on which this Schedule comes into force in relation to the development).

This timing provision is a very important one because, in many cases, the supporting documents which are provided with applications will have taken months to compile.

297

> This is particularly so with reports relating to ecology because, of course, some of the input data is seasonal.

(4) This paragraph is subject to paragraphs 6 and 7.

6 If—

(a) a person carries on activities on land on or after 30 January 2020 otherwise than in accordance with—

(i) planning permission, or

(ii) any other permission of a kind specified by the Secretary of State by regulations, and

(b) as a result of the activities the biodiversity value of the onsite habitat referred to in paragraph 5(1) is lower on the relevant date than it would otherwise have been,

the pre-development biodiversity value of the onsite habitat is to be taken to be its biodiversity value immediately before the carrying on of the activities.

> The objective of this provision is, of course, to ensure that a developer or landowner does not run down the application site in order to create an artificially low base level. It might, at first blush, appear that this would be a difficult provision to apply in practice because, of course, the relevant habitat will have been destroyed or degraded. However, local planning authorities have experience of reconstructing the past in connection with certificates of lawfulness and enforcement proceedings, and so they should have some tools to hand to deploy in this task (for example, by collecting eye-witness evidence of the previous condition of the site). In many cases, it will be found that there is some form of photographic evidence. References to the prior condition of the site may also be made in contemporaneous documents.

7 Where planning permission is granted in respect of land which is registered in the biodiversity gain site register under section 100 of the Environment Act 2021, the pre-development biodiversity value of the land is the total of—

(a) the biodiversity value of the onsite habitat on the relevant date, and

(b) to the extent that it is not included within that value, the biodiversity value of the habitat enhancement which is, on that date, recorded in the register as habitat enhancement to be achieved on the land.

Post-development biodiversity value

8(1) In relation to any development for which planning permission is granted, the post-development biodiversity value of the onsite habitat is the projected value of the onsite habitat as at the time the development is completed.

(2) That value is to be calculated by taking the pre-development biodiversity value and—

(a) if at the time the development is completed the development will, taken as a whole, have increased the biodiversity value of the onsite habitat, adding the amount of that increase, or

(b) if at the time the development is completed the development will, taken as a whole, have decreased the biodiversity value of the onsite habitat, subtracting the amount of that decrease.

This is subject to paragraph 9.

Paragraph 1738 of the Explanatory Memorandum states:

"1738 Paragraph 8 defines the post-development biodiversity value of habitat on the development site as the projected value of habitats on the development site. The value needs to be projected because a planning authority will need to use this figure before development starts to determine whether the development will achieve the net gain objective. In practice, the post development biodiversity value of habitats on the development site will be determined by applying the metric to the developer's plan for the development site as detailed in the biodiversity gain plan."

All of this depends, of course, on the ability of the local planning authority to secure the delivery of the biodiversity gain plan in reality.

9(1) This paragraph applies in relation to any development for which planning permission is granted where—

(a) the person submitting the biodiversity gain plan for approval proposes to carry out works in the course of the development that increase the biodiversity value of the onsite habitat, and

(b) the planning authority considers that the increase is significant in relation to the pre-development biodiversity value.

(2) The increase in biodiversity value referred to in sub-paragraph (1) is to be taken into account in calculating the post-development biodiversity value of the onsite habitat only if the planning authority is satisfied that the condition in sub-paragraph (3) is met.

(3) The condition is that any habitat enhancement resulting from the works referred to in sub-paragraph (1)(a) will, by virtue of—

(a) a condition subject to which the planning permission is granted,

(b) a planning obligation, or

(c) a conservation covenant,

be maintained for at least 30 years after the development is completed.

There is a considerable difference between a statutory provision requiring habitat enhancement to be maintained for at least 30 years after the completion of the development and actually ensuring that this maintenance period is delivered in practice. In reality, this leads one to look beyond statutory remedies and to ask how security for future maintenance can be delivered in the real world. In the majority of cases, one is drawn to consider the use of financial securities such as bonds or guarantees. This, of course, rules out the use of a planning condition for this purpose. Nor is there anything in the provisions relating to conservation covenants which allows for the imposition of financial securities. So far as our town and country planning is concerned, one tends to be drawn down to the use of planning obligations for this purpose.

---

(4) The Secretary of State may by regulations amend sub-paragraph (3) so as to substitute for the period for the time being specified there a different period of at least 30 years.

Registered offsite biodiversity gains

10(1) 'Registered offsite biodiversity gain' means any habitat enhancement, where—

(a) the enhancement is required to be carried out under a conservation covenant or planning obligation, and

(b) the enhancement is recorded in the biodiversity gain site register (as to which, see section 100 of the Environment Act 2021).

This provision provides that conservation covenant agreements and planning obligations which secure offsite biodiversity net gain must be not only registered as local land charges but also placed on the biodiversity gain site register. This could be a trap for the unwary. Paragraph 1740 of the Explanatory Memorandum states:

> *"1740 Paragraph 10 defines what can be counted towards 'registered offsite biodiversity gain' in relation to a development. This relates to gain achieved on land other than the development site. Where a developer makes an agreement with a third party to do so, or enters into an agreement to do so themselves, this gain can be allocated to the development to be counted towards meeting the biodiversity objective. The biodiversity gain and its allocation to a development must be recorded on the biodiversity gains site register."*

(2) References to the allocation of registered offsite biodiversity gain are to its allocation in accordance with the terms of the conservation covenant or planning obligation referred to in sub-paragraph (1)(a).

(3) The biodiversity value of registered offsite biodiversity gain is measured, under the biodiversity metric, in relation to development to which it is allocated.

Biodiversity credits

11 'Biodiversity credits' means credits under section 101 of the Environment Act 2021.

General

12(1) In relation to development for which planning permission is granted—

'onsite habitat' means habitat on the land to which the planning permission relates;

'planning authority' means the local planning authority, except that—

(a) in a case where the planning permission is granted by Mayoral development order under section 61DB, 'planning authority' means such of the Mayor of London or the local planning authority as may be specified in the order;

(b) in a case where the planning permission is granted by the Secretary of State under section 62A, 76A or 77, 'planning authority' means such of the Secretary of State or the local planning authority as the Secretary of State may determine;

(c) in a case where the planning permission is granted on an appeal under section 78, 'planning authority' means such of the person determining the appeal or the local planning authority as that person may direct.

(2) 'Habitat enhancement' means enhancement of the biodiversity of habitat.

This is a difficult provision to interpret because the phrase "'*Habitat enhancement' means enhancement of the biodiversity of habitat*" is circular. Not only this, but enhancing the biodiversity of a habitat is very different from enhancing a habitat per se. The former would involve an attempt to measure the immeasurable, or almost immeasurable, because any selected habitat may be inhabited by innumerable different species which, in turn, fluctuate from time to time.

(3) References to the grant of planning permission include the deemed grant of planning permission.

This provision will, in the main, be relevant where planning permission is deemed to be granted by the GPDO.

PART 2

CONDITION OF PLANNING PERMISSION RELATING TO BIODIVERSITY GAIN

General condition of planning permission

13(1) Every planning permission granted for the development of land in England shall be deemed to have been granted subject to the condition in sub-paragraph (2).

When read in the context provided by the Town and Country and Planning Act 1990, the word "*development*" includes not only built development but also material changes of use and mining operations. This might pose considerable difficulties where, for example, the application is for a material change of use of an inner city building which does not have the benefit of any onsite habitat at all. Arguably, this is one of the problems which must be addressed by the Secretary of State in providing detailed regulations: see the Consultation Document.

(2) The condition is that the development may not be begun unless—

(a) a biodiversity gain plan has been submitted to the planning authority (see paragraph 14), and

(b) the planning authority has approved the plan (see paragraph 15).

This is a "*pre-commencement condition*" (aka a "*Grampian*" type condition) and is therefore subject to a complicated set of rules: see Chapter 20 above.

Biodiversity gain plan

14(1) For the purposes of paragraph 13(2)(a), a biodiversity gain plan is a plan which—

(a) relates to development for which planning permission is granted, and

(b) specifies the matters referred to in sub-paragraph (2).

In practice, one would anticipate that the developer will have provided a draft biodiversity gain plan as part of their application documents so that it can be taken into account in the balancing exercise which will be applied by the local planning authority in coming to its decision. Defra is currently consulting on a draft template for biodiversity gain plan: see the Consultation Document.

(2) The matters are—

(a) information about the steps taken or to be taken to minimise the adverse effect of the development on the biodiversity of the onsite habitat and any other habitat,

This is the first step in the application of the *"biodiversity hierarchy"*: see Chapter 9 above.

(b) the pre-development biodiversity value of the onsite habitat,

(c) the post-development biodiversity value of the onsite habitat,

The post-development biodiversity value of the onsite habitat will include the value of any enhancements to, or additions to, existing onsite habitats.

(d) any registered offsite biodiversity gain allocated to the development and the biodiversity value of that gain in relation to the development,

"Registered offsite biodiversity gain" as per allocations in the biodiversity register: see paragraph 12.

(e) any biodiversity credits purchased for the development, and

See Chapter 13 and section 101 above for *"Biodiversity Credits"*.

(f) such other matters as the Secretary of State may by regulations specify.

(3) The Secretary of State may by regulations make provision about—

(a) any other matters to be included in a biodiversity gain plan;

(b) the form of a biodiversity gain plan;

(c) the procedure to be followed in relation to the submission of a biodiversity gain plan (including the time by which a plan must be submitted);

(d) persons who may or must submit a biodiversity gain plan.

Again, see the Consultation Document.

Approval of biodiversity gain plan

15(1) For the purposes of paragraph 13(2)(b) a planning authority to which a biodiversity gain plan is submitted must approve the plan if, and only if, it is satisfied as to the matters specified in sub-paragraph (2).

(2) The matters are—

(a) that the pre-development biodiversity value of the onsite habitat is as specified in the plan,

(b) that the post-development biodiversity value of the onsite habitat is at least the value specified in the plan,

(c) that, in a case where any registered offsite biodiversity gain is specified in the plan as allocated to the development—

(i) the registered offsite biodiversity gain is so allocated (and, if the allocation is conditional, that any conditions attaching to the allocation have been met or will be met by the time the development begins), and

(ii) the registered offsite biodiversity gain has the biodiversity value specified in the plan in relation to the development,

(d) that any biodiversity credits specified in the plan as purchased for the development have been so purchased,

(e) that the biodiversity gain objective is met, and

(f) any other matters specified in the plan under paragraph 14(2)(f).

Regulations about determinations

16 The Secretary of State may make regulations as to—

(a) the procedure which a planning authority is to follow in determining whether to approve a biodiversity gain plan(including the time by which a determination must be made);

(b) factors which may or must be taken into account in making such a determination;

(c) appeals relating to such a determination.

The appeal provision in (c) is an important safeguard for applicants, and it should mean that local planning authorities will have to deal with applications expeditiously.

Exceptions

17 Paragraph 13 does not apply in relation to—

(a) development for which planning permission is granted—

(i) by a development order, or

(ii) under section 293A (urgent Crown development), or

(b) development of such other description as the Secretary of State may by regulations specify.

Among other things, the exemption in (a) will apply to permitted development. Paragraph 1749 of the Explanatory Memorandum states:

"1749 Paragraph 17 exempts all development granted planning permission by the Secretary of State using a development order, or under provisions for urgent Crown development, from the application of the general condition. This includes development granted permission by the General Permitted Development Order, which allows various types of development to proceed without requiring a planning application. Paragraph 17 also gives the Secretary of State the power to exempt development from the requirement to apply the general condition."

Modifications for irreplaceable habitat

18(1) The Secretary of State may by regulations make provision modifying or excluding the application of this Part of this Schedule in relation to any development for which planning permission is granted where the onsite habitat is 'irreplaceable habitat' as defined in the regulations.

(2) Regulations under this paragraph must make provision requiring, in relation to any such development, the making of arrangements for the purpose of minimising the adverse effect of the development on the biodiversity of the onsite habitat.

(3) Regulations under this paragraph may confer powers and duties, including powers and duties in relation to the giving of guidance, on Natural England.

Paragraphs 1750 and 1751 of the Explanatory Memorandum state:

"1750 A net gain in biodiversity cannot be achieved on areas of development which result in the loss of irreplaceable habitat, such as ancient woodland. In recognition of this paragraph 18 allows the Secretary of State to make regulations that modify or exclude the application of the general condition to irreplaceable habitat. Existing strong planning policy protections for irreplaceable habitat will remain, and will not be replaced or in any way undermined by the biodiversity gain requirement or any regulations to be made in relation to irreplaceable habitat. Sub-paragraph(2) specifies that, where development does impact irreplaceable habitats, regulations must require measures to be taken to minimise the negative impacts of this development on those habitats, and that those measures should be agreed with the planning authority where they are not made by the planning authority in the first place. Sub-paragraph (3) allows regulations to confer powers and duties on Natural England in relation to giving guidance on the treatment of irreplaceable habitat in development.

1751 Whilst it is generally agreed in practice that development cannot claim biodiversity net gain in cases when development results in land take from statutory protected sites (such as Sites of Special Scientific Interest, Special Protection Areas, Special Areas of Conservation, and Ramsar sites), development on such sites is not specifically exempted from the net gain requirement. The biodiversity metric does not address impacts on species, recognise the significance of site designations, or take account of indirect impacts, cumulative impacts or in-combination impacts. In recognition of these limitations, the biodiversity net gain requirement for development on such sites is additional to any existing legal or policy requirements for statutory protected areas and their features, including restoration and conservation of designated features and the achievement of favourable conservation status and favourable condition. These requirements will need to be dealt with separately by the developer and planning authority."

Modifications for particular kinds of planning permission

19(1) The Secretary of State may by regulations make provision modifying the application of this Part of this Schedule in relation to—

(a) the grant of outline planning permission, where the reservation of matters for subsequent approval has the effect of requiring or permitting development to proceed in phases, or

(b) the grant of any kind of planning permission, where the grant is subject to conditions (whether requiring the subsequent approval of any matters or otherwise) having that effect.

(2) Regulations under this paragraph may include provision for a grant of planning permission referred to in sub-paragraph (1)(a) or (b) to be subject to conditions relating to meeting the biodiversity gain objective referred to in paragraph 2.

20(1) The Secretary of State may by regulations make provision modifying or excluding the application of this Part of this Schedule in relation to development for which—

(a) planning permission is granted under section 73A (planning permission for development already carried out), or

(b) planning permission is granted by an order under section 102 (orders requiring discontinuance of use etc).

(2) Regulations under this paragraph may in particular include provision—

(a) for paragraph 13 not to apply in relation to the grant of planning permission referred to in sub-paragraph (1)(a) or (b);

(b) for the grant of any such planning permission to be subject to other conditions relating to meeting the biodiversity gain objective.

(3) The conditions referred to in sub-paragraph (2)(b) may include conditions requiring—

(a) habitat enhancement on the land to which the planning permission relates;

(b) the allocation of registered offsite biodiversity gain to any development for which the planning permission is granted;

(c) the purchase of biodiversity credits for any such development.

Further application of this Part

21 The Secretary of State may by regulations make provision to apply this Part of this Schedule in relation to development for which planning permission is granted under section 141 or 177(1), with such modifications or exclusions as may be specified in the regulations."

PART 2

CONSEQUENTIAL AMENDMENTS

3(1) The Town and Country Planning Act 1990 is amended as follows.

(2) In section 56 (time when development begins), in subsection (3), at the end insert "and paragraph 13 of Schedule 7A".

(3) In section 69 (register of applications etc)—

(a) in subsection (1), at the end insert—

"(e) applications for approval of biodiversity gain plans under Part 2 of Schedule 7A.";

(b) in subsection (2)(a), for "and (aza)" substitute ", (aza) and (e)".

(4) In section 70 (determination of applications: general considerations), in subsection (1)(a), after "section 62D(5)" insert ", paragraph 13 of Schedule 7A".

(5) In section 73 (determination of applications to develop land after non-compliance),after subsection (2A) insert—

"(2B) Nothing in this section authorises the disapplication of the condition under paragraph 13 of Schedule 7A (biodiversity gain condition).

(2C) Subsection (2D) applies where—

(a) for the purposes of paragraph 13 of Schedule 7A a biodiversity gain plan was approved in relation to the previous planning permission('the earlier biodiversity gain plan'),

(b) planning permission is granted under this section, and

(c) the conditions subject to which the planning permission is granted under this section do not affect the post-development biodiversity value of the onsite habitat as specified in the earlier biodiversity gain plan.

(2D) Where this subsection applies, the earlier biodiversity gain plan is regarded as approved for the purposes of paragraph 13 of Schedule 7A in relation to the planning permission granted under this section."

(6) In section 74A (deemed discharge of planning permission conditions), after subsection (2) insert—

"(2A) But this section does not apply to the condition under paragraph 13 of Schedule 7A (biodiversity gain condition)."

(7) In section 76C (provisions applying to applications made under section 62A), in subsection (2), after "Schedule 1" insert ", or by regulations under paragraph 14(3)or 16 of Schedule 7A,".

(8) In section 84 (simplified planning zone schemes: conditions and limitations on planning permission), at the end insert—

"(5) A simplified planning zone scheme may not disapply the condition under paragraph 13 of Schedule 7A (biodiversity gain condition)."

(9) In section 88 (enterprise zones), after subsection (3) insert—

"(3A) Subsection (3) is subject to paragraph 13 of Schedule 7A (biodiversity gain condition)."

(10) In section 96A (power to make non-material changes to planning permission), after subsection (3) insert—

"(3A) The conditions referred to in subsection (3)(b) do not include the condition under paragraph 13 of Schedule 7A (biodiversity gain condition)."

(11) In section 97 (revocation or modification of planning permission), at the end insert—

"(7) Subsection (1) does not permit the revocation or modification of the condition under paragraph 13 of Schedule 7A (the biodiversity gain condition), subject as follows.

(8) The Secretary of State may by regulations make provision—

(a) for the condition under paragraph 13 of Schedule 7A to apply in relation to the modification of planning permission under this section, subject to such modifications as may be specified in the regulations;

(b) for planning permission modified under this section to be subject to other conditions relating to meeting the biodiversity gain objective referred to in paragraph 2 of Schedule 7A (including conditions of a kind referred to in paragraph 20(3) of that Schedule)."

(12) In section 100ZA (restriction on power to impose planning conditions in England),in subsection (13)(c), after "limitation" insert "but do not include the condition under paragraph 13 of Schedule 7A (biodiversity gain condition)".

(13) In section 106 (planning obligations), in subsection (1), in the words before paragraph (a), after "106C" insert ", Schedule 7A".

(14) In section 106A (modification and discharge of planning obligations), after subsection (6) insert—

"(6A) Except in such cases as may be prescribed, the authority may not under subsection (6) discharge or modify the planning obligation if the authority considers that doing so would—

(a) prevent the biodiversity gain objective referred to in paragraph 2 of Schedule 7A from being met in relation to any development, or

(b) give rise to a significant risk of that objective not being met in relation to any development."

(15) In section 333 (regulations and orders), after subsection (3A) insert—

"(3AA) No regulations may be made under paragraph 2(4) of Schedule 7A (biodiversity gain condition) unless a draft of the instrument containing the regulations has been laid before, and approved by a resolution of, each House of Parliament."

SCHEDULE 18 SECTION 130

DISCHARGE OR MODIFICATION OF OBLIGATIONS UNDER ONSERVATION COVENANTS

PART 1

DISCHARGE BY UPPER TRIBUNAL

Power to discharge on application by landowner or responsible body

1(1) The Upper Tribunal may, on the application of a person bound by, or entitled to the benefit of, an obligation under a conservation covenant by virtue of being the holder of an estate in land, by order discharge the obligation in respect of any of the land to which it relates.

(2) The Upper Tribunal must add as party to the proceedings on an application under sub-paragraph (1) the responsible body under the covenant.

2(1) The Upper Tribunal may, on the application of the responsible body under a conservation covenant, by order discharge an obligation under the covenant in respect of any of the land to which it relates.

(2) The Upper Tribunal must add as party to the proceedings on an application under sub-paragraph (1) any person who, by virtue of being the holder of an estate in land, is bound by, or entitled to the benefit of, the obligation to which the application relates.

Deciding whether to discharge

3(1) The Upper Tribunal may exercise its power under paragraph 1(1) or 2(1) if it considers it reasonable to do so in all the circumstances of the case.

(2) In considering whether to exercise its power under paragraph 1(1) or 2(1), the matters to which the Upper Tribunal is to have regard include—

(a) whether there has been any material change of circumstance since the making of the original agreement, in particular—

(i) change in the character of the land to which the obligation relates or of the neighbourhood of that land;

(ii) change affecting the enjoyment of the land to which the obligation relates;

(iii) change affecting the extent to which performance of the obligation is, or is likely in future to be, affordable;

(iv) change affecting the extent to which performance of the obligation is, or is likely in future to be, practicable;

Items (iii) and (iv) would seem to open the discussion to include matters of economic viability, but it is difficult to reconcile these provisions with paragraph 3(4) below.

(b) whether the obligation serves any conservation purpose it had—

(i) when the original agreement was entered into, or

(ii) if the obligation has since been modified (whether by agreement or by the Upper Tribunal), when the obligation was modified, as the case may be; and

(c) whether the obligation serves the public good.

This *"public good"* test is very subjective and, therefore, problematic.

(3) In considering whether to exercise its power under paragraph 1(1), the matters to which the Upper Tribunal is to have regard also include—

(a) whether any conservation purpose which the obligation in question had when the original agreement was entered into could be served equally well by an obligation relating to different land in respect of which the applicant holds a qualifying estate; and

(b) whether, if an order under paragraph 1(1) were made, such an alternative obligation could be created by means of a conservation covenant.

The phrase *"to have regard to"* means that the list in (a) and (b) is not exhaustive. These matters are not criteria but material considerations which should not exclude other material considerations.

(4) In considering, for the purposes of this paragraph, affordability or practicability in relation to performance of an obligation, change in the personal circumstances of a person bound by the obligation is to be disregarded.

This would seem to close the discussion regarding matters of economic viability. It is difficult to reconcile this provision with paragraph 3(2) above, which includes *"change affecting the extent to which performance of the obligation is, or is likely in future to be, affordable"*.

(5) In this paragraph references to the original agreement, in relation to an obligation under a conservation covenant, are to the agreement containing the provision which gave rise to the obligation.

Supplementary powers

4(1) The Upper Tribunal may include in an order under paragraph 1(1) or 2(1) provision requiring the applicant to pay compensation in respect of loss of benefit resulting from the order.

(2) Compensation under sub-paragraph (1) shall be payable to such person at such time and be of such amount as the order may provide.

5(1) The Upper Tribunal may, if it considers it reasonable to do so in connection with the discharge under paragraph 1(1) of an obligation under a conservation covenant, include in the order discharging the obligation provision making the discharge conditional on the entry by the applicant and the responsible body under the covenant into a conservation covenant agreement containing such provision as the order may specify.

(2) The power under sub-paragraph (1) is exercisable only with the consent of the applicant and the responsible body.

PART 2

MODIFICATION BY UPPER TRIBUNAL

Power to modify on application by landowner or responsible body

6(1) The Upper Tribunal may, on the application of a person bound by, or entitled to the benefit of, an obligation under a conservation covenant by virtue of being the holder of an estate in land, by order modify the obligation in respect of any of the land to which it relates.

(2) The Upper Tribunal must add as party to the proceedings on an application under sub-paragraph (1) the responsible body under the covenant.

7(1) The Upper Tribunal may, on the application of the responsible body under a conservation covenant, by order modify an obligation under the covenant in respect of any of the land to which it relates.

(2) The Upper Tribunal must add as party to the proceedings on an application under sub-paragraph (1) any person who, by virtue of being the holder of an estate in land, is bound by, or entitled to the benefit of, the obligation to which the application relates.

8 The power under paragraph 6(1) or 7(1) does not include power to make a change to an obligation which, had it been included in the original agreement, would have prevented

the provision of the agreement which gave rise to the obligation being provision in relation to which the conditions in section 117(1)(a) were met.

Deciding whether to modify

9(1) The Upper Tribunal may exercise its power under paragraph 6(1) or 7(1) if it considers it reasonable to do so in all the circumstances of the case.

(2) In considering whether to exercise its power under paragraph 6(1) or 7(1), the matters to which the Upper Tribunal is to have regard include—

(a) whether there has been any material change of circumstance since the making of the original agreement, in particular—

(i) change in the character of the land to which the obligation relates or of the neighbourhood of that land;

(ii) change affecting the enjoyment of the land to which the obligation relates;

(iii) change affecting the extent to which performance of the obligation is, or is likely in future to be, affordable;

(iv) change affecting the extent to which performance of the obligation is, or is likely in future to be, practicable;

Items (iii) and (iv) would seem to open the discussion to include matters of economic viability, but it is difficult to reconcile these provisions with paragraph 9(3) below.

(b) whether the obligation serves any conservation purpose it had—

(i) when the original agreement was entered into, or

(ii) if the obligation has since been modified (whether by agreement or by the Upper Tribunal), when the obligation was modified,

as the case may be; and

(c) whether the obligation serves the public good.

(3) In considering, for the purposes of this paragraph, affordability or practicability in relation to performance of an obligation, change in the personal circumstances of a person bound by the obligation is to be disregarded.

> This would seem to close the discussion regarding matters of economic viability. It is difficult to reconcile this provision with paragraph 9(2) above, which includes *"change affecting the extent to which performance of the obligation is, or is likely in future to be, affordable"*.

Supplementary powers

10(1) The Upper Tribunal may include in an order under paragraph 6(1) or 7(1) provision requiring the applicant to pay compensation in respect of loss of benefit resulting from the order.

(2) Compensation under sub-paragraph (1) shall be payable to such person at such time and be of such amount as the order may provide.

11(1) The Upper Tribunal may, if it considers it reasonable to do so in connection with the modification under paragraph 6(1) of an obligation under a conservation covenant, include in the order modifying the obligation provision making the modification conditional on the entry by the applicant and the responsible body under the covenant into a conservation covenant agreement containing such provision as the order may specify.

(2) The power under sub-paragraph (1) is exercisable only with the consent of the applicant and the responsible body.

Effect of modification

12(1) The modification of an obligation by an order under this Part binds—

(a) the parties to the proceedings in which the order is made, and

(b) any person who, as respects any of the land to which the modification relates, becomes a successor of a person bound by the modification.

(2) For the purposes of sub-paragraph (1) "successor of a person bound by the modification" means a person who holds, in respect of any of the land to which the modification relates—

(a) the estate held by the person so bound when the order modifying the obligation was made, or

(b) an estate in land derived (whether immediately or otherwise) from that estate after the order modifying the obligation was made.

Interpretation

13 In this Part, references to the original agreement, in relation to an obligation under a conservation covenant, are to the agreement containing the provision which gave rise to the obligation.

Index

T

U

W